Get started in Russian

Rachel Farmer

For UK order enquiries: please contact Bookpoint Ltd, 130 Milton Park, Abingdon, Oxon OX14 4SB. *Telephone:* +44 (0) 1235 827720. Fax: +44 (0) 1235 400454. Lines are open 09.00–17.00, Monday to Saturday, with a 24-hour message answering service. Details about our titles and how to order are available at www.teachyourself.com

For USA order enquiries: please contact McGraw-Hill Customer Services, PO Box 545, Blacklick, OH 43004-0545, USA. *Telephone:* 1-800-722-4726. Fax: 1-614-755-5645.

For Canada order enquiries: please contact McGraw-Hill Ryerson Ltd, 300 Water St, Whitby, Ontario L1N 9B6, Canada. *Telephone:* 905 430 5000. Fax: 905 430 5020.

Long renowned as the authoritative source for self-guided learning – with more than 50 million copies sold worldwide – the *Teach Yourself* series includes over 500 titles in the fields of languages, crafts, hobbies, business, computing and education.

British Library Cataloguing in Publication Data: a catalogue record for this title is available from the British Library.

Library of Congress Catalog Card Number: on file.

First published in UK 1996 as Teach Yourself Beginner's Russian by Hodder Education, part of Hachette UK, 338 Euston Road, London NW1 3BH.

First published in US 1996 by The McGraw-Hill Companies, Inc.

This edition published 2010.

Previously published as Teach Yourself Beginner's Russian

The *Teach Yourself* name is a registered trade mark of Hodder Headline.

Typeset by MPS Limited, A Macmillan Company.

Printed in Great Britain for Hodder Education, an Hachette UK Company, 338 Euston Road, London NW1 3BH.

The publisher has used its best endeavours to ensure that the URLs for external websites referred to in this book are correct and active at the time of going to press. However, the publisher and the author have no responsibility for the websites and can make no guarantee that a site will remain live or that the content will remain relevant, decent or appropriate.

Hachette UK's policy is to use papers that are natural, renewable and recyclable products and made from wood grown in sustainable forests. The logging and manufacturing processes are expected to conform to the environmental regulations of the country of origin.

Impression number 10 9 8 7 6 5 4

Year 2014 2013 2012

Contents

Credits

Front cover: Stockbyte/Getty Images

Back cover and pack: © Jakub Semeniuk/iStockphoto.com, © Royalty-Free/Corbis, © agencyby/iStockphoto.com, © Andy Cook/iStockphoto.com, © Christopher Ewing/iStockphoto.com, © zebicho - Fotolia.com, © Geoffrey Holman/iStockphoto.com, © Photodisc/Getty Images, © James C. Pruitt/iStockphoto.com, © Mohamed Saber - Fotolia.com

Pack: © Stockbyte/Getty Images

Only got a minute?

Millions of people visit Russia every year, and many more visit other Russian-speaking countries and communities.

Russia offers a vast and impressive spectrum of scenery, with its 11 time zones spanning the frozen Arctic Ocean, tundra, steppe, forest, mountains, deserts, volcanoes, lakes, rivers and semi-tropical coastline.

Its centres of population are scarcely less diverse, ranging from huge cosmopolitan cities reflecting the rapid economic development of the country to tiny villages where life has hardly changed for centuries.

If you have the benefit of understanding and speaking just a little Russian, you will find that the people of this vast country will appreciate your effort and take you to their hearts. Russians may sometimes appear rather stern in public but when they are amongst friends they certainly know how to enjoy themselves, and their hospitality is legendary.

Get started in Russian approaches the language in a straightforward and logical way, building your confidence step by step and encouraging you to practise your new skills in everyday situations: meeting people, finding your way around, shopping, eating out, organizing accommodation and leisure activities. You even learn how to complain, call the emergency services and go to the doctor's, so you will be equipped for everything!

This course will not ask you to spend time studying grammar. Any rules you need are explained in simple terms with helpful examples. You don't even need to master the Russian alphabet immediately: the first half of the course spells everything out in English letters as well, until you are used to the Russian letters. In one way Russian is easier than English in that once you can read the Russian alphabet all you have to do is say the sounds and people will understand you. There are no nasty surprises with spellings. Or, at least, hardly any!

So, whether you are a beginner or are wanting a refresher course, **Get started in Russian** is the user-friendly course for you.

5 Only got five minutes?

Russia is famously a land of extremes and paradoxes. It is the world's largest country in terms of area, and yet it is sparsely populated and has no natural boundaries, so much of its history has been shaped by defending itself against threats from outside its borders.

Russia holds nearly half the world's reserves of oil, gas and coal and yet its climate makes their extraction very challenging. Similarly much of Russia's vast land mass cannot be cultivated because of the weather conditions, ranging from permafrost to desert. Because of Russia's size and climate, with 11 time zones and temperatures ranging from +40° to −50°, transport is inevitably time-consuming, but the country's more than 1,000 airports make it as efficient as possible.

Russia's history has seen great swings from inward-looking autocracy to outward-looking westernization. The impact of Peter the Great's drive for westernization can be seen in the magnificent city of St Petersburg, built on the marshes at huge human cost. In the twentieth century Russia's population was dragged out of its largely rural way of life into a programme of rapid industrialization with startling results, including both ecological disasters and marvels such as the palatial Moscow metro system.

In the late twentieth and early twenty-first century Russia has enjoyed strong economic growth based on its natural resources, and there have been vast improvements in some of the infrastructure. The country is now much more geared to receiving foreign visitors, whether tourists or entrepreneurs. Business opportunities in Russia have presented some complications but there are great rewards for those who are prepared to be patient with the bureaucratic systems and to work hard at building relationships. Russia's rollercoaster history of political and economic crises means that people take events such as the global financial crisis in their stride.

Russia's belief systems have been varied and paradoxical, ranging from paganism, Orthodox Christianity, Communism and official state atheism, with a recent flourishing again of Orthodoxy. Of course, this summary is a simplification and Russia actually has great diversity in its religious beliefs and believers, including Muslims, Buddhists, Catholics and Protestants. There is also great diversity in nationalities, each having their own traditions, religions, languages and cultures, united only by their shared citizenship, state and official language. Unlike the USA, Russia has not become a melting pot.

Strong traces of superstition remain in this culture in spite of its scientific and medical advances. Perhaps because of the extremes in their environment, Russians have a depth of emotional expression not seen everywhere, being inclined to extremes of melancholy and celebration: all part of the complex Russian soul. Their attitude to things such as time, the truth, the law, the environment and money is complex, too, which makes a fascinating study for students of Russian.

There is also the vast wealth of Russian literature, music, architecture, ballet, theatre, film, museums and galleries to enjoy, as well as the natural beauties of the Russian outdoors. Winter sports are very popular and it is exciting for foreigners to see how Russians from a very young age enjoy the snow and ice.

Moscow is a city where historical buildings such as the Kremlin, with its many museums and churches, sit side by side with state-of-the-art modern developments. The legendary Red Square and St Basil's cathedral are awe-inspiring to visitors.

St Petersburg, with its beautiful European architecture and network of canals, delights visitors with its palaces and famous Hermitage museum.

Wherever you go in Russia and whatever you do, you will be reminded of Churchill's statement about Russia that it is a riddle, wrapped in a mystery, inside an enigma.

Speaking Russian opens up to you the opportunity to explore independently and to get to know the people who live here and in other Russian-speaking countries. *Get started in Russian* approaches the language in a straightforward and logical way, building your confidence step by step and encouraging you to practise your new skills in everyday situations: meeting people, finding your way around, shopping, eating out, organizing accommodation and leisure activities.

This course will not ask you to spend much time studying grammar. Any rules you need are explained in simple terms with helpful examples. You don't even need to master the Russian alphabet immediately: the first half of the course spells everything out in English letters as well, until you are used to the Russian letters. So, whether you are a beginner or are wanting a refresher course, *Get started in Russian* is the user-friendly course for you. It can open a window on this fascinating world or it can prepare you to move on to more concentrated study of Russian.

Dedication

To Peter, Lucy and Catherine

....

Meet the author

I graduated in Russian, French and Serbo-Croat at the University of Birmingham, and then gained a teaching qualification at the University of Nottingham.

I went on to teach languages, particularly Russian, to learners in schools, colleges, prisons: anywhere I could inspire and cultivate an interest in the Russian language and culture.

For ten years I taught Russian at the University of Nottingham, during which time I wrote my PhD thesis on the contemporary Russian writer Voinovich, who became a lifelong friend.

Over the years I have visited and worked in Russia at every opportunity and now deliver training and coaching in cross-cultural issues, and leadership and management to national and international managers in Russian-speaking countries. I also train, coach and carry out research for European businesses which have links with Russia.

Russia has exerted a strong influence on my life ever since I first studied the language at school, and it colours many of my interests. I have always loved reading, especially Russian fiction, and I enjoy writing fiction myself, with a Russian flavour of course.

My other interests include travel, walking, cinema, family and friends. I am based in Nottingham.

Introduction

Get started in Russian is the course to use if you are a complete beginner or have just a smattering of Russian. It is a self-study course, and will help you to speak, understand and read the language sufficiently for you to visit Russia or receive Russian visitors at home.

The course works best with the accompanying recording, but it is not essential. The recorded dialogues and exercises will give you practice in understanding the language and in pronouncing it correctly, and will give you confidence to speak out loud. Each unit contains at least one activity which requires the recording, but the material will always be covered by other activities as well. If you don't have the recording, use the **Pronunciation guide** to help you pronounce the words correctly. Always read the words and dialogues out loud in a strong, clear voice.

How the units work

In Units 1–2 you will learn to read the Russian alphabet, and in Units 3–10 you will learn the basic structures of the language which you will need in different situations. In Unit 11 you will learn to read the handwritten Russian script and to write it if you choose, and in Units 12–20 you will learn how to cope with practical situations in more detail.

Within each unit you will find:

- A list of things you can expect to learn.
- **Insight boxes** with tips to help you with your learning or basic background information on Russian customs and way of life relevant to the unit. You should bear in mind that in recent times there have been many changes in

Russian life and even in the language as it absorbs many new international words. You may therefore find if you visit Russia that details of everyday life have changed. This is particularly likely to be true with matters relating to the economic state of the country.

- **Key words and phrases** which will be used in the unit. Try to learn them by heart as they will help you with the rest of the unit and will often appear again later in the book. In Units 3–10, while you are getting used to the Russian alphabet, each word will have its pronunciation in English letters next to it. Try not to become dependent on this, but just use it to check any sounds you are not sure of.

- If you have the recording, listen to the dialogue **ДиалОг** once or twice to try and get the gist of it. Then use the pause button to break it up into phrases and repeat each phrase out loud to develop your accent. If you only have the book, read the dialogue through several times before you look up the words and say the phrases out loud. As you become more confident, you could cover up part of the dialogue and try to remember what to say.

- All languages work by following certain patterns, and the **Mechanics of the language** section shows you examples of the mechanics of constructing Russian. Once you have become used to the patterns you can make up sentences yourself by changing words or their endings.

- The exercises allow you to practise the language which you have just learned in the **Mechanics of the language** section. For some of the exercises you need the recording. It is important to do the exercises and to check your answers in the back of the book so that you are sure you understand the language in one unit before moving on.

- In the later units you may find a short Russian anecdote or joke.

- At the end of each unit (except for Unit 11) you will find short revision sections entitled **Test yourself**, intended to allow you to decide if you're ready to move on to the next unit.

How to succeed in learning Russian

1 Spend a little bit of time on Russian each day, rather than a marathon session once a week. It is most effective to spend no more than 20–30 minutes at a time.
2 Go back and revise words and language patterns regularly until things which seemed difficult become easier.
3 Say the words and phrases out loud and listen to the recording whenever you can.
4 Take every opportunity to use the language. Try to meet a Russian speaker or join a class to practise with other people.
5 Don't worry if you make mistakes. The most important thing is to communicate, and by jumping in at the deep end and trying things out, you may surprise yourself with how well you can make yourself understood!

Symbols and abbreviations

◀) The recording is needed for the following section.

(m) masculine   (n) neuter   (f) feminine   (pl) plural
(sing) singular

At the back of the book

At the back of the book is a reference section which contains:

- Answers
- Numbers
- A brief summary of Russian language patterns
- An English–Russian vocabulary list
- A Russian–English vocabulary list containing all the words in the course

Pronunciation guide

First, here are a few tips to help you acquire an authentic accent:

1 Listen carefully to the recording or Russian speaker, and whenever possible, repeat words and phrases loudly and clearly.
2 Make a recording of yourself and compare it with the one provided.
3 Ask a Russian speaker to listen to your pronunciation and tell you how to improve it.
4 Practise specific sounds which you find difficult.
5 Make a list of words which give you trouble and practise them.
6 Listen to Russian whenever you can, for example on the Internet, radio or podcasts. Even if you aren't concentrating or you don't understand the meaning, it will help you to become more familiar with the sounds of the language.

Russian sounds

Most English speakers can pronounce most Russian sounds without difficulty. What is more, reading Russian is often easier than reading English with its complicated spelling, e.g. *enough, plough, cough*. In Russian, what you see is more or less what you get, and if you join together the sound of the individual letters you will usually end up with the sound of the whole word. The first two units will take you through the sounds in detail, but here is a reference guide to help you.

Consonants

Б	б	b	as in *bag*
В	в	v	as in *visitor*
Г	г	g	as in *good*
Д	д	d	as in *duck*

Ж	ж	zh	as in *pleasure*
З	з	z	as in *zoo*
К	к	k	as in *kiss*
Л	л	l	as in *lane*
М	м	m	as in *moon*
Н	н	n	as in *note*
П	п	p	as in *pin*
Р	р	r	as in *rabbit*
С	с	s	as in *sit*
Т	т	t	as in *tennis*
Ф	ф	f	as in *funny*
Х	х	ch	as in *loch*
Ц	ц	ts	as in *cats*
Ч	ч	ch	as in *chicken*
Ш	ш	sh	as in *ship*
Щ	щ	shsh	as in *Spanish sherry*

When you listen to spoken Russian, you may notice that the first six consonants in the list will change their sound if they occur at the end of a word. Don't worry about this, but try to get into the habit of imitating the way that Russians speak.

Б	б	b	at the end of a word sounds like **p**
В	в	v	at the end of a word sounds like **f**
Г	г	g	at the end of a word sounds like **k**
Д	д	d	at the end of a word sounds like **t**
Ж	ж	zh	at the end of a word sounds like **sh**
З	з	z	at the end of a word sounds like **s**

Vowels

If a word has more than one syllable there will be one vowel which is pronounced more strongly than the others. This is called a stressed vowel. When vowels are stressed they are pronounced clearly and strongly. When they are in an unstressed position they are pronounced more weakly. Listen to the recording whenever possible and notice what happens to vowels in different positions as you repeat the words.

А	**a**	**a**	as in *father*
Е	**е**	**ye**	as in *yesterday*
Ё	**ё**	**yo**	as in *yonder*
И	**и**	**ee**	as in *street*
Й	**й**	**y**	as in *toy*
О	**о**	**o**	as in *born*
У	**у**	**oo**	as in *boot*
	ы		sounds rather like **i** in *ill* (say it by keeping your mouth very slightly open and drawing your tongue back as far as it will go).
Э	**э**	**e**	as in *leg*
Ю	**ю**	**yoo**	as in *universe*
Я	**я**	**ya**	as in *yard*

The soft and hard signs

ь   The soft sign has the effect of softening the preceding consonant, as if adding a soft **y** sound to it.

ъ   The hard sign is rare, is not pronounced, and makes a tiny pause between syllables.

1

....

The Russian alphabet

In this unit you will learn
- *How to read 20 letters of the Russian alphabet*
- *How to ask where something is*
- *How to show where something is*
- *How to thank someone*

Before you start

You may think that Russian will be difficult to learn because of its different alphabet, but you will probably be surprised how quickly you can learn to recognize the letters. The Russian alphabet is called the Cyrillic alphabet after the monk, St Cyril, who invented it. In order to follow this course, you will need to know how to read Russian in its printed form, so that is what you will concentrate on for the first two units. Later, in Unit 11, you will have the chance to see how Russian is written by hand. One of the good things about Russian is that words are pronounced more or less as they are written, so in that way it is easier than English with its complicated spellings.

If you have the recording, make sure you have it handy as you'll be using it to practise the pronunciation of the words. Russian has some sounds which will be new to you, but if you listen carefully and repeat the words clearly, you should soon make progress. It might be helpful to record yourself and compare what you sound like with the recording. If you don't have the recording, use the **Pronunciation guide** in the Introduction.

Remember that it is more effective to study little and often than to try and do a long session every now and then. Your concentration will probably be best in 20-minute bursts.

The Russian alphabet

The Russian alphabet has 33 letters. These can be divided into four groups of letters: those which look and sound like English letters; 'false friends' which look like English letters but sound different; a group of unfamiliar letters with familiar sounds; and those which are quite unlike English letters.

English look- and sound-alikes

◀ CD 1, TR 1, 01:37

The first group (those which look and sound like their English counterparts) contains five letters:

A	a	sounds like	a	in	*father*
T	т	sounds like	t	in	*tennis*
O	o	sounds like	o	in	*born*
M	м	sounds like	m	in	*moon*
K	к	sounds like	k	in	*kiss*

With these letters you can already read the following Russian words:

Атом	atom
мАма	mum
кот	cat

You will notice that a capital letter has been used for the first vowel, the letter a in **Атом** and **мАма**. This is to show you which syllable to emphasize in words of more than one syllable. Remember that every syllable has a vowel and it is the vowel sound that is capitalized to show you the correct stress. In English, if we capitalized every stressed syllable, it would look like this: *the piAno plAyer wants to recOrd a rEcord*. Of course you will still see capital letters as normal at the start of sentences and when showing names of people and places.

When you are speaking Russian, put lots of energy into the stressed syllable and pronounce it clearly. The vowels in unstressed syllables are underplayed and do not need to be pronounced so clearly. For example, in the syllable before the stress, **o** will sound like **a** in *father*, and in any other position it will sound like **a** in *asleep*. You will soon get used to where the stress falls on words which you use often, but to help you the stress will be shown throughout the book. When you are reading real Russian text you won't know which syllable to stress, but don't worry. You will probably be understood, even if you get it wrong.

False friends

◆》 CD 1, TR 1, 02:01

The next group of letters contains seven letters:

C	**c**	sounds like	**s**	in	*sit*	
P	**p**	sounds like	**r**	in	*rabbit*	
E	**e**	sounds like	**ye**	in	*yesterday* (when unstressed, like **yi** or **i**)
B	**в**	sounds like	**v**	in	*visitor*	
H	**н**	sounds like	**n**	in	*note*	
Y	**y**	sounds like	**oo**	in	*boot*	
X	**x**	sounds like	**ch**	in	*loch* (Scots)

Reading practice

To practise the 12 letters which you have now met, see if you can read the words in the following exercises. They are mostly international words, so you should recognize them without too much difficulty. When you have done this, listen to them on the recording if you have it, and repeat them. Then try reading them again without looking at the English meaning until you can say them easily.

1 First, we have five cities. See if you can match them up with their English names.

◀) CD 1, TR 1, 02:17

If you decide that **a** is Tomsk, write **a ii**. You can check the answers in the back of your book. Don't forget to say the words out loud.

a Томск **b ТорОнто** **c ВЕна** **d Омск** **e МУрманск**

i *Vienna* **ii** *Tomsk* **iii** *Murmansk* **iv** *Toronto* **v** *Omsk*

2 Now try to identify these five Russian names.

◀) CD 1, TR 1, 02:36

a СвЕта **b АнтОн** **c ВЕра** **d РомАн** **e Анна**

i *Anna* **ii** *Vera* **iii** *Sveta* **iv** *Anton* **v** *Roman*

3 Imagine you are walking around Moscow and you see the following places signposted. What are they?

◀) CD 1, TR 1, 02:50

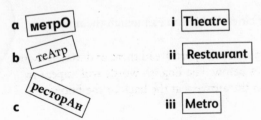

a метрО   i **Theatre**

b теАтр   ii **Restaurant**

c ресторАн   iii **Metro**

4 A Russian friend gives you a shopping list. What do you need to buy?

◀) CD 1, TR 1, 03:04

a сОус	i cocoa
b какАо	ii sauce
c сАхар	iii rum
d ром	iv sugar

If you have managed to read these words out loud and have practised them until you are fairly confident, you are ready to move on to another group of letters.

Unfamiliar letters with familiar sounds

◀) CD 1, TR 1, 03:20

The next group of letters contains 13 new letters. To make it easier, you are going to meet only five of them to begin with.

П	п	sounds like	p	in	*pin*
Л	л	sounds like	l	in	*lane*
И	и	sounds like	ee	in	*street*
З	з	sounds like	z	in	*zoo*
Д	д	sounds like	d	in	*duck*

Now see if you can read words containing the 17 letters you have met so far. Remember to say them all out loud, and check your pronunciation with the recording if you have it.

Reading practice

5 These words are to do with sport. Read them and match them up with the pictures below. The English words will appear in the correct order in the answers at the back of the book.

◀) **CD 1, TR 1, 03:29**

тЕннис   снУкер   стадиОн   крИкет

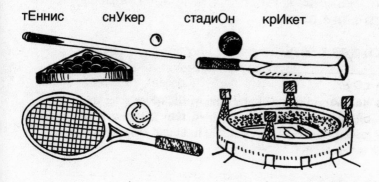

Now match up the remaining words about sport with the English words below.

старт	нокАут	трЕнер	рекОрд
атлЕтика	спорт	спортсмЕн	
record	*knockout*	*sport*	*trainer*
start	*sportsman*	*athletics*	

6 Next, can you identify the names of the nine cities around the world? Draw lines linking the Russian and English names.

◀) **CD 1, TR 1, 03:57**

a Минск	**i** *Moscow*
b МосквА	**ii** *Samarkand*
c АмстердАм	**iii** *Tokyo*
d КИев	**iv** *London*
e ТОкио	**v** *Madrid*
f ЛОндон	**vi** *Minsk*
g ОдЕсса	**vii** *Kiev*
h МадрИд	**viii** *Amsterdam*
i СамаркАнд	**ix** *Odessa*

7 Match up these four words connected with travel and transport with their English equivalents below

🔊 **CD 1, TR 1, 04:23**

вИза	трАктор	пАспорт	таксИ
taxi	*passport*	*tractor*	*visa*

8 In this grid you will find nine words which refer to occupations or leisure activities. They are written in capital letters. Read them out loud and pronounce them clearly.

🔊 **CD 1, TR 1, 04:36**

Д	И	П	Л	О	М	А	Т					
						У			Д			
						Р			О		Т	
				Х	И	М	И	К	Т		Р	
						С			О		А	
К	О	С	М	О	Н	А	В	Т			К	
	Т							О			Т	
	У							Р			О	
А	Д	М	И	Н	И	С	Т	Р	А	Т	О	Р
	Е										Р	
	Н										И	
	Т					К	А	П	И	Т	А	Н

14

Here they are again in lower-case letters. You will notice that in their printed form, most Russian capital letters are just bigger versions of lower-case letters. Check their meanings against the list in English, which again is in the wrong order.

дипломАт турИст космонАвт хИмик студЕнт
администрАтор дОктор трактОрист капитАн
administrator captain diplomat doctor student (male)
tractor driver tourist cosmonaut chemist

9 Below is a list of ten Russian names, five for men and five for women. The women's names are the ones ending in -a. See if you can read them all out loud, and underline the feminine ones.

◄》 CD 1, TR 1, 05:04

ИвАн НИна АлексАндр ВладИмир ЕкатерИна
ЛИза Лев ИрИна ВалентИн ЛарИса

10 You overhear a conversation between **ВЕра** (VyEra) and **АлексАндр** (AlexAnder). **ВЕра** cannot find her friend, and asks **АлексАндр** if he knows where she is. Listen to the conversation and repeat it. Otherwise, read it out loud. You will hear three unfamiliar words.

◄》 CD 1, TR 1, 05:27

где?	pronounced	gdye	*where is?*
вот	pronounced	vot	*there is*
спасИбо	pronounced	spasEEba	*thank you*

ВЕра	АлексАндр, где ИрИна?
АлексАндр	Вот ИрИна.
ВЕра	СпасИбо, АлексАндр.

11 Your next set of words is all to do with science. See if you can read them. Don't look at their meanings in English until you have finished.

◀) CD 1, TR 1, 05:42

Атом комЕта метеОр клИмат механИзм микроскОп
спУтник килО литр планЕта лунА киломЕтр
*kilo microscope sputnik comet litre atom kilometre
planet mechanism moon meteor climate*

12 Now see if you can recognize these pieces of technical equipment. There is one word in this list which doesn't belong. Underline it, and don't forget to pronounce all the words clearly. Cover up the English version until you have tried to read the Russian.

◀) CD 1, TR 1, 06:12

QUICK VOCAB	

телевИзор	*radio*
кассЕта	*printer*
монитОр	*television*
кинокАмера	*cassette*
лимонАд	*cine camera*
рАдио	*monitor*
прИнтер	*lemonade*

Unfamiliar letters with familiar sounds — three more!

◀) CD 1, TR 1, 06:37

Once you are confident reading the 17 letters you have met so far, you are ready to learn three more from the group of unfamiliar letters with familiar sounds.

Ф	ф	sounds like	f	in	*funny*
Ю	ю	sounds like	yoo	in	*universe*
Г	г	sounds like	g	in	*good*

Reading practice

13 Here are some signs which might help you as you walk around a Russian town if you do not have a **план** (plan) a town plan. Match them up with their English meanings. Remember that they would not normally have a capital letter to show where the stress is.

◀)) CD 1, TR 1, 06:45

stadium park Internet café telephone casino kiosk zoo sauna café institute antiques grocer's (gastronom) university

парк   киОск   гастронОм

зоопАрк   стадиОн   кафЕ

сАуна   телефОн   институт   казинО

интернЕт-кафЕ   университЕт   антиквариАт

14 Nina is always getting lost. She supports the football team **ДинАмо** (DeenAmo) and she is looking for the stadium. If you have the recording, listen to the conversation and repeat it. If not, try to read it out loud.

НИна	ИвАн, где стадиОн?
ИвАн	СтадиОн? Вот стадиОн.
НИна	А, вот стадиОн. СпасИбо, ИвАн.

◀ CD 1, TR 1, 07:23

When Nina says «**А**» it is like saying *Aah* in English.

15 You are visiting friends in their flat (**квартИра** kvartEEra) in a block of flats (**дом** dom). You hear them mention the following domestic objects as they show you around. Try to read them out loud before looking at the English equivalents to check the meaning.

◄) **CD 1, TR 1, 07:45**

лАмпа стул коридОр дивАн мИксер вАза
тОстер газ лифт

gas corridor lamp mixer vase toaster lift
sofa (divan) chair

16 As you listen carefully to their conversation, you hear the following words and realize they are interested in music.

◄) **CD 1, TR 1, 08:16**

саксофОн композИтор гитАра пианИно оркЕстр
солИст Опера пианИст компАкт-дИск
хЕви металл-рОк

piano opera composer pianist saxophone
compact disc orchestra guitar soloist
heavy metal rock

17 You are in a concert hall when you hear a pianist asking his colleague, the composer, for help in finding something. Repeat the conversation. What has the pianist lost?

◄) CD1, TR 1, 08:42

ПианИст	ВладИмир, где пианИно?
КомпозИтор	ПианИно? Где, где пианИно? А, вот пианИно, ВалентИн!
ПианИст	А, вот пианИно! СпасИбо.

18 Now you are in a restaurant looking at a menu. Work out what is on it and underline the drinks. Read out the whole list as if you were giving your order to the waiter. The menu is below.

◆ CD 1, TR 1, 09:24

МенЮ	
омлЕт	салАт
вИски	фрукт
кОфе	мЮсли
котлЕта	винО
Пепси-кОла	суп министрОне

Pepsi-cola   muesli   salad   coffee   wine   minestrone soup
whisky   omelette   cutlet (flat meatball)   fruit

Congratulations! You can now read 20 letters of the Cyrillic alphabet, and you have only 13 more to learn. Before you move on, read back over all the Russian words you have met and say them out loud without looking at the English. Check your pronunciation with the recording if you have it. Then read the English words and see if you can remember them in Russian. Don't worry if you don't get them all exactly right.

TEST YOURSELF

Now here are ten questions to see if you feel confident with what you have learned. Take your time and look back over the unit if you need to.

1 How many letters does the Russian alphabet have?

2 Which five Russian letters look and sound the same as their English counterparts?

3 What is the English name of this city? ЛОндон

4 What does this word mean? РесторАн

5 What is the English equivalent of this Russian name? НИна

6 What does где mean? It is a question word.

7 What would you do with лимонАд?

8 What would you do at a стадиОн?

9 What would you do with a гитАра?

10 Where would you find a менЮ?

Well done! Now you really are ready to move on to Unit 2 where you will learn to read the rest of the whole alphabet. Good luck!

2

The remainder of the alphabet

In this unit you will learn
- *How to read the remaining 13 letters of the Russian alphabet*
- *How to say you don't know*
- *How to ask who someone is*
- *How to say 'no'*

Before you start

Make sure that you can read and say all the Russian words in Unit 1. Remember to use the recording if you have it, and say each new word out loud to practise your pronunciation.

More letters and sounds

You already know these 20 letters of the Russian alphabet:

- those which look and sound like English letters: **а т о м к**
- the 'false friends' which look like English letters but sound different: **с р е в н у х**
- and the unfamiliar letters with familiar sounds: **п л и з д ф ю г**

Unfamiliar letters with familiar sounds — the last five

There are still five letters to learn in the group of unfamiliar letters with familiar sounds, and we will begin with these.

Б	б	sounds like	b	in	*bag*
Э	э	sounds like	e	in	*leg*
Й	й	sounds like	y	in	*toy*
Ё	ё	sounds like	yo	in	*yonder*
Я	я	sounds like	ya	in	*yak* (except in the syllable before the stress, when it sounds like *yi*.)

The letter **я** on its own means *I*, so that is another word to add to your repertoire! To practise these new letters along with those you already know, see if you can read the words in the following exercises. Try to work out what they mean before you look at the English meanings. If you have the recording, listen to the words and repeat them carefully. Remember to emphasize each syllable which has a stress mark. Wherever **ё** appears in a word, that syllable will always be stressed.

Reading practice

1 First try matching up these cities with their English names.

a БерлИн		**i**	*Sofia*
b Ялта		**ii**	*Baghdad*
c Санкт-ПетербУрг		**iii**	*Berlin*
d СофИя		**iv**	*St Petersburg*
e БухарЕст		**v**	*Bucharest*
f БагдАд		**vi**	*Yalta*

You can check the answers in the back of your book.

2 All these words are to do with travel and transport. Write the correct letter next to each English word to show that you have understood.

◀》 CD 1, TR 2, 00:40

a	стюардЕсса		*trolleybus*
b	платфОрма		*airport*
c	экскУрсия		*signal*
d	автОбус		*express*
e	трамвАй		*stewardess*
f	аэропОрт		*Aeroflot*
g	экспрЕсс		*platform*
h	сигнАл		*tram*
i	АэрофлОт		*excursion*
j	троллЕйбус		*bus*

3 If you want to read the sports pages of a Russian newspaper, here are some words which will be useful. Match them up with the English words that follow.

◀》 CD 1, TR 2, 01:11

футбОл	волейбОл	бадминтОн
марафОн	*Армрестлинг*	*бокс*
гимнАстика	пинг-пОнг	**сЕрфинг**
финАл	рЕгби	**пэйнтбОл**
хоккЕй	баскетбОл	*бОдибилдинг*

rugby *marathon* *boxing* *volleyball* *football* *ice hockey*
basketball *final* *surfing* *badminton* *ping-pong* *arm-
wrestling* *bodybuilding* *gymnastics* *paintball*

4 You are visiting your music-loving Russian friends again. This time their conversation is about music, theatre and books, and you hear them mention the following words. Try to read them out loud before looking at the English words to check their meaning.

🔊 **CD 1, TR 2, 01:47**

симфОния	балерИна	поЭт	актрИса
бестсЕллер	актЁр	балЕт	трИллер
best-seller	*actress*	*ballet*	*symphony*
ballerina	*thriller*	*poet*	*actor*

5 You pick up a magazine about science, and work out the following words.

🔊 **CD 1, TR 2, 02:18**

энЕргия	киловАтт	атмосфЕра
килогрАмм	электрОника	эксперимЕнт
kilogram	*experiment*	*atmosphere*
energy	*kilowatt*	*electronics*

6 Your friends have an atlas, and you browse through it recognizing these names.

🔊 **CD 1, TR 2, 02:40**

АмЕрика	МЕксика	Африка	ПакистАн
АргентИна	Англия	РоссИя	УкраИна
КанАда	Индия	АвстрАлия	НорвЕгия
Argentina	*Mexico*	*Russia*	*Australia*
America	*Norway*	*England*	*Ukraine*
Canada	*Pakistan*	*India*	*Africa*

7 You play a game with their little girl, **ЛЕна** (LyEna). You ask her where certain countries are on a world map and she shows you. Occasionally she doesn't know and then she says:

Я не знАю (Ya nye znAyoo) *I don't know.*

Listen to the conversation or read it out loud.

CD 1, TR 2, 03:15

·You	ЛЕна, где КанАда?
ЛЕна	КанАда? Вот КанАда.
You	Где РоссИя?
ЛЕна	Вот РоссИя, и вот МосквА.
You	Где Англия?
ЛЕна	Англия? Я не знАю. Где Англия?
You	Вот Англия, и вот ЛОндон.

Did you work out what **и** means?

и   (ee) *and*

The last eight letters and sounds

◀ CD 1, TR 2, 03:45

Once you are happy with those new letters you are ready to move on to learn the remaining eight letters of the Russian alphabet, which are quite unlike English letters. The first five letters of this group make sounds which will be familiar to you, but in English you would need more than one letter to show the whole sound.

Ж	ж	sounds like	zh	as in	*pleasure*
Ц	ц	sounds like	ts	as in	*cats*
Ч	ч	sounds like	ch	as in	*chicken*
Ш	ш	sounds like	sh	as in	*ship*
Щ	щ	sounds like	shsh	as in	*Spanish sherry*

The last three letters of the group never occur at the beginning of a word. They are:

ы sounds rather like **i** in *ill*, but with the tongue further back in the mouth

ь is a 'soft sign' which adds a soft 'y' sound to the letter before it. Think of how you would pronounce the **p** in *pew*. When you see a Russian word written using English letters in this book, a soft sign will be indicated by an apostrophe '. So, for example, the word for computer **компьЮтер** will be written **kamp'yOOter**.

ъ is a 'hard sign'. This is very rare, and makes a tiny pause between syllables.

Now you have met all the letters of the Russian alphabet. The Russian alphabet is shown in its correct order in your **Alphabet guide** in Unit 7. Remember that Russian spelling and pronunciation are simpler than English, and if you just join together every letter in a word you will come fairly close to pronouncing it correctly. Now have a go at reading some more words in which any letter of the alphabet may appear! Good luck!

Reading practice

8 Imagine you are walking around the centre of Moscow. You see these signs outside some of the buildings. What are they?

◆) **CD 1, TR 2, 04:25**

a бар   **b** МелОдия   **c** ПИцца Хат   **d** музЕй   **e** цирк   **f** банк
g библиотЕка   **h** Кремль   **i** пОчта   **j** БольшОй теАтр

9 Signs outside some other buildings tell you what you can find inside. Match the signs and the English words.

◀) CD 1, TR 2, 04:52

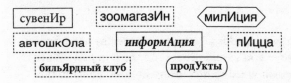

сувенИр	зоомагазИн	милИция
автошкОла	информАция	пИцца
бильЯрдный клуб	продУкты	

information   souvenirs   pet shop   pizza   driving school
provisions   militia (police)   billiard club

10 Traditional Russian cookery is delicious, and includes such
dishes as **борщ** (borshsh) which is beetroot soup, and **щи**
(shshee) which is cabbage soup. They are often served with
bread **хлеб** (khlyep) and sour cream **сметАна** (smitAna).
ВОдка (vOtka) vodka is a traditional Russian drink, and **чай**
(chai) tea is also frequently drunk, usually without milk and
sometimes with a slice of lemon. However, many Russians
enjoy Western-style food as well. See if you can match the
words with the pictures.

◀) CD 1, TR 2, 05:23

a чИзбургер   **b** банАн   **c** кОфе каппучИно
d пИцца сУпер супрИм

11 Many words to do with the world of work are also familiar. What are these?

◀ CD 1, TR 2, 05:54

a мЕнеджер **b** факс **c** брИфинг **d** мАркетинг
e флОппи диск **f** бизнесмЕн **g** нОу-хау **h** брОкер
i уИк-энд **j** компьЮтер **k** нОутбук

12 Here is a family portrait. It has been labelled for you. Can you read who everyone is?

◀ CD 1, TR 2, 06:31

бАбушка   кот   дЕдушка   мАма   пАпа   сын   дочь

Pointing to the picture and speaking out loud, answer the following questions. (In answer to the first one you would say: «Вот мАма».)

Где мАма?	Где дочь?
Где сын?	Где дЕдушка?
Где бАбушка?	Где кот?
Где пАпа?	

The children are described in Russian as **сын** (syn) *son* and **дочь** (doch') *daughter*. You could also describe them as **брат** (brat) *brother* and **сестрА** (sistrA) *sister*.

13 Just as many English words are familiar to Russians, names of many famous Russians are familiar to us. Can you work out who these people are?

◀)) **CD 1, TR 2, 07:08**

Writers	*Composers*	*Political leaders*
a ЧЕхов	d ЧайкОвский	g ЛЕнин
b ТолстОй	e РахмАнинов	h Горбачёв
c ПУшкин	f ШостакОвич	i Ельцин

Writers: i *Pushkin* ii *Tolstoy* iii *Chekhov*
Composers: i *Rachmaninov* ii *Tchaikovsky* iii *Shostakovich*
Political leaders: i *Lenin* ii *Yeltsin* iii *Gorbachev*

14 For your last alphabet reading exercise, imagine you have to visit the doctor in Russia. Let's hope it never happens, but if it does here are some words which might prove useful:

◀)) **CD 1, TR 2, 07:37**

a температУра **b** бактЕрия **c** антибиОтик **d** массАж
e таблЕтка **f** диАгноз **g** пенициллИн **h** инфЕкция

Well done! You have managed to read words containing any letter of the Russian alphabet except for the hard sign **ъ**. That is because it is so rare, but just for good luck, here is a word which contains a hard sign: **объЕкт** (ob-yEkt) *object*. So now there is nothing which can surprise you! With every new word, just say each sound in order, emphasizing the stressed syllable, and you should be pronouncing it well enough for a Russian to understand you.

Mechanics of the language

Now that you can pronounce Russian and feel confident with the sounds, you'll be glad to know that it is a logical language and that all you need to make up your own sentences is an understanding of the patterns of the language. Before learning any more words and phrases, here are some key points on starting to use those patterns. While some things may seem to be more complicated than English, some things are definitely easier.

1 'The' and 'a'

The good news is that there are no words in Russian for *the* or *a*. So студЕнт means either *the student* or *a student*.

2 'To be'

More good news! In Russian the verb 'to be' is not used when you are talking about things happening now. So you do not need to learn to say *I am, you are, he is* and so on. In English you would say *I am a businessman*, but in Russian this is simply Я – бизнесмЕн, literally *I businessman*. This may sound like Tarzan speaking, but don't worry, it is real Russian. So if you hear АнтОн – студЕнт, it means *Anton is a student*. Note that written Russian may use a dash to replace the verb 'to be'.

3 *Gender of nouns*

A noun is a word that names someone or something: **мЕнеджер** *manager*, **ЛарИса** *Larisa*, **РоссИя** *Russia*, **автОбус** *bus*, **кот** *cat*, **электрОника** *electronics*. Russian nouns are divided randomly into three groups called 'gender groups': masculine, feminine and neuter. Later it will be helpful to know which group a noun belongs to. As you might expect, **бизнесмЕн** *businessman* is masculine and **балерИна** *ballerina* is feminine, but even non-living things in Russian have a gender. The good thing is that you do not have to memorize which gender each noun has. You can tell simply by looking at the ending. Here are the most common endings.

Masculine
Most masculine nouns end in a consonant or -**й**. (Look at your **Pronunciation guide** if you are not sure what a consonant is.) So **стадиОн** *stadium*, **чИзбургер** *cheeseburger*, **ЛОндон** *London*, and **дом** *house* or *block of flats* are all masculine. So are **музЕй** *museum*, and **трамвАй** *tram*.

Feminine
Most feminine nouns end in -**а** or -**я**. So **шкОла** *school*, **ОдЕсса** Odessa, **Англия** *England*, and **энЕргия** *energy* are all feminine. If you meet a word like **студЕнтка** which ends in -**а**, you know that this must be a female student. A male student, as you know, is **студЕнт**. (There are exceptions to this rule, e.g. **пАпа** *Dad* which ends in -**а** but which is masculine because of its meaning.)

Neuter
Most neuter nouns end in -**о** or -**е**. So **метрО** *metro*, **винО** *wine* and **кафЕ** *café* are all neuter.

Soft sign ь

There is also a small group of nouns ending in a soft sign ь. These may be either masculine or feminine, and you have to learn which gender they are. **Кремль** (Kryeml') *Kremlin* is masculine and **медАль** (medAl') *medal* is feminine. **Дочь** *daughter* is, of course, feminine. Every time you meet a new noun ending in ь it will have (*m*) or (*f*) next to it to show you whether it is masculine or feminine.

To summarize:

Masculine nouns end in	a consonant	парк
	й	музЕй
	ь	Кремль
Feminine nouns end in	**а**	студЕнтка
	я	энЕргия
	ь	дочь
Neuter nouns end in	**о**	метрО
	е	кафЕ

Exercises

15 Listen to the recording to find out what jobs people do. Match up the numbers and the letters. So if you think Nina is an actress write *a iv*.

◄)) CD 1, TR 2, 08:01

a	НИна	**i**	бизнесмЕн
b	АлексАндр	**ii**	поЭт
c	Анна	**iii**	администрАтор
d	ВладИмир	**iv**	актрИса
e	БорИс	**v**	стюардЕсса

16 Look at the following pictures and make up a sentence about each person, using the words in brackets. For example, **ЛарИса – студЕнтка** (*Larisa is a student*).

Игорь   ЛарИса   АнтОн   НатАша   БорИс

(теннисИст, студЕнтка, футболИст, балерИна, турИст)

17 НатАша is at a party. She is rather short-sighted so she asks ЛарИса for help in spotting her friends. But ЛарИса doesn't know them all. In this conversation you will meet two new words:

Кто? (Kto?) *Who?*

Нет (Nyet) *No*

НатАша	ЛарИса, где АнтОн?
ЛарИса	АнтОн? Кто АнтОн?
НатАша	АнтОн – студЕнт.
ЛарИса	А, вот АнтОн.
НатАша	СпасИбо, ЛарИса. Где Анна?
ЛарИса	Анна? Кто Анна? АктрИса?
НатАша	Нет. Анна – балерИна.
ЛарИса	БалерИна? А, вот Анна.

CD 1, TR 2, 08:28

18 Read this list of words and decide which are masculine, feminine and neuter. Write (m), (f) or (n) in the brackets at the side to show their gender.

a Атом	( )	**c** салАт	( )	**e** АмЕрика	( )
b платфОрма	( )	**d** пианИно	( )	**f** теАтр	( )
g трамвАй	( )	**i** кинО	( )	**k** волейбОл	( )
h информАция	( )	**j** дочь	( )	**l** винО	( )

19 These words are grouped according to gender, but there is one word in each group which has the wrong gender. Find the odd one out in each group and underline it.

Masculine	Feminine	Neuter
суп	гитАра	метрО
Кремль	Англия	кафЕ
план	медАль	рАдио
пАспорт	вОдка	саксофОн
сестрА	стадиОн	какАо
трамвАй	шкОла	пианИно

20 You are in a restaurant ordering three items. Can you find them hidden in the string of letters below?

абресуптономлетхалисалаткуд

Which gender are all three things which you ordered?

21 See if you can decipher these jumbled words using the clues. The first letter of each word is in bold print. They are all feminine.

a тасре**с** (a relative)
b фими**с**оян (orchestral music)
c г**А**нетиран (a country)
d аке**б**итбило (a place for bookworms)
e урме**т**ерпата (this is high if you are feverish)

Did you know that you can already say and read more than 350 words in Russian? When you are confident that you understand everything in these first two units, you are ready to move on to Unit 3.

TEST YOURSELF

But first, try this short test to make quite sure you are ready.

1 How do you pronounce the individual letters ч, б, я?

2 What is the name of this country in English? АвстрАлия

3 What does this mean? Я не знАю

4 Who is дЕдушка?

5 How many genders of nouns are there in Russian?

6 If a noun ends in the letter a, which gender is it?

7 Which gender is the word трамвАй?

8 Which gender is the word винО?

9 What does this mean? БорИс – мЕнеджер.

10 What does this mean? Кто Это?

Well done! You may not be sure yet why you need to know the gender of nouns, but it will make things easier later on so be patient! Now you are ready to move on to Unit 3, where you will start trying out real conversations.

3

ДОбрый день!
Good day!

In this unit you will learn
- *How to say 'hello' and 'goodbye'*
- *How to greet and address someone*
- *How to say you don't understand*
- *How to ask if anyone speaks English*

Before you start

It is very important for you to read the **Introduction** to the course. This gives some useful advice on studying alone and how to make the most of the course. If you are working with the recording, keep it handy as you will need it for the **Key words** and **Dialogue** sections. If you don't have the recording, use the **Pronunciation guide** in the Introduction.

Insight
Russian names

If you have ever seen a Russian play or read a Russian book in English you will have noticed that one Russian person may appear to have many names. Actually, Russians have three names each.

Their first name **Имя** (EEmya) is their given name, for example, **ИвАн** (EevAn) or **НИна** (NEEna). Then they have a 'patronymic' name, **Отчество** (Ochistvo). This is formed from their father's first name plus a special ending: **-ович** (oveech) or **-евич** (yeveech) for boys and **-овна** (ovna) or **-евна** (yevna) for girls. Finally they have a family name, **фамИлия** (famEEliya), which has the same function as our surname. So you would be able to work out that **ВладИмир ИвАнович КозлОв** (VladEEmir EevAnovich KazlOf) had a father called **ИвАн** (EevAn), and **ЕлЕна АлексАндровна ПопОва** (IlyEna AliksAndrovna PapOva) had a father called **АлексАндр** (AliksAndr). Notice that the man's name has masculine endings (consonants) and the woman's name has feminine endings (**-а**).

QUICK VOCAB

Имя	EEmya	*given name*
Отчество	Ochistvo	*patronymic*
фамИлия	famEEliya	*family name*

How to address Russians

Adult Russians who are on formal terms may call each other by their first name and patronymic. This is a mark of respect, and young people may address older people in this way, for example, a schoolchild may address a teacher as **ГалИна МихАйловна** (GalEEna MikhAilovna). In Soviet times, another official form of address was **товАрищ** (tavArishsh) *comrade*, used either with the surname or on its own to address someone whose name was not known. Nowadays, **товАрищ** has lost popularity and the pre-Revolutionary **господИн** (guspadEEn) *sir* and **госпожА** (guspazhA) *madam* have reappeared. Sometimes people use the words **мужчИна** (mooshchEEna) *man* and **жЕнщина** (zhEnshsheena) *woman* to address strangers. The phrase *ladies and gentlemen* in Russian is **ДАмы и господА** (dAmy i guspadA). If you want to address an audience you will say **уважАемые дАмы и господА** (uvazhAemye dAmy i guspadA) *respected ladies and gentlemen.*

Adult Russians who are close friends will call each other by their first name, and children will usually be addressed by their first name. People on first-name terms will often use 'diminutive' forms. This is like using Mike for Michael or Annie for Annabel, but each Russian name has lots of possible diminutives. For example, **ЕлЕна** (IlyEna) might be called **ЛЕна** (LyEna) for short, **ЛЕночка** (LyEnuchka) or **ЛенУся** (LyinOOsya) affectionately, **ЛенОк** (LyinOk) jokingly, **ЛЕнка** (LyEnka) perhaps by an angry parent, and more rarely but affectionately, **Алёна** (AlyOna) and **Алёнушка** (AlyOnooshka).

ДиалОг 1 Dialogue 1

ДОброе Утро	DObroye OOtra	*Good morning*
ДОбрый день	DObry dyen'	*Good day*
ДОбрый вЕчер	DObry vyEcher	*Good evening*
ЗдрАвствуйте	ZdrAstvooeetyi	*Hello*
До свидАния	Da sveedAnya	*Goodbye*

ДиалОг 2 Dialogue 2

МенЯ зовУт	MinyA zavOOt	*I am called*
Очень приЯтно	Ochen' preeyAtna	*Pleased to meet you (literally: very pleasant)*
Как вас зовУт?	Kak vas zavOOt?	*What are you called?*
Как делА?	Kak dyilA?	*How are things?*
хорошО	khurashO	*good, well*

ДиалОг 3 Dialogue 3

извинИте	eezveenEEtye	*excuse me/I'm sorry*
молодОй человЕк	maladOy chilavyEk	*young man*
вы	vy	*you*
нет	nyet	*no*
я	ya	*I*
не	nye	*not*
дЕвушка	dyEvushka	*young woman/miss*
да	da	*yes*

ДиалОг 4 Dialogue 4

Я не понимАю	Ya nye paneemAyoo	*I don't understand*
МЕдленнее, пожАлуйста	MyEdlyn-ye-ye, pazhAloosta	*slower, please*
Вы говорИте по-англИйски?	Vy gavarEEtye pa-anglEEsky?	*Do you speak English?*
Я говорЮ по-рУсски	плОхоYa gavaryOO pa-rOOsky plOkha	*I speak Russian badly*

Dialogues

Listen to the dialogues on the recording, or read them through several times until you feel comfortable with them. Pretend to be one of the people in each dialogue and try to memorize what they say. Pause the recording and say your part out loud. Then check your pronunciation with the recording or with the pronunciation given in the **Quick vocab** box. If you are not working with a recording, remember to emphasize the stressed syllables and to underplay the unstressed ones.

ДИАЛОГ 1 Dialogue 1

In this dialogue people are greeting each other and saying 'goodbye' in Russian at different times of day.

ВИктор	ДОброе Утро, НатАша.
НатАша	ДОброе Утро, ВИктор.
БорИс	ДОбрый день, Анна.
Анна	ДОбрый день, БорИс.
СвЕта	ДОбрый вЕчер, ЛЕна.
ЛЕна	ДОбрый вЕчер, СвЕта.
ИрИна	ЗдрАвствуйте!
АнтОн	ЗдрАвствуйте!
ТАня	До свидАния, ИвАн.
ИвАн	До свидАния, ТАня.

CD 1, TR 3, 00:17

Now cover up the text and see if you can remember how to say:

a good morning **b** good evening **c** hello **d** good day **e** goodbye.

ДИАЛОГ 2 *Dialogue 2*

◀)) **CD 1, TR 3, 01:40**

In this dialogue Igor and Alison meet and introduce themselves.

Igor	**Alison**
ДОбрый вЕчер. МенЯ зовУт Игорь.	Очень приЯтно.
Как вас зовУт?	МенЯ зовУт Алисон.
Очень приЯтно. Как делА, Алисон?	ХорошО, спасИбо.

Practise the dialogue, then imagine that you are Alison. Cover up the right-hand side of the dialogue. Say you are pleased to meet Igor, and answer his questions. Now cover up the left-hand side and practise Igor's part of the conversation.

ДИАЛОГ 3 *Dialogue 3*

In connection with an advert about a flat, Volodya has arranged to meet a young man called Sasha and his girlfriend Nastya outside a metro station. (Incidentally, **ВолОдя** is a diminutive of **ВладИмир**, **САша** is a diminutive of **АлексАндр** and **НАстя** is a diminutive of **АнастАсия**.) Read their conversation carefully.

ВолОдя	ИзвинИте, молодОй человЕк, вы САша?
МИша	Нет, я не САша.
ВолОдя	ИзвинИте. . . . ДЕвушка, вы не НАстя?
ВЕра	НАстя? Нет, я не НАстя.
ВолОдя	ИзвинИте, вы САша и НАстя?
САша и НАстя	Да. Вы ВолОдя?
ВолОдя	Да, я ВолОдя. Очень приЯтно, САша. Очень приЯтно, НАстя.

CD 1, TR 3, 02:45

Repeat the dialogue, and check that you know how to say *excuse me* or *sorry*, and how to address an unknown young man or woman.

ДИАЛОГ 4 *Dialogue 4*

In the second dialogue in this unit, Alison managed to understand what Igor said to her. Andrew is not quite so lucky and has a few problems understanding a new acquaintance at a party.

НиколАй	ЗдрАвствуйте.
Andrew	ЗдрАвствуйте.
НиколАй	Как вас зовУт?
Andrew	МЕдленнее, пожАлуйста.
НиколАй	Как вас зовУт?
Andrew	ИзвинИте, я не понимАю.
НиколАй	Как вас зовУт? МенЯ зовУт НиколАй ПетрОвич. Как вас зовУт?
Andrew	А, менЯ зовУт Андрю. Вы говорИте по-англИйски?
НиколАй	Да, я говорЮ по-англИйски.
Andrew	Oh good! ХорошО! Я плОхо понимАю по-рУсски.

CD 1, TR 3, 03:36

Practise the dialogue several times until you are happy with the new words.

Mechanics of the language

1 *Two ways of saying 'you'*

In Russian, as in many languages, there are two different words
for *you*. English used to have two words – *you* and *thou* – but
now we nearly always use *you*. The two Russian words are **вы**
(vy) and **ты** (ty). **Вы** is used whenever you are speaking to more
than one person, or to an adult with whom you are on formal or
polite terms. **Ты** is used whenever you are speaking informally to
one person only. So you would nearly always use **ты** to address
a child or a close friend or relation. (Let your Russian friends
decide whether to use **вы** or **ты** with you. The younger generation
often prefer the less formal **ты** while older people may feel more
comfortable using **вы** even when they have known you for years.)

There are also two ways of saying *hello*, depending on whether
you call someone **вы** or **ты**. If you are talking to more than one
person or formally to one adult, you say **здрАвствуйте** as you have
already learned, but if you are talking to a child, close friend or
relative, you say **здрАвствуй**, missing off the last two letters. So, if
you picked up the phone and heard your Russian boss calling, you
might say: **ЗдрАвствуйте, ВладИмир ИвАнович. Где вы?** *Hello,
VladEEmir EevAnuvich. Where are you?*

If, on the other hand, it was your long-lost friend, you would say:
ЗдрАвствуй, ЛЕна. Где ты? *Hello, LyEna. Where are you?*

2 *Asking questions*

A statement can easily be turned into a question in Russian simply
by varying the rise and fall of your voice. If you make a statement
in Russian, your voice should fall:

ИвАн – студЕнт. *Ivan is a student.*

If you want to make the statement into a question, your voice should rise:

ИвАн – студЕнт? *Is Ivan a student?*

If the question contains a question word, like *who? what? where? why? when? how?* then your voice should rise on the question word itself:

Как делА? *How are things?*

3 *To do or not to do*

You have already met people saying that they can and can't do things, and you have probably noticed the little word **не** (nye) which means *not*. In Unit 2, little **ЛЕна** said **Я не знАю** *I don't know*. In the last dialogue, Andrew said **Я не понимАю** *I don't understand*. **НиколАй** told him: **Я говорЮ по-англИйски** *I speak English*. So you can work out that:

Я знАю	Ya znAyoo	means	*I know*
Я понимАю	Ya paneemAyoo	means	*I understand*
Я говорЮ	Ya gavaryOO	means	*I speak*

If you want to say that you can't do any of these things, simply slip **не** *not* between **я** and the word which says what you are doing.

Я не знАю	*I don't know*
Я не понимАю	*I don't understand*
Я не говорЮ	*I don't speak*

The action words *to know, to understand, to speak* may be described as verbs. If you want to say that you do any of these things well or badly, slip **хорошО** *well* or **плОхо** *badly* between **я** and the verb.

Я хорошО знАю Алисон	*I know Alison well*
Я хорошО понимАю Андрю	*I understand Andrew well*
Я плОхо говорЮ по-рУсски	*I speak Russian badly*

By the end of the course you should be able to say truthfully *I speak Russian well*. Why not try it out now! **Я хорошО говорЮ по-рУсски.**

4 Who's who?

You already know how to say *I* (**я**) and *you* (**ты** or **вы**) in Russian. Now you should be ready to learn *he*, *she*, *we* and *they*.

In Russian, *he* is **он** (on). So you could say: **Он – поЭт.** *He is a poet.*

She is similar to *he* but has a feminine ending: **онА** (anA). So you could say: **ОнА – балерИна.** *She is a ballerina.*

We is **мы** (my), rhyming with **ты** and **вы**. So you might hear: **Мы – мАма и пАпа.** *We are Mum and Dad.*

They is **онИ** (anEE). So you might say: **ОнИ – САша и НАстя.** *They are Sasha and Nastya.*

Now you can refer to anyone in a conversation, even if you don't know what they are called.

я	*I*	мы	*we*
ты	*you* (one person, familiar)	**вы**	*you* (more than one person, or formal acquaintance)
он	*he*		
онА	*she*	**онИ**	*they*

Exercises

1 Imagine you have to fill in a form for a male Russian friend. Match the names provided with the blanks on the form.

a Имя _____   **i** ВладИмирович
b Отчество _____   **ii** СмирнОв
c фамИлия _____   **iii** БорИс

Now do the same for a female Russian friend.

a Имя _____   **i** НИна
b Отчество _____   **ii** Горбачёва
c. фамИлия _____   **iii** БорИсовна

What is the first name of your male friend's father? And your female friend's father?

2 How would you say 'hello' at these times of day?
a 9.15
b 14.45
c 20.30

3 You meet a Russian who asks you what your name is: **Как вас зовУт?** How do you answer: *My name is . . .?*

М——— з——— Stuart.

He says he is pleased to meet you. How does he say that in Russian?

О——— п———.

4 Imagine that you are working in Russia and an old friend and colleague Анна МихАйловна calls to see you. What should you say?

a Как вас зовУт? **b** Я не понимАю **c** ДЕвушка
d До свидАния **e** ЗдрАвствуйте **f** ИзвинИте

5 a You want to attract the attention of the young man serving behind the counter of a crowded shop in St Petersburg. How do you address him?
  b You step on someone's foot. What do you say?
  c You want to ask the girl at the cash-desk a question. How do you address her?
  d You think you recognize a girl called Nina whom you met on the tram yesterday. What do you say to her?

Choose your answers from the suggestions below:

i ДЕвушка! **ii** ИзвинИте, вы НИна? **iii** МолодОй человЕк!
iv ИзвинИте!

6 How do you pronounce these words and phrases?

◀) **CD 1, TR 3, 04:30**

a ЗдрАвствуйте	**e** Где БорИс?
b СпасИбо	**f** Я не знАю
c Я говорЮ по-англИйски	**g** МЕдленнее, пожАлуйста
d ХорошО	**h** ИзвинИте

What do they all mean?

7 Draw lines to link the matching phrases in Russian and English.

a Я говорЮ по-англИйски.	**i** I don't know.
b Я не понимАю.	**ii** I understand Russian well.
c Я хорошО понимАю по-рУсски.	**iii** I speak English.
d Я не знАю.	**iv** I understand.
e Я понимАю.	**v** I don't understand.

8 Which word is missing? Refer to the words in brackets below if you need to.

a МенЯ _____ ИвАн.
b _____ вЕчер.
c Я _____ понимАю.
d Вы _____ по-англИйски?
e МолодОй _____.

(ДОбрый, человЕк, зовУт, не, говорИте)

9 Using the recording, check that you understand which is the right answer.

◀) CD 1, TR 3, 05:27

a The speaker says **i** good morning **ii** good day **iii** good evening.
b She is called **i** Nina Petrovna **ii** Nina Borisovna **iii** Anna Petrovna.
c She **i** speaks English **ii** doesn't speak English **iii** speaks English well.

10 Match up the questions and answers so that they make sense.

a Кто он?   **i** ОнИ – бАбушка и дЕдушка.
b Кто ты?   **ii** ОнА – стюардЕсса.
c Кто онА?   **iii** Мы – брат и сестрА.
d Кто вы?   **iv** Он – студЕнт.
e Кто онИ?   **v** Я – космонАвт.

TEST YOURSELF

You have arrived at the end of Unit 3. Now you know how to say 'hello' and 'goodbye', find out who people are and exchange greetings. You also know how to cope if you don't understand.

What do these words and phrases mean?

1 здрАвствуйте

2 до свидАния

3 извинИте

4 как вас зовУт?

5 вы говорИте по-англИйски?

How would you say the following phrases in Russian? They all appear in this unit. You obviously can't write the answers yet, but say them out loud and check the answers in the back of the book.

6 say you don't understand

7 say 'you' if you were talking to a child

8 say 'you' if you were talking to your boss

9 say you are pleased to meet someone

10 ask someone to speak more slowly

You'll find the answers to these questions at the end of the book. If most of them are correct you are ready to move on to the next unit. If you still need practice, spend some more time revising this unit until you feel confident enough to move on.

4

Где банк?
Where's the bank?

In this unit you will learn

- *How to name some important places in a town*
- *How to ask and say where things are*
- *How to describe things that you see*
- *How to understand a Russian address*
- *How to count to ten*

Before you start

Look back at Unit 2 to make sure that you can recognize whether a noun is masculine, feminine or neuter. Just to check, write *m, f,* or *n* in the brackets following these words: **автОбус** (   ) **Опера** (   ) **пианИно** (   ) **метрО** (   ) **мАма** (   ) **банк** (   ).

ПассажИрский трАнспорт *(passazhEErsky trAnsport)*
passenger transport

Passenger transport in Russian cities includes the **автОбус** (aftOboos) *bus,* **трамвАй** (tramvAy) *tram* and **троллЕйбус** (trallyEiboos) *trolleybus* and, in some cities, an underground system **метрО** (mitrO). Each city has its own system for buying and using tickets.

A **талОн** (talOn) *ticket* (pictured opposite) for the bus, tram and trolleybus services may generally be bought from the driver or in advance and must be validated when it is used. In some cities you will meet a **кондУктор** (kondOOktur) *conductor* who sells tickets on the bus.

автОбус, троллЕйбус, трамвАй и метрО

ГУП «МОСГОРТРАНС»

25 РУБ. ИСП. ПО 30.09.09 И364Ø249221

ТАЛОН на одну поездку
в АВТОБУСЕ, ТРАМВАЕ, ТРОЛЛЕЙБУСЕ
в г. Москве

Для реализации водителем

Без отметки о гашении недействителен. В автобусах 300-х и
400-х маршрутов билет недействителен. Сохранять до конца поездки.
Подделка или использование заведомо подложных проездных документов преследуется по закону.

To gain access to the metro a ticket **билЕт** (beelyEt) to the value of a given number of journeys, valid up to a given date, has to be inserted into an entry barrier or, in the case of magnetic tickets, touched against the entry barrier. In some cities each metro station has an automated information and assistance point on the platform. Some metro systems have maps showing the station names in both the Cyrillic and Latin alphabets.

You can buy a ticket for a period of time that will be valid on any form of transport or on all of them. This is called a **проезднОй** (praiznOi).

In Moscow, more than seven million passengers a day use the metro system with its nearly 180 stations. The system is constantly being developed and new stations added.

МаршрУтка (marshrOOtka) is a *minibus taxi* which follows a fixed route for a fare that costs more than a bus ticket but less than a taxi fare. You pay the driver directly for this service.

Taxis (**таксИ**) and private drivers offering unregistered taxi services for a negotiated fare complete the picture of passenger transport in Russian cities.

Russian addresses

Russian addresses are written in a different order from most of Europe, starting with the city **гОрод** (gOrat), then the street **Улица** (OOleetsa), the number of the block of flats **дом** (dom), the building section number **кОрпус** (kOrpoos) and finally the flat number **квартИра** (kvartEEra). If a name is included, this will be written after the rest of the address with the surname first. So a typical address **Адрес** (Adryes) might look like this:

МосквА,
БотанИческая Улица,   (Botanical Street)
дом 8, кОрпус 4, квартИра 10.

ДиалОг 1

москвИч/ москвИчка	maskvEEch/ maskvEEchka	Muscovite (m, f)
Это	Eto	it is/is it?
вон там	von tam	over there

ДиалОг 2

кинотеАтр	keenotiAtr	cinema
спрАвочное бюрО	sprAvuchnoye byurO	information office
НЕ за что!	NyE za shto!	Don't mention it!

ДиалОг 3

здесь	zdyes'	here, around here
он/онА/онО	on/onA/anO	it (m/f/n)
скажИте	skazhEEtye	tell me
гостИница	gastEEneetsa	hotel

ДиалОг 4

какОй Это гОрод?	kakOy Eto gOrat?	What sort of city is it?
какОй/какАя/ какОе	kak-Oy/-Aya/ -Oye gOrat	what sort of (m/f/n)?

большОй/большАя/ большОе	bol'sh-Oy/-Aya/ -Oye	big (m/f/n)
красИвый/красИвая/ красИвое	krasEEv-y/-aya/ -oye	beautiful (m/f/n)

ДиалОг 5

хорОший/хорОшая/ хорОшее	kharOsh-y/-aya/ -eye	good (m/f/n)
там	tam	there

ДиалОг 6

мАленький/ мАленькая/ мАленькое	mAlyen'-ky/ -aya/-oye	little (m/f/n)

Dialogues

ДИАЛОГ 1

Andrew's Russian is getting better every day, and he has gone out to find his way around Moscow. First he needs to change some money.

Andrew	ИзвинИте, пожАлуйста, Это банк?
МосквИчка	Нет, Это пОчта.
Andrew	Где банк?
МосквИчка	Банк вон там.

ДИАЛОГ 2

He has read in the paper that there is a good film on at the «КОсмос» cinema.

Andrew	МолодОй человЕк, Это кинотеАтр «КОсмос»?
МосквИч	Нет, Это кинотеАтр «ПланЕта».
Andrew	Где кинотеАтр «КОсмос»?
МосквИч	ИзвинИте, я не знАю.
Andrew	Где спрАвочное бюрО?
МосквИч	Вон там.
Andrew	СпасИбо.
МосквИч	НЕ за что! До свидАния.

ДИАЛОГ 3

Andrew is feeling hungry, but can't make up his mind whether to eat at a restaurant, hotel or café.

Andrew	ИзвинИте, где здесь ресторАн?
МосквИч	Вот он.
Andrew	СкажИте, пожАлуйста, где здесь гостИница?
МосквИч	Вот онА.
Andrew	СпасИбо. Где здесь кафЕ?
МосквИч	Вот онО.

ДИАЛОГ 4

While he is having lunch, he asks a Muscovite what sort of city Moscow is.

| Andrew | СкажИте, какОй Это гОрод? |
| МосквИч | Это большОй, красИвый гОрод. |

54

ДИАЛОГ 5

Meanwhile, Volodya asks Sasha and Nastya about the flat in the advert.

CD 1, TR 4, 01:46

ВолОдя СкажИте, какАя Это квартИра?
СAша Это большАя, хорОшая квартИра. Там лифт, телефОн и красИвый балкОн.

ДИАЛОГ 6

The pianist from Unit 1 has found his piano, but he is disappointed with it, and complains to the composer.

CD 1, TR 4, 02:05

ПианИст Это Очень мАленькое пианИно!
КомпозИтор Нет, Это не мАленькое пианИно. ПианИно – большОе, красИвое.

Numerals 0–10

CD 1, TR 4, 02:33

0 ноль	nol'			
1 одИн	adEEn	**6 шесть**	shest'	
2 два	dva	**7 семь**	syem'	
3 три	tree	**8 вОсемь**	vOsyem'	
4 четЫре	chitYrye	**9 дЕвять**	dyEvyat'	
5 пять	pyat'	**10 дЕсять**	dyEsyat'	

Number practice

Read all the numbers aloud or listen to the recording and repeat the numbers after you hear them spoken. Try to say the first three numbers without looking, then add another three until you can say them all without looking. If you have a pack of playing cards shuffle the pack and then turn over a card at a time calling out the number, or throw some dice, calling out the score each time. Do this until you can say the numbers up to ten in random order as soon as you see them. Then read these numbers out loud in the right order.

пять дЕвять четЫре два шесть ноль вОсемь
одИн дЕсять три семь

Now try reciting the numbers from 10 down to 0.

Mechanics of the language

1 Это *This is*

You already know that you do not need a verb *to be* in Russian if you are talking about things happening now. For example, **АнтОн студЕнт** *Anton is a student*. But there is a very useful word in Russian meaning *this is* or *these are*: **Это**. So, **Это телефОн** means *This is a telephone*. You can also use **Это** as a question word: **Это телефОн?** *Is this a telephone?*

Это ресторАн? Нет, Это не ресторАн. Это кафЕ.

2 Он, Она, Оно *It*

In English we use *it* to refer to anything we have already mentioned which is not a person, for example, *it (the bus) is late*. In Russian, every time you want to use *it* you must think whether the noun you are referring to is masculine, feminine or neuter. Look back at Unit 2 to remind yourself how to tell whether a word is masculine, feminine or neuter. You already know that **он** means *he* and **онА** means *she*. **Он** and **онА** also mean *it* when referring to a masculine and feminine noun respectively. **ОнО** is what you use to refer to a neuter noun. Notice that the endings of these words do what you would expect: the masculine **он** ends in a consonant, the feminine **онА** ends in **-а** and the neuter **онО** ends in **-о**.

Где автОбус?	*Where is the bus?*	**Вот он.**	*(m)*	*There it is.*
Где вАза?	*Where is the vase?*	**Вот онА.**	*(f)*	*There it is.*
Где рАдио?	*Where is the radio?*	**Вот онО.**	*(n)*	*There it is.*

3 КакОй Это . . .? *What sort of . . .?*

Just as there are three similar words for *it* in Russian, so there are also three forms of the word meaning *What sort of . . .?* when you are asking about a singular noun. Again you choose which to use by remembering whether the noun you are referring to is masculine, feminine or neuter.

КакОй? means *what sort of?* when it refers to a masculine noun.
КакАя? means *what sort of?* when it refers to a feminine noun.
КакОе? means *what sort of?* when it refers to a neuter noun.

Notice that **какОй** has a typical masculine ending in **-й**, **какАя** has a typical feminine ending in **-я**, and **какОе** has a typical neuter ending in **-е**.

КакОй Это суп? *What sort of soup is it?* *(m)*
КакАя Это гитАра? *What sort of guitar is it?* *(f)*
КакОе Это винО? *What sort of wine is it?* *(n)*

4 Adjectives

When you want to describe a singular noun, possibly in answer to a question like **КакОй Это суп?** you will need to choose a masculine, feminine or neuter ending for the adjective (or describing word) you want to use. Again this will depend on the gender of the noun to which you are referring. This is called making the adjective 'agree' with the noun. If you want to describe something as beautiful, work out which gender the noun is, and use the correct ending to make the adjective agree.

Masculine	Feminine	Neuter
Это крас**Ивый** парк.	Это крас**Ивая** в**А**за.	Это крас**Ивое** р**А**дио.
It's a beautiful park.	*It's a beautiful vase.*	*It's a beautiful radio.*

Look at the other adjectives in your word list. You will notice that the most common endings are -**ый** (*m*), -**ая** (*f*) and -**ое** (*n*). Sometimes, as in м**А**ленький, the masculine ending will be spelt -**ий** because of a spelling rule which need not concern us here (see **Summary of language patterns**). Similarly, the neuter form may sometimes be spelt -**ее** as in хор**О**шее. Finally, any masculine adjective with the last syllable stressed will have the ending -**Ой** as in больш**Ой**. In your word lists from now on, adjectives will appear in singular masculine form only, unless there is anything unusual about them. Don't worry – even if you get the endings wrong you will still be understood!

Insight

How are you getting on with reading Russian? It's a great feeling when you start to pick out words. I am looking at the home page of the BBC Russian service and out of 15 headings there are 11 international words that you would recognize. For example, there is **спорт**, **р**А**дио**, **культ**У**ра**, **шоу-б**И**знес** and **Росс**И**я**, just to mention a few.

Exercises

1 Look at the map of part of Moscow and imagine that you are a tourist asking someone where certain places are. So you might ask out loud: **Где здесь парк?** Now imagine what the reply will be and say it aloud: **Вот он.** Carry on until you can say where everything on the map is.

Здесь (zdyes') means *here*, and if you include it in the question, it implies that you do not have a particular park in mind, or you do not know if you are looking in the right area, but you just want to know where there might be a park around here.

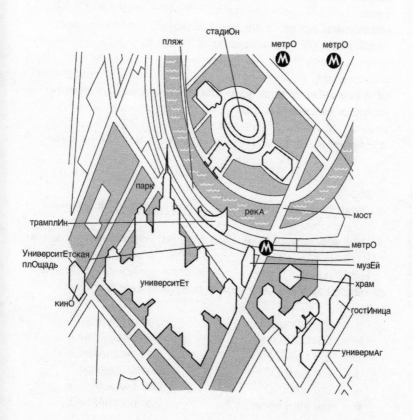

Ключ Klyooch Key		
рекА	ryikA	river
мост	most	bridge
стадиОн	stadeeOn	stadium
музЕй	moozyEy	museum
парк	park	park
метрО	mitrO	metro
храм	khram	church
универмАг	oonivermAk	department store
гостИница	gastEEnitsa	hotel
кинО	keenO	cinema
университЕт	ooniversityEt	university
трамплИн	tramplEEn	ski jump
пляж	plyash	beach
университЕтская плОщадь (f)	ooniversityEtskaya plOshshad'	university square

2 Here are some more signs that you might see. Try to work out what they mean.

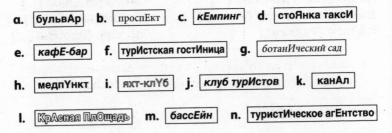

a. бульвАр **b.** проспЕкт **c.** кЕмпинг **d.** стоЯнка таксИ

e. кафЕ-бар **f.** турИстская гостИница **g.** ботанИческий сад

h. медпУнкт **i.** яхт-клУб **j.** клуб турИстов **k.** канАл

l. КрАсная ПлОщадь **m.** бассЕйн **n.** туристИческое агЕнтство

3 Underline the correct answer to each of these questions:

a	Где вокзАл?	Вот он/онА/онО.
b	Где стАнция?	Вот он/онА/онО.
c	Где трамвАй?	Вот он/онА/онО.
d	Где метрО?	Вот он/онА/онО.
e	Где шкОла?	Вот он/онА/онО.
f	Где университЕт?	Вот он/онА/онО.

g Где гостИница?   Вот он/онА/онО.
h Где спрАвочное бюрО?   Вот он/онА/онО.

4 What are these numbers? Say them out loud.

> 4   5   *10*   ² 8
> *0*   6   1   7   **3**   9

5 Listen to the recording and write down the scores of these
entirely fictional, amazingly high-scoring international football
matches as you hear them. The countries involved are Russia,
Italy, Spain, France and England.

◀) **CD 1, TR 4, 03:08**

МеталлИст (РоссИя) [   ]   ЮвЕнтус (ИтАлия) [   ]
РеАл (ИспАния) [   ]   ДинАмо (РоссИя) [   ]
Нант (ФрАнция) [   ]   СпартАк (РоссИя) [   ]
Астон ВИлла (Англия) [   ]   ЛАцио (ИтАлия) [   ]
НьюкАсл юнАйтед (Англия) [   ]   АтлЕтик (ИспАния) [   ]
НАполи (ИтАлия) [   ]   ТорпЕдо (РоссИя) [   ]

6 Listen to the recording and fill in the columns to say which
number bus, tram or trolleybus people are looking for.

◀) **CD 1, TR 4, 03:59**

автОбус   трамвАй   троллЕйбус

a
b
c
d

7 A Russian tourist speaks to you:

a **Где спрАвочное бюрО?** *Tell him it's over there.*

b **Где троллЕйбус?** *Tell him you are sorry, you don't know.*

c **Это библиотЕка?** *Tell him no, it's the post office.*

d **СпасИбо.** *Tell him not to mention it.*

8 Try out a few new adjectives. They are all colours.

крАсный	krAsny	*red*
бЕлый	byEly	*white*
жЁлтый	zhOlty	*yellow*
зелЁный	zilyOny	*green*
чЁрный	chOrny	*black*

In the box above, each adjective is in its masculine form. Below you have the same adjectives in different forms: masculine, feminine and neuter. They have become separated from their nouns. See if you can match them up.

9 Rearrange the following information into an address, and read it out loud including the numbers.

   a квартИра 3
   b КраснодАр
   c кОрпус 7
   d ВостОчная Улица (*East Street*)
   e дом 5

10 See if you can unjumble the Russian sentences below to put this conversation into Russian.

Tourist	*Excuse me. Where is the park?*
Tour guide	*There it is. Over there.*
Tourist	*What sort of park is it?*
Tour guide	*It is a beautiful big park!*
Tourist	*Thank you. Goodbye.*

   a КакОй Это парк? **b** СпасИбо. До свидАния.
   c Вот он. Вон там. **d** ИзвинИте. Где парк?
   e Это красИвый, большОй парк!

TEST YOURSELF

By now you know about the public transport system in Russian cities, you can read a Russian address, and you can request and give information about where places are. You can also give a description of something, and you can count to ten. To test yourself, try these ten quick questions.

1 Which form of transport is this? троллЕйбус

2 What are these three separate numbers? три, пять, дЕсять

3 In an address, what does квартИра mean?

4 What does this question mean? какОй Это гОрод?

5 What does this mean? Это крАсное винО

How do you say these words and phrases in Russian? They all appear in this unit. You obviously can't write the answers yet, but say them out loud and check the answers in the back of the book.

6 Six

7 Two

8 Where is the metro?

9 Is this a bank?

10 Where is the restaurant? There it is.

If you managed those questions and the exercises in this unit, you are now ready to move on. If you need to spend more time on this unit don't worry – there's a lot to absorb. It is best to work slowly and be sure of things before you move on to new information.

5

ИдИте прЯмо
Go straight ahead

In this unit you will learn
- *How to ask for and give directions*
- *How to ask whether things are available*
- *How to make plural forms*
- *How to say whether somewhere is open or closed*
- *How to count from 10 to 30*

Before you start

If you are at all unsure about how to tell whether a noun is masculine, feminine or neuter, go back to Unit 2 again.

Look back at Unit 4 and reread the section on how to choose adjective endings, as you will have the chance to practise this later in this unit.

Revise your numbers 0–10 in Unit 4, as this will help you to learn the numbers up to 30.

In this unit you will be asking for directions. Remember that in real life, the Russians whom you ask for directions probably won't have read this book, and they may give you rather complicated answers! Don't panic, but just try to pick out the essential words. Remember that you can always ask them to speak more slowly, and in this unit you will also learn how to ask someone to repeat something.

Insight
ТелефОн-автомАт (TilifOn-aftamAt) Pay phone

To use a public telephone, you will need to buy a
телефОнная кАрта (tilifOnnaya kArta) *phone card*. Pay
phones are not widely used these days as the use of mobile
phones grows. You can buy a **сим-кАрта** (sim-kArta)
SIM card and top up your account either at a kiosk or at a
machine. When you get through to a home number, if the
person you want does not pick up the phone, ask **САша
дОма?** (SAsha dOma?) *Is Sasha at home?*

КиОск (KiOsk) Kiosk

Kiosks can be found on many city streets in Russia, especially
near metro stations. They sell all manner of goods, including
theatre tickets, newspapers, maps, flowers, confectionery and
tobacco. Look out for the following signs: **театрАльные
билЕты** (tiatrAl'nye beelyEty) for theatre tickets, **печАть**
(pichAt') for newspapers and magazines and **цветЫ** (tsvitY)
for flowers. Russians love to give and receive flowers, but
you should remember to give an odd number of blooms on
happy occasions as an even number is associated with sad
events. In winter you may see glass cases of flowers for sale
on the streets, with candles burning inside to stop the flowers
from freezing. **ТабАк** (TabAk) means that cigarettes are for
sale, and, especially in small towns and villages, you may still
see people smoking a version of a cigarette called **папирОса**
(papirOsa) which has a cardboard mouthpiece.

ДиалОг 1

как попАсть в. . .?	kak papAst' v . . .?	How do I/you get to?
центр	tsentr	the centre
идИте	eedEEtye	go
прЯмо	pryAma	straight ahead
потОм	patOm	then
налЕво	nalyEva	to the left
крАсный	krAsny	red
плОщадь (f)	plOshshad'	square
повторИте	pavtarEEtye	repeat

ДиалОг 2

КудА вы идёте?	KoodA vy eedyOtye?	Where are you going?
Я идУ в . . .	Ya eedOO v . . .	I am going to . . .
далекО	dalyikO	far, a long way
недалекО	nidalyikO	not far
напрАво	naprAva	to the right
интерЕсный	intiryEsny	interesting

ДиалОг 3

закрЫт/а/о	zakrYt/zakrYta/ zakrYto	closed
на ремОнт	na rimOnt	for repairs
Ой, как жаль!	Oy, kak zhal'!	Oh, what a pity!
галерЕя	galiryEya	gallery
открЫт/а/о	atkrYt/atkrYta/ atkrYto	open

ДиалОг 4

У вас есть . . .?	Oo vas yest' . . .?	Do you have . . .?
сувенИр/ сувенИры	soovinEEr/ soovinEEry	souvenir/s
матрёшка/ матрёшки	matryOshka/ matryOshky	set/s of stacking wooden dolls
конфЕта/конфЕты	konfyEta/konfyEty	sweet/s
рУсский	rOOsky	Russian

QUICK VOCAB

америкАнский	amirikAnsky	American
кнИга/кнИги	knEEga/knEEgy	book/s
Дом КнИги	dom knEEgy	House of the Book (bookshop)

Dialogues

ДИАЛОГ 1

Andrew is still exploring Moscow. Now he is heading for Red Square and the Kremlin.

◆ CD 1, TR 5

Андрю	ДЕвушка, извинИте, как попАсть в центр?
ДЕвушка	В центр? ИдИте прЯмо, потОм налЕво, и там КрАсная ПлОщадь и Кремль.
Андрю	ПовторИте, пожАлуйста.
ДЕвушка	ИдИте прЯмо, потОм налЕво.
Андрю	СпасИбо.

ДИАЛОГ 2

Alison is looking for the museum when Igor sees her.

◆ CD 1, TR 5, 00:44

Игорь	ЗдрАвствуйте, Алисон. КудА вы идёте?
Алисон	Я идУ в музЕй. Это далекО?
Игорь	Нет, Это недалекО. ИдИте прЯмо, и музЕй напрАво. МузЕй Очень интерЕсный.
Алисон	СпасИбо. До свидАния.

ДИАЛОГ 3

As Alison sets off, Igor suddenly remembers something.

Игорь	Алисон, музЕй закрЫт. ЗакрЫт на ремОнт.
Алисон	Ой, как жаль!
Игорь	Но галерЕя открЫта. И галерЕя Очень интерЕсная.
Алисон	Как попАсть в галерЕю?
Игорь	ИдИте налЕво, потОм напрАво, и галерЕя прЯмо. Это недалекО.

ДИАЛОГ 4

A tourist called Colin is asking a **киоскёр** *(kioskyOr) stall-holder about the souvenirs she is selling.*

КОлин	У вас есть сувенИры?
Киоскёр	Да. Вот матрёшки и конфЕты. Здесь кассЕты и там рУсская вОдка и рУсское винО.
КОлин	Это рУсский шоколАд?
Киоскёр	Нет, америкАнский. Очень хорОший шоколАд.
КОлин	А у вас есть кнИги?
Киоскёр	Нет, идИте в Дом КнИги. Это недалекО.
КОлин	Где Дом КнИги?
Киоскёр	ИдИте налЕво, потОм прЯмо, и Дом КнИги напрАво.

Numerals 11–30

🔊 **CD 1, TR 5, 02:41**

11 одИннадцать	adEEnatsat'	18 восемнАдцать	vasyemnAtsat'
12 двенАдцать	dvyenAtsat'	19 девятнАдцать	dyevitnAtsat'
13 тринАдцать	treenAtsat'	20 двАдцать	dvAtsat'
14 четЫрнадцать	chitYrnatsat'	21 двАдцать одИн	dvAtsat' adEEn
15 пятнАдцать	pitnAtsat'	22 двАдцать два	dvAtsat' dva
16 шестнАдцать	shesnAtsat'	23 двАдцать три	dvAtsat' tree
17 семнАдцать	syemnAtsat'	30 трИдцать	trEEtsat'

Number practice

Read all the numbers out loud or listen to the recording and repeat them. You will notice that 11–19 are made up more or less of the numbers 1–9 plus the ending -**надцать** which is a contracted form of **на дЕсять** *on ten*. To practise numerals this time, you could add 10 or 20 to the numbers on your playing cards or dice. Or make up sums:

13 + 8 = 21   тринАдцать плюс вОсемь – двАдцать одИн
30 – 11 = 19   трИдцать мИнус одИннадцать – девятнАдцать

Mechanics of the language

1 Как попАсть в . . .? *How do I get to . . .?*

To ask how to get somewhere in Russian, simply say **как попАсть в** . . . *How to get to?* and add the place to which you want to go. This simple rule works for masculine and neuter nouns, like **теАтр** and **кафЕ,** but for feminine words you should try to remember to change the ending of the noun from -**а** to -**у** and -**я** to -**ю**. (For those people with an interest in grammar, these endings are called *accusative* endings, and you use them after **в** and **на** when movement to a place is indicated.)

Masculine	Feminine	Neuter
Как попАсть в теАтр?	Как попАсть в библиотЕку? Как попАсть в галерЕю?	Как попАсть в кафЕ?

When talking about going to a certain place, occasionally you need to use **на** instead of **в** to mean *to*: for example, **Как попАсть на стадиОн?** *How do I get to the stadium?* **Как попАсть на пОчту?** *How do I get to the post office?*

If you meet a new word in the **Quick vocab** list which needs **на** instead of **в** you will see (**на**) next to it.

2 КудА?/Где? *Where to?/Where?*

You already know the word **Где?** *Where?* In **ДиалОг 2** you met a different word which you use to ask *Where to?* **КудА?**

Где музЕй? *Where is the museum?*
КудА вы идёте? *Where are you going to?*

In the same dialogue, you also met part of the verb *to go*. This refers to going somewhere on foot, not by transport.

я идУ *I am going*   **вы идёте** *you are going*

3 Открыт/закрыт *Open/Closed*

Note that these words have different endings depending on the gender of the noun they refer to.

Masculine	Feminine	Neuter
МедпУнкт открЫт.	ПОчта открЫта.	СпрАвочное бюрО открЫто.
БассЕйн закрЫт.	ГостИница закрЫта.	КафЕ закрЫто.

4 *Plural forms of nouns*

To make a plural form in English we usually add -*s*: *rabbit/rabbits*. In Russian, to make the plural forms of masculine nouns you usually add -**ы** unless the spelling rule (see **Summary of language patterns**) makes you use -**и** instead. For feminine plural forms, you remove the last letter (usually -**а** or -**я**) and then add -**ы** or -**и**. You will remember that nouns ending in a soft sign -**ь** may be either masculine or feminine, and these also lose the last letter before adding **-и**.

Masculine	Feminine
ресторАн/ресторАны	**гостИница/гостИницы** *hotel/s*
restaurant/s	
киОск/киОски *kiosk/s*	**библиотЕка/библиотЕки** *library/ libraries*
рубль/рублИ *rouble/s*	**плОщадь/плОщади** *square/s*

Neuter nouns also lose their last letter before adding **-a** or **-я** to make the plural form, so **Утро** *morning* becomes **Утра**. But most of the neuter nouns which you have met so far (**бюрО, какАо, кафЕ, килО, кинО, метрО, пианИно, рАдио**) do not change their form at all when they become plural. This is because neuter nouns which have been borrowed directly from other languages are exempt from all the usual rules. So you have to try to tell from the context whether there is one piano or many!

Exercises

1 Look at the town plan and its key opposite. Only new words are shown in English. Make sure you know how to say all the places in Russian. Then sit yourself down with a Russian friend in the window of a café in the left-hand corner and ask whether the places shown on the plan are far away or not, for example:

ГостИница далекО?	Да, Это далекО.
ИнститУт далекО?	Нет, Это недалекО.

2 Now you can try asking your friend for directions. **Как попАсть в библиотЕку?** *How do I get to the library?* To begin with, all the places that you ask about are feminine, so you will need to change **-a** to **-y** and **-я** to **-ю**. Underline the correct form of the question.

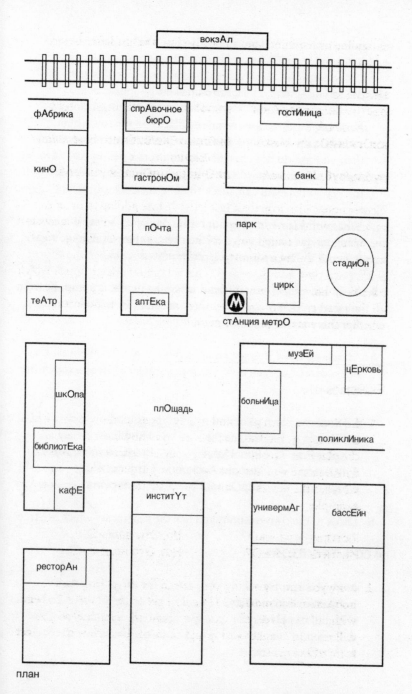

a Как попАсть . . . **i** на пОчту? **ii** на пОчта?

b Как попАсть . . . **i** в гостИница? **ii** в гостИницу?

c Как попАсть . . . **i** в поликлИника? **ii** в поликлИнику?

d Как попАсть . . . **i** на фАбрику? **ii** на фАбрика?

Now ask for directions to all the places on the town plan, including the masculine and neuter places, remembering that their endings do not change: **Как попАсть в ресторАн?** *How do I get to the restaurant?* Ask your questions in the order given in the key so that you can check them in the back of the book.

What will your friend say in reply? Make up suitable answers using **идИте напрАво** *go to the right*, **идИте налЕво** *go to the left*, and **идИте прЯмо** *go straight ahead*.

3 Now ask your Russian friend where he or she is going: **КудА вы идёте?** *Where are you going?* and supply suitable answers. **Я идУ в гостИницу** *I am going to the hotel*.

4 Match up these nouns and adjectives to make sentences. Use one word from each column, for example: **a) Игорь хорОший футболИст.**

a Игорь	рУсская	гОрод
b ЛЕна	большОй	кафЕ
c Хард-Рок	красИвая	газЕта (*newspaper*)
d ЛОндон	америкАнское	футболИст
e ПрАвда	хорОший	балерИна

5 Listen to the conversations and tick the statements which are true.

🔊 **CD 1, TR 5, 03:35**

a МузЕй открЫт.

b БиблиотЕка закрЫта.

c КафЕ открЫто.

d РесторАн закрЫт.

e ПОчта открЫта.

1	ресторАн	15	цирк
2	институт	16	стАнция метрО (на)
3	универмАг		(stAntseeya metrO)
4	бассЕйн		metro station
5	кафЕ	17	пОчта (на)
6	библиотЕка	18	парк
7	шкОла	19	стадиОн (на)
8	плОщадь (на)	20	кинО
9	поликлИника	21	гастронОм
	(polyklEEnika) *health*	22	банк
	centre	23	фАбрика (на)
10	цЕрковь (f) (tsErkov')		(fAbreeka) *factory*
	church	24	спрАвочное бюрО
11	больнИца (bal'nEEtsa)	25	гостИница
	hospital	26	вокзАл (на) (vakzAl)
12	музЕй		*train station*
13	теАтр		
14	аптЕка (aptyEka)		
	pharmacy		

6 Match up these questions with suitable answers.

a У вас есть кнИги?

b У вас есть кОфе?

c У вас есть таблЕтки?

d У вас есть продУкты?

e У вас есть сувенИры?

f У вас есть котлЕта и салАт?

i Нет, идИте в аптЕку.

ii Нет, идИте в киОск.

iii Нет, идИте в гастронОм.

iv Нет, идИте в кафЕ.

v Нет, идИте в ресторАн.

vi Нет, идИте в библиотЕку.

7 Read Ivan's shopping list on the next page, and wherever he wants more than one of something (e.g. bananas), put a tick. The first one has been done for you.

ГастронОм	АптЕка	ТабАк	КиОск	ТеАтр
банАны ✓	таблЕтки	сигарЕты	цветЫ	билЕт
кОфе		и папирОсы	конфЕты	
сАхар				
фрУкты				

8 When you are reasonably confident with your numbers, listen to the recording and jot down the missing numbers from each six-digit phone number **нОмер телефОна** as it is read out. The numbers will be read in pairs: 17-25-10 **семнАдцать – двАдцать пять – дЕсять**.

🔊 **CD 1, TR 5, 04:30**

a 12 – _____ – 1___
b 25 – _____ – ___7
c 14 – 3___ – _____
d 1___ – _____ – 24
e _____ – _____ – 12

If you do not have the recording or if you want more practice, you could make up and jot down some more phone numbers, and read them out clearly.

9 Look at these road signs and see if you can match them up with their captions opposite. You do not need to understand every word to do this.

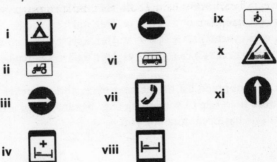

a инвалИды

b движЕние прЯмо

c телефОн

d кЕмпинг

e гостИница/мотЕль

f больнИца

g автОбусы

h движЕние напрАво

i разводнОй мост

j трАкторы

k движЕние налЕво

10 You are visiting another town. Read the instructions below to identify the buildings on your new plan. Match up the letters with the numbers.

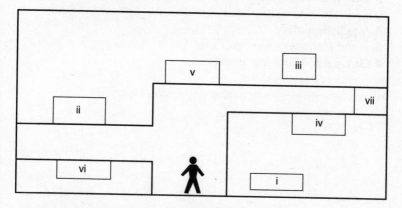

a ТеАтр прЯмо.

b ИдИте прЯмо, потОм напрАво и библиотЕка напрАво.

c ИдИте налЕво, и гастронОм напрАво.

d ИдИте прЯмо, потОм напрАво, и вокзАл налЕво.

e ИдИте налЕво, и ресторАн налЕво. Это недалекО.

f ИдИте прЯмо, потОм напрАво, и гостИница прЯмо.

g Вот кафЕ, напрАво.

11 See if you can put the following phrases into Russian. If your memory needs jogging, the answers are written below, but in the wrong order.

1 Excuse me, how do I get to the restaurant?
2 Go straight ahead, then to the left and the restaurant is on the right.
3 Is it far? No, it's not far.
4 Is the museum open?
5 Do you have any chocolate?

i МузЕй открЫт?
ii ИзвинИте, как попАсть в ресторАн?
iii Это далекО? Нет, Это недалекО.
iv У вас есть шоколАд?
v ИдИте прЯмо, потОм налЕво, и ресторАн напрАво.

TEST YOURSELF

Now you should be able to find your way around a Russian town happily understanding numbers up to 30, never rattling a shop door which says **закрЫт**, and finding out what is available in shops which are open! Well done! To test yourself, try these ten quick revision questions.

What do these words and phrases mean?

1 Как попАсть в центр?

2 У вас есть цветЫ?

3 МузЕй закрЫт.

4 ПовторИте, пожАлуйста.

5 Это далекО?

How do you say these words and phrases in Russian? As usual, you have met them all in this unit. Say them out loud to yourself and then check the answers in the back of the book.

6 26, 13, 30

7 restaurants

8 How do I get to the museum?

9 Go straight ahead.

10 Where are you going to?

How did you manage? If you feel reasonably confident with your results then you are ready to move on to Unit 6. However, now that you have completed five units, you may decide it would be helpful to look back over everything you have done so far. If nothing else, you may find that things which seemed difficult at first now seem easier!

6

Что вы хотИте?
What do you want?

In this unit you will learn
- *How to say what you want*
- *How to pay for something in a shop*
- *How to say that something belongs to you*
- *How to make plural forms of adjectives*
- *How to count from 30 to 100*

Before you start

You have already spent two units finding your way around a Russian city. In this unit you will learn more things to say when you finally find the shop or café you were looking for. Since you already know lots of words and phrases you could try rehearsing them in your own environment. Be as active in your language learning as possible.

Every time you talk to a friend, colleague, salesperson or waiter in your own language, try to repeat the transaction to yourself in Russian. Wherever you are, try to name what you see around you in Russian. When you are going somewhere, even if it is just down the corridor, pretend to give directions to a visiting Russian. Say telephone numbers, bus numbers and number plates to yourself in Russian.

If there was anything you didn't understand in an earlier unit, look back at it before you go on. It may be clearer now that you understand more.

Revise your numbers 0–30 in the **Numbers** section at the back of the book, as this will make learning the higher numbers much easier.

УнивермАг (OonivermAk) *Department store*

The most famous Russian department store is **ГУМ (ГосудАрственный универсАльный магазИн)** *GOOM State department store* in Red Square in Moscow. In Soviet times this used to be centrally run, but since perestroika it has been divided up into individual shops which are leased out to leading Russian and Western retailers. A modern shopping centre is called торгОвый центр (torgOvy tsentr).

РЫнок (RYnok) *Market*

If you want to buy fresh vegetables and fruit **Овощи и фрУкты** (Ovashshee ee frOOkty), milk and dairy produce молокО (mulakO) and meat and fish мЯсо и рЫба (myAsa ee rYba) the local markets are a good source of supply, although in the winter months there is inevitably less choice.

КафЕ (kafEh) *Café*

The waiter **официАнт** (afitsiAnt) and waitress **официАнтка** (afitsiAntka) in a café or restaurant may be addressed as **молодОй человЕк** and **дЕвушка**, forms of address which apply to anyone up to about fifty years of age!

КАсса (KAssa) *Cash desk*

In some shops you may need to pay for your purchases at a cash desk **кАсса** (kAssa), and then take your receipt **чек** (chek) back to the counter to collect your goods. This is an unusual system now but you may still find it being used in some small towns and old-fashioned shops.

ДиалОг 1

что?	shto?	*what?*
Что вы хотИте купИть?	Shto vy khatEEtye koopEEt'?	*What do you want to buy?*
подАрок/подАрки	padArak/padArki	*present/presents*
я хочУ	ya khachOO	*I want*
балалАйка	balalAika	*balalaika (stringed instrument)*
ПойдЁм	paeedyOm	*Let's go*

ДиалОг 2

покажИте	pukazhEEtye	*show (me)*
СкОлько стОит?	SkOl'ka stOeet?	*How much is it?*
Сто пятьдесЯт рублЕй	Sto pidisyAt rooblyEi	*150 roubles*
Где платИть?	Gdye platEEt'?	*Where do I pay?*
кАсса	kAssa	*cash desk*

ДиалОг 3

фруктОвый сок	frooktOvy sok	*fruit juice*
Или	EEly	*or*
официАнтка	afitsiAntka	*waitress*
идИте сюдА	eedEEtye syoodA	*come here*
Что у вас есть?	Shto oo vas yest'?	*What have you got?*
минерАльная водА	minirAl'naya vadA	*mineral water*
с	s	*with*
с лимОном	s leemOnum	*with lemon*
с сАхаром	s sAkharum	*with sugar*
с молокОм	s mulakOm	*with milk*
сейчАс	seychAs	*now, right away*

ДиалОг 4

ваш/вАша/вАше/вАши	vash/vAsha/vAshe/vAshy	*your (m/f/n/pl)*
мой/моЯ/моё/моИ	moy/mayA/mayO mayEE	*my (m/f/n/pl)*
джаз	dzhaz	*jazz*

Insight

The first language skills that a little child picks up come from listening. Speaking, reading and writing come later. Listen to Russian whenever you can and, even if you don't understand it, you will get used to the sounds of the language and will learn how to imitate it.

Dialogues

ДИАЛОГ 1

Peter is visiting Russia on business, but before returning home he goes shopping for presents with a colleague, Anton Pavlovich. Anton Pavlovich speaks some English, but they have agreed to speak only Russian in the morning and English in the afternoon.

АнтОн ПАвлович	Что вы хотИте купИть, ПИтер?
ПИтер	СувенИры и подАрки.
АнтОн ПАвлович	КакИе сувенИры и подАрки?
ПИтер	Я хочУ купИть кнИги, матрЁшки, шоколАд, вОдку и балалАйку.
АнтОн ПАвлович	ХорошО. ПойдЁм в Дом КнИги.

CD 1, TR 6

ДИАЛОГ 2

In Дом КнИги *Peter soon gets into his stride.*

ПИтер	МолодОй человЕк, у вас есть кнИга «Анна КарЕнина»?
МолодОй человЕк	Да.
ПИтер	ПокажИте, пожАлуйста.
МолодОй человЕк	Вот онА.
ПИтер	СкОлько стОит?
МолодОй человЕк	Сто пятьдесЯт рублЕй.

CD 1, TR 6, 00:53

ПИтер	Где платИть?
МолодОй человЕк	ИдИте в кАссу.
ПИтер	СпасИбо.

ДИАЛОГ 3

Later in the morning, Peter and Anton Pavlovich pop into a café.

CD 1, TR 6, 01:23

АнтОн ПАвлович	Что вы хотИте, ПИтер?
ПИтер	Я хочУ фруктОвый сок Или чай, пожАлуйста.
АнтОн ПАвлович	ДЕвушка, идИте сюдА, пожАлуйста. У вас есть фруктОвый сок?
ОфициАнтка	ИзвинИте, нет.
АнтОн ПАвлович	Что у вас есть?
ОфициАнтка	Чай, кОфе, минерАльная водА, Пепси-кОла.
ПИтер	ДАйте, пожАлуйста, чай с лимОном и с сАхаром.
АнтОн ПАвлович	И кОфе с молокОм.
ОфициАнтка	Чай с лимОном и с сАхаром, и кОфе с молокОм. СейчАс.

ДИАЛОГ 4

While they wait for their drinks, Peter and Anton Pavlovich look at their purchases.

CD 1, TR 6, 02:14

АнтОн ПАвлович	Что у вас есть?
ПИтер	Вот кнИга «Анна КарЕнина» и матрёшки.
АнтОн ПАвлович	Как хорошО. Это Очень красИвые матрёшки. ПИтер, Это вАша кассЕта?
ПИтер	Да, Это моЯ кассЕта, «РУсский джаз».

АнтОн ПАвлович	И вот мой компАкт-дИск. Опера «БорИс ГодунОв».
ОфициАнтка	Вот чай и кОфе.
ПИтер	СпасИбо.
АнтОн ПАвлович	Oh look, it's twelve o'clock. We can speak English now!

Numerals 10–100

◀)) CD 1, TR 6, 03:03

10 дЕсять	dyEsyat'
20 двАдцать	dvAtsat'
30 трИдцать	trEEtsat'
40 сОрок	sOrak
50 пятьдесЯт	pidisyAt
60 шестьдесЯт	shesdisyAt
70 сЕмьдесят	syEmdyesyat
80 вОсемьдесят	vOsyemdyesyat
90 девянОсто	dyevinOsta
100 сто	sto
146 сто сОрок шесть	sto sOrak shest' etc.

If you are hoping to visit Russia, you will need to learn relatively high numbers to cope with the prices in roubles.

A rouble is **рубль** in Russian, and you may hear it in different forms: **рубль, рублЯ, рублЕй**. As long as you recognize the number which goes with it this should be no problem, and if you do get confused, you could carry a notepad and ask salespeople to write down the price for you: **НапишИте, пожАлуйста** (napeeshEEtye, pazhAloosta), *write, please*. Practise the numbers in this unit until you can say them almost without thinking. Every time you see a number in your daily life, say it in Russian, as long as doing so doesn't distract you from driving or working!

Language patterns

1 Plural adjectives

In English, the adjective form is the same whether you are describing one or several items: *big blue balloon, big blue balloons*. In Russian, you will remember that there are three forms of singular adjectives to match the singular nouns: masculine, feminine and neuter. (See Unit 4.) Now that you know how to form plural nouns (e.g. **конфЕты** *sweets*), you may want to use adjectives with them. This is easy as it doesn't matter if the plural noun you are referring to is masculine, feminine or neuter. There is only one type of plural adjective ending: **-ые**. This may also be written **-ие** if the spelling rule applies (see **Summary of language patterns**).

красИвые кнИги	*beautiful books*
хорОшие конфЕты	*good sweets*
большИе пИццы	*big pizzas*

The same ending is used with the plural form **какИе...?** *what sort of...?*

КакИе сувенИры и подАрки?   *What sort of souvenirs and presents?*

2 My balalaika and your balalaika

In the same way as there are masculine, feminine, neuter and plural forms of adjectives and nouns, there are also different forms of the words *my* and *your*.

Masculine	Feminine	Neuter	Plural
мой пАспорт	**моЯ** балалАйка	**моё** пианИно	**моИ** цветЫ
my passport	*my balalaika*	*my piano*	*my flowers*
ваш пАспорт	**вАша** балалАйка	**вАше** пианИно	**вАши** цветЫ
your passport	*your balalaika*	*your piano*	*your flowers*

As you would expect, these words use the typical endings: -**й** and the consonant -**ш** for masculine forms, -**я** and -**а** for feminine forms, -**ё** and -**е** for neuter forms, and -**и** for plurals.

3 I want to buy a balalaika

Did you notice what happens to the endings of the feminine nouns in **ДиалОг 1**? Peter says: **Я хочУ купИть кнИги, матрёшки, шоколАд, вОдку и балалАйку**. **ВОдка** and **балалАйка** have changed to **вОдку** and **балалАйку**. Once again, this is the accusative form. It will occur when a feminine noun is the person or thing which has something done to it, or, in grammatical terms, is the direct object of a verb. By direct object, we mean that a noun answers the question *what?* asked after the verb. Here are some examples of direct objects in English:

She baked **bread**.	She baked **what?**	**Bread**.
He likes **opera, books, wine**.	He likes **what?**	**Opera, books and wine**.
He plays the **balalaika**.	He plays **what?**	**The balalaika**.

And some in Russian:

Я хочУ купИть **балалАйку**.	You want to buy **what?**	**A balalaika**.
Я хочу **Пепси-кОлу**.	You want **what?**	**Pepsi-cola**.

4 Imperatives: do this, do that!

Did you realize that you can already give people eight different orders or requests in Russian? **ЗдрАвствуйте** *hello* was the first one you learned, and it means literally *Be healthy!*

Others which you know are:

извинИте	*excuse (me)*	покажИте	*show (me)*
повторИте	*repeat*	идИте	*go*
напишИте	*write*	дАйте	*give (me)*
скажИте	*tell (me)*		

Add **пожАлуйста** to be polite, and you should be able to get things done!

Exercises

1 Choose a question word from the list below to complete these dialogues.

a ———— теАтр?   Вот он.
b ———— вас зовУт?   МенЯ зовУт НИна.
c ———— вы идЁте?   Я идУ на пОчту.
d ———— вы хотИте?   Я хочУ суп, хлеб и вОдку.
e ———— Это?   Это САша. Он – мой сын.

Как? Что? Где? Кто? КудА?

2 You work in a Russian kiosk. You cannot keep everything on display, but you have a list so that you know what is tucked away in boxes. A tourist comes up and asks if you have various items. Carry out an imaginary conversation with the tourist. If you have the items he asks for, tell him all about them. If not, say **ИзвинИте, нет**. Here is your list.

хорОшие банАны

билЕты в теАтр

рУсская вОдка

компАкт-дИски

конфЕты

кОфе

лимонАд

матрЁшки

папирОсы и сигарЕты

план

сувенИры

цветЫ

The first example has been done for you.

a Tourist   У вас есть сувенИры?
    You   Да, есть. Вот красИвые рУсские матрЁшки.
b Tourist   У вас есть балалАйка?
c Tourist   У вас есть сигарЕты? КакИе? РУсские Или
               америкАнские?
d Tourist   У вас есть банАны?

Now carry on the conversation. You could ask him if he wants any sweets, or he could ask you how much something costs.

3 Say the following phone numbers, and check them off below.

a 65 – 43 – 74   **b** 14 – 58 – 92   **c** 123 – 89 – 12
d 135 – 91 – 36   **e** 117 – 54 – 22

  i   сто семнАдцать – пятьдесЯт четЫре – двАдцать два
 ii   сто двАдцать три – вОсемьдесят дЕвять – двенАдцать
iii   сто трИдцать пять – девянОсто одИн – трИдцать шесть
 iv   шестьдесЯт пять – сОрок три – сЕмьдесят четЫре
  v   четЫрнадцать – пятьдесЯт вОсемь – девянОсто два

4 Which orders or requests would you use in the following circumstances? You want someone to:

a repeat something   **c** give you something
b show you something   **d** go somewhere

e tell you something   **g** excuse you
f write something

i идИте, пожАлуйста **ii** повторИте, пожАлуйста **iii** скажИте, пожАлуйста **iv** покажИте, пожАлуйста **v** напишИте, пожАлуйста **vi** извинИте, пожАлуйста **vii** дАйте, пожАлуйста

5 You are in a possessive mood. Every time Boris claims that an item belongs to him, you contradict him and say it is yours.

БорИс Это мой микроскОп.
Вы Нет, Это не ваш микроскОп. Это мой микроскОп.

Choose from **мой/моЯ/моё/моИ** and **ваш/вАша/вАше/вАши** to fill in the blanks.

a БорИс Это моЁ рАдио. **Вы** Нет, Это не в_____ рАдио. Это м_____ рАдио.

b БорИс Это моЯ кнИга. **Вы** Нет, Это не в_____ кнИга. Это м_____ кнИга.

c БорИс Это моИ гитАры. **Вы** Нет, Это не в_____ гитАры. Это м_____ гитАры.

d БорИс Это мой билЕт. **Вы** Нет, Это не в_____ билЕт. Это м_____ билЕт.

For more practice, you could try the same thing in a more generous mood, adding your own ideas.

БорИс Это вАши сигарЕты?
Вы Нет, Это не моИ сигарЕты. Это вАши сигарЕты.

6 Listen to find out what people want. Tick off the items on the list below as you hear them mentioned. Then listen again and underline each feminine item asked for. These will have changed their endings from -a to -y and -я to -ю. If you don't have the recording, make up sentences on this model: **Я хочУ котлЕту, салАт и кОфе с молокОм.**

◀) CD 1, TR 6, 03:41

винО ✓	конфЕты ✓	чай с лимОном ✓
вОдка ✓	пИцца ✓	кОфе с сАхаром ✓
суп ✓	сметАна ✓	омлЕт ✓
борщ ✓	фрУкты ✓	Пепси-кОла ✓

7 Link each adjective to a suitable noun by joining them with a line.

БольшОй	сад
мАленькое	конфЕты
красИвые	человЕк
рУсские	винО
интерЕсная	папирОсы
молодОй	теАтр
ботанИческий	кнИга
хорОшие	рАдио
бЕлое	цветЫ

8 Use this grid to work on your numbers. Cover up all but one line of numbers, and read out the ones you see. Try it again in a day or two, and see if you are any quicker.

1	14	36	97	12
8	122	3	88	45
64	199	20	17	150
7	13	65	10	63
144	21	19	5	111

9 There are many situations which you could now handle if you were visiting Russia. Look at the pictures and answer these questions to make sure.

1 Что вы хотИте?
2 КудА вы идЁте?
3 Что Это?
4 МетрО закрЫто?
5 Это ваш билЕт? *(Yes)*.

TEST YOURSELF

Now you can shop, order food and drinks, say who things belong to and talk about plural balalaikas as well as one single balalaika! Well done. Before you move on to the next unit, just try these ten quick questions to make sure you feel confident with what you have learned.

What do these words and phrases mean?

1 Что вы хотИте купИть?

2 Что у вас есть?

3 ПокажИте, пожАлуйста.

4 СкОлько стОит?

5 ДАйте, пожАлуйста, кОфе.

How would you say these words and phrases in Russian? Say your answers out loud and check the answers in the back of the book.

6 *tea with lemon*

7 *120*

8 *my passport*

9 *repeat, please*

10 *young man*

В гостИнице

At the hotel

In this unit you will learn

- *How to give your particulars when booking into a hotel*
- *How to say the letters of the alphabet and fill in a form*
- *How to say what nationality you are and what you do*
- *How to say where you work*
- *How to specify 'this' or 'that'*
- *How to count from 100 to 1,000*

Before you start

If you are thinking of visiting Russia at any time you will need somewhere to stay. You may be fortunate enough to have friends there, or you may need to book into a **гостИница** (gastEEnitsa) *hotel*. The language in this unit will enable you to do this, and it will also be useful whenever you need to give or ask for personal details. You may find it particularly helpful to be able to use the alphabet in case anyone asks **Как Это пИшется?** (Kak Eta pEEshetsa?) *How is that written?* In this unit, you will also learn to count up to 1,000, so make sure you know your numbers up to 100 first.

Insight
Hotel accommodation

If you are travelling to Russia you will need a tourist or business visa. When you arrive at your hotel you will meet the **администрАтор** *administrator* at the **ресЕпшн** (risEpshn) *reception desk*. Each floor of a big hotel may also have a woman on duty called a **дежУрная** (dyizhOOrnaya). In big hotels most signs are in English as well as Russian.

....

Saying the alphabet in Russian

◀) **CD 1, TR 7, 00:19**

In Russian, as in English, the name of a letter sometimes sounds different from the sound that the letter makes. If you had not thought of this before, say *h*, *w*, or *y* out loud in English and think how confusing the letter names might be to a foreign visitor. You may need to know the names of Russian letters to spell something, for example your name or the name of your home town, so here they are, in the correct order. Familiarize yourself with them before you move on to the dialogues. You will see the letter first, for example **C c**. Then you see the name of the letter in Russian **эс** and finally the English transliteration of the letter name (es). You can listen to them on your recording.

Alphabet guide
Glance back through the book, picking a few words at random and spelling them out loud.

....

А а	**а**	**a**
Б б	**бэ**	(beh as in bed)
В в	**вэ**	(veh)
Г г	**гэ**	(geh)
Д д	**дэ**	(deh)
Е е	**е**	(yeh)
Ё ё	**ё**	(yoh)

Ж ж	жэ	(zheh)
З з	зэ	(zeh)
И и	и	(ee)
Й й	и крАткое	(ee krAtkoye, short и)
К к	ка	(ka)
Л л	эль	(el')
М м	эм	(em)
Н н	эн	(en)
О о	о	(o)
П п	пэ	(peh)
Р р	эр	(air)
С с	эс	(es)
Т т	тэ	(teh)
У у	у	(oo)
Ф ф	эф	(ef)
Х х	ха	(kha)
Ц ц	цэ	(tse)
Ч ч	че	(che)
Ш ш	ша	(sha)
Щ щ	ща	(shsha)
ъ	твёрдый знак	(tvyOrdy znak, hard sign)
ы	ы	(iy)
ь	мЯгкий знак	(myAkhky znak, soft sign)
Э э	э	(eh)
Ю ю	ю	(yoo)
Я я	я	(ya)

ДиалОг 1

ОднУ минУточку	AdnOO minOOtuchkoo	(Wait) one moment
СлУшаю вас	SlOOshayoo vas	I'm listening to you
кОмната	kOmnata	room
нОмер	nOmyer	hotel room/number
ЗапОлните Этот бланк	ZapOlneetye Etot blank	Fill in this form
МОжно?	MOzhna?	Is it possible/Would you mind?

так	tak	*so*
но	no	*but*
я пишУ	ya peeshOO	*I write*
Как Это пИшется?	Kak Eta pEEshetsa?	*How is that spelled?*
Англия	Angleeya	*England*
Кто вы по профЕссии?	Kto vy pa prafyEssee?	*What are you by profession?*
учИтельница/ учитель	oochEEtyelneetsa/ oochEEtyel	*teacher (f/m)*
я рабОтаю	ya rabOtayoo	*I work*
в	v	*in*
шкОла	shkOla	*school*
граждАнство	grazhdAnstva	*nationality/ citizenship*
англичАнка	angleechAnka	*Englishwoman*
багАж	bagAsh	*luggage*
чемодАн	chimadAn	*suitcase*
сУмка	sOOmka	*bag*
аккордеОн	akordeOn	*accordion*
ключ	klyooch	*key*

ДиалОг 2

душ	doosh	*shower*
вАнная	vAnnaya	*bathroom*
туалЕт	tooalyEt	*toilet*
буфЕт	boofyEt	*snack bar*
внизУ	vneezOO	*downstairs*

ДиалОг 3

Где вы живёте?	Gdye vy zheevyOtye?	*Where do you live?*
Где вы рабОтаете?	Gdye vy rabOtayetye?	*Where do you work?*
инженЕр	eenzhinyEr	*engineer*
нЕмец	nyEmyets	*German man*
францУженка	frantsOOzhenka	*French woman*
я живУ	ya zheevOO	*I live*

продавЕц/	pradavyEts/	shop assistant (m/f)
продавщИца	pradavshshEEtsa	
конЕчно	kanyEshna	of course
рУсский/рУсская	rOOskee/rOOskaya	Russian man/ woman
америкАнец	amyirikAnyets	American man
врач	vrach	doctor
испАнка	eespAnka	Spanish woman

Dialogues

ДИАЛОГ 1

Fiona arrives at a hotel where she has reserved a room.

ФиОна	ЗдрАвствуйте.
АдминистрАтор	ОднУ минУточку. Да, слУшаю вас.
ФиОна	МенЯ зовУт ФиОна ХАрисон. Я хочУ кОмнату, пожАлуйста.
АдминистрАтор	*(looks through bookings)* ФиОна ХАрисон? Да, вот вАша фамИлия. ВАша кОмната нОмер 38 (трИдцать вОсемь).
ФиОна	СпасИбо.
АдминистрАтор	ЗапОлните Этот бланк.
ФиОна	*(handing the form to the administrator for help)* МОжно, пожАлуйста? Я говорЮ по-рУсски, но плОхо пишУ.
АдминистрАтор	МОжно. Как вАша фамИлия?
ФиОна	ФамИлия ХАрисон, и Имя ФиОна.
АдминистрАтор	Так, ХАрисон. Как Это пИшется, ФиОна?
ФиОна	Ф – и – о – н – а.
АдминистрАтор	КакОй у вас Адрес?

ФиОна	Англия, ШЕлтон, Улица КрОсли, дом 13 (тринАдцать).
АдминистрАтор	И кто вы по профЕссии?
ФиОна	Я учИтельница. Я рабОтаю в шкОле в ШЕлтоне.
АдминистрАтор	КакОе у вас граждАнство?
ФиОна	Я англичАнка.
АдминистрАтор	Ваш пАспорт, пожАлуйста.
ФиОна	Вот он.
АдминистрАтор	СпасИбо. У вас есть багАж?
ФиОна	Да, вот мой чемодАн, моЯ сУмка и мой аккордеОн.
АдминистрАтор	Вот ваш ключ.

ДИАЛОГ 2

Fiona is shown to her room.

АдминистрАтор	Вот вАша кОмната. Вот у вас телевИзор, телефОн и балкОн. И в коридОре душ, вАнная и туалЕт.
ФиОна	СпасИбо. СкажИте, в гостИнице есть рестирАн?
АдминистрАтор	Да, рестирАн, буфЕт и бар. Но рестирАн сейчАс закрЫт.
ФиОна	Как жаль! Как попАсть в буфЕт?
АдминистрАтор	БуфЕт напрАво. Это недалекО.
ФиОна	И бар?
АдминистрАтор	Бар внизУ.

CD 1, TR 7, 02:52

ДИАЛОГ 3

As you may have guessed from her luggage, Fiona has come to Moscow to an international conference of accordion players. At their first meeting, Fiona gets the ball rolling by asking everyone to introduce themselves and say where they work.

ФиОна	Кто вы по профЕссии? Где вы живёте и где вы рабОтаете?
Карл	МенЯ зовУт Карл. Я инженЕр. Я рабОтаю в институтЕ в БерлИне. Я нЕмец.
БрижИт	ЗдрАвствуйте, менЯ зовУт БрижИт. Я францУженка. Я учИтельница и я живУ в ЛиОне. Я там рабОтаю в шкОле.
СергЕй	МенЯ зовУт СергЕй. Я продавЕц и я рабОтаю в магазИне здесь в МосквЕ. Я, конЕчно, рУсский.
Грег	ЗдрАвствуйте, я америкАнец и менЯ зовУт Грег. Я актёр и я живУ в Нью ЙОрке.
ИрИна	Я врач. Меня зовУт ИрИна. Я рабОтаю в поликлИнике в НОвгороде. Я рУсская.
ХуанИта	МенЯ зовУт ХуанИта. Я продавщИца и рабОтаю в магазИне. Я живУ в БарселОне. Я испАнка.

Numerals 100–1,000

100 сто	sto		600 шестьсОт	shes-sOt
200 двЕсти	dvyEstee		700 семьсОт	syemsOt
300 трИста	trEEsta		800 восемьсОт	vasyemsOt
400 четЫреста	chitIryesta			
500 пятьсОт	pitsOt		900 девятьсОт	dyevitsOt
1,000 тЫсяча	tYsyacha			
1,539 тЫсяча пятьсОт трИдцать дЕвять			tYsyacha pitsOt trEEtsat' dyEvyat'	

Practise these numbers until you are confident with them, testing yourself with numbers which you see around you every day.

Mechanics of the language

1 How to say 'in'

You will remember that in Unit 5 you met the words в and на, meaning *to*, as in **Как попАсть в теАтр?** *How do I get to the theatre?* There the words в and на triggered the accusative case in the following word. However, when в and на mean *in* or *at* a certain place, they trigger a different case, known as the *prepositional case*, in the following word. Again, you use в unless you see (на) next to the word in your vocabulary list. You saw в used a good deal in **ДиалОг 3**. Did you notice what happened to the ending of each word following в?

Masculine	**Feminine**
(инститУт) в инститУте	(шкОла) в шкОле
(теАтр) в теАтре	(поликлИника) в поликлИнике
(НОвгород) в НОвгороде	(МосквА) в МосквЕ

Masculine words generally add the ending -e and feminine words replace the ending -a with -e.

2 How to say which one you mean (demonstrative pronouns)

Did you notice in **ДиалОг 1** that Fiona was told to fill in *this* form, **ЗапОлните Этот бланк? Этот** is the word for *this* or *that* which is used to point out masculine words. So, **ДАйте, пожАлуйста, Этот чемодАн** would mean *Please give me that suitcase*. If you want to refer to a feminine noun, use **Эта** instead. *This girl is my daughter* would be **Эта дЕвушка – моЯ дочь.** For neuter words you need to use **Это**, as in **ПокажИте, пожАлуйста, Это рАдио** *Please show me that radio*. To refer to plural nouns use **Эти**, as in **Эти билЕты – моИ.** *These tickets are mine.*

3 ГРАЖДАНСТВО (Grazhdanstva) Nationality

In **ДиалОг 3** you met people of different nationalities. As you would expect, there are different words in Russian to refer to the male and female of a particular nationality, so a Russian man is **рУсский** and a Russian woman is **рУсская**. In the chart below you can see the name of the country, the words for a man and woman of that nationality, and finally the language which they speak. You could make up sentences to practise: **Вы рУсский? Вы, конЕчно, говорИте по-рУсски!**

◀) CD 1, TR 7, 05:42

	Country	Man	Woman	Language
	(странА)	(мужчИна)	(жЕнщина)	(язЫк)
Russia	**РоссИя**	**рУсский**	**рУсская**	**по-рУсски**
	RassEEya	rOOsky	rOOskaya	pa-rOOsky
England	**Англия**	**англичАнин**	**англичАнка**	**по-англИйски**
	Angleeya	angleechAnin	angleechAnka	pa-anglEEsky
America	**АмЕрика**	**америкАнец**	**америкАнка**	**по-англИйски**
	AmyEreeka	amereekAnyets	amereekAnka	pa-anglEEsky
Japan	**ЯпОния**	**япОнец**	**япОнка**	**по-япОнски**
	YapOniya	yapOnyets	yapOnka	pa-yapOnsky
Spain	**ИспАния**	**испАнец**	**испАнка**	**по-испАнски**
	EespAniya	eespAnyets	eespAnka	pa-eespAnsky
France	**ФрАнция**	**францУз**	**францУженка**	**по-францУзски**
	FrAntsiya	frantsOOs	frantsOOzhenka	pa-frantsOOzsky
Germany	**ГермАния**	**нЕмец**	**нЕмка**	**по-немЕцки**
	GermAniya	nyEmyets	nyEmka	pa-nemyEtsky

Exercises

1 You are staying in St Petersburg when a friend calls you asking for the phone numbers of hotels in the city. You look in a directory and read out the names and numbers of the following hotels. The line is poor so you have to spell them out clearly. Read them out loud and check them on the recording.

◀) **CD 1, TR 7, 07:28**

i	АстОрия	311–42–06
ii	ЕврОпа	312–00–72
iii	КарЕлия	226–35–15
iv	ОлИмпия	119–68–00
v	Санкт-ПетербУрг	542–94–11
vi	КоммодОр	119–66–66

2 Tony, a visiting sports coach, has to fill in a registration form **анкЕта** at the hotel reception desk. Match the information required with his personal details. His written Russian is not very good, so he spells out his details for the **администрАтор**. Read the spellings out loud.

> **АнкЕта**
>
> **a** ФамИлия
> **b** Имя
> **c** Адрес
> **d** ГраждАнство
> **e** ПрофЕссия
> **f** НОмер пАспорта

i АngличАнин **ii** КАртер **iii** ТрЕнер **iv** Антони **v** Р 243569 О
vi Англия, СтОкпорт, Эдуард Стрит, дом 35.

3 See if you can guess what nationality these people are.

a шотлАндец/шотлАндка **b** португАлец/португАлка
c ирлАндец/ирлАндка **d** норвЕжец/норвЕжка

4 Below you have a jumbled up table of information about four people. You are told their **Имя** *name*, **граждАнство** *nationality*, **профЕссия** *job* and **где рабОтает** *where he or she works*. See if you can sort out the information so that it makes sense, i.e. so that a French person with a French name is working in a French city. Make up a sentence about each person. The first one has been done for you: **a** МарИ – францУженка. ОнА врач. ОнА рабОтает в больнИце в ПарИже.

Имя	ГраждАнство	ПрофЕссия	Где рабОтает
a МарИ	**i** рУсский	**1** учИтель	**A** в теАтре в АрхАнгельске
b Ханс	**ii** францУженка	**2** актёр	**B** в шкОле в БерлИне
c БорИс	**iii** англичАнка	**3** продавщИца	**C** в больнИце в ПарИже
d ДжЕнни	**iv** нЕмец	**4** врач	**D** в магазИне в БирмингЕме

5 Match up the questions and answers so that they make sense.

a Где вы рабОтаете?

b Кто вы по профЕссии?

c Как попАсть в буфЕт?

d Вы говорИте по-англИйски?

e Как вАша фамИлия?

f МагазИн открЫт?

g Как вас зовУт?

i МоЯ фамИлия БрАдли.

ii ИдИте прЯмо и буфЕт налЕво.

iii Я рабОтаю в шкОле.

iv Нет, магазИн закрЫт.

v Я врач.

vi МенЯ зовУт СергЕй.

vii Нет, я говорЮ по-францУзски.

6 Remembering that after **в** and **на** (meaning *in* or *at*) you have to change the ending of the following word, choose the correct form in these sentences.

a Я рабОтаю в больнИца / больнИце в АрхАнгельске / АрхАнгельск.

b – Где футболИсты? – ФутболИсты на стадиОн / стадиОне.

c В гостИнице / гостИница есть буфЕт?

d – МолодОй человЕк, где здесь бар? – Бар внизУ, в ресторАн / ресторАне.

7 Underline the correct demonstrative form (**Этот, Эта, Это, Эти**) in the following sentences.

(**Этот, Эта, Это, Эти**) кнИга Очень интерЕсная.
ПокажИте, пожАлуйста, (**Этот, Эта, Это, Эти**) пАспорт.
(**Этот, Эта, Это, Эти**) сигарЕты не моИ. ОнИ вАши.
ДАйте, пожАлуйста, (**Этот, Эта, Это, Эти**) рАдио.

8 Read out loud the following selection of international dialling codes from Russia. Try to work out which countries are represented, and match them up with their English equivalents.

a	АвстрАлия	61	**i**	*Germany*
b	БанглаДеш	880	**ii**	*Canada*
c	БолгАрия	359	**iii**	*Fiji*
d	ГайАна	592	**iv**	*Israel*
e	ГермАния	49	**v**	*Ethiopia*
f	ИзрАиль	972	**vi**	*Australia*
g	КанАда	1	**vii**	*Bulgaria*
h	СингапУр	65	**viii**	*Guyana*
i	ФИджи	679	**ix**	*Singapore*
j	ЭфиОпия	251	**x**	*Bangladesh*

9 The dialogue below, between a hotel administrator and a tourist called Richard Rigby, has been written down in the wrong order. Unscramble it, beginning with the phrase in bold print.

АдминистрАтор	РИчард РИгби
1 Вы америкАнец?	**2** У вас есть кОмната?
3 ЗапОлните Этот бланк, пожАлуйста.	**4** ЗдрАвствуйте.
5 СлУшаю вас.	**6** Нет, я англичАнин.
7 Да. Как вас зовУт?	**8** МенЯ зовУт РИчард РИгби.

10 Try saying your own name with a Russian accent, and then spell out the sound of your name in Russian letters. Some sounds are tricky to reproduce, but here are a few clues from common English names.

Carol	КЭрол	*George*	Джордж
Catherine	КАтрин	*Hugh*	Хью
Jane	Джейн	*John*	Джон
Susan	СьЮзан	*Simon*	САймон
Wendy	УЭнди	*William*	УИльям

TEST YOURSELF

Now you know how to book yourself into a hotel and have a conversation about where you are from and what you do. You can also count up to a thousand! Just before you move on to the next unit, try these 10 questions to make sure you have remembered what you have learned. Don't worry if you have forgotten a few things – words and phrases will get easier to remember the more times you use them.

What do these words and phrases mean?

1 МОжно?

2 Где вы рабОтаете?

3 Я живУ в МосквЕ.

4 Как Это пИшется?

5 Я рУсский.

How would you say these words and phrases in Russian? Say your answers out loud and check the answers in the back of the book.

6 One moment.

7 I work in a shop.

8 Do you speak English?

9 Is the shop open?

10 596

КотОрый час?

What time is it?

In this unit you will learn
- *How to tell the time*
- *How to say the days of the week*
- *How to talk about meals and daily routine*
- *How to make arrangements*

Before you start

If you go to Russia, or meet Russians at home, you need to understand when things are happening and at what time public places open and close. For this, you need to be able to tell the time and know the days of the week. With the structures introduced in this unit you will be able to make arrangements and feel in control.

ЗАвтрак, обЕд, Ужин *Breakfast, dinner, supper*

ЗАвтрак (zAftrak) *breakfast* may be **кАша** (kAsha) *porridge*, meat, cheese, fish or eggs and tea or coffee. There is nearly always bread on a Russian meal table as well. At midday you may have a second breakfast if your main meal is to be in the evening.

ОбЕд (abyEt) *dinner* is the main meal and may be eaten at any time from midday to late evening. It may include **закУски** (zakOOsky) *starters*, a soup and a main dish, followed by cake and tea or coffee.

Ужин (OOzhin) *supper* is a light meal, served in the evening.

Telling the time

◀️ **CD 1, TR 8**

To ask the time, you say:

КотОрый час? (KatOry chas?) literally *Which hour?* or **СкОлько сейчАс врЕмени?** (SkOl'ka syeychAs vryEmyinee?) literally *How much now time?*

Insight

Telling the time on the hour is easy.

| **СейчАс час.** | SyeychAs chas | *Now it's one o'clock.* |
| **СейчАс два часА.** | SyeychAs dva chasA | *Now it's two o'clock.* |

3.00	**Три часА**	tree chasA
4.00	**ЧетЫре часА**	chitYrye chasA
5.00	**Пять часОв**	pyat' chasOf
6.00	**Шесть часОв**	shest' chasOf
7.00	**Семь часОв**	syem' chasOf
8.00	**ВОсемь часОв**	vOsyem' chasOf
9.00	**ДЕвять часОв**	dyEvyat' chasOf
10.00	**ДЕсять часОв**	dyEsyat' chasOf
11.00	**ОдИннадцать часОв**	adEEnatsat' chasOf
12.00	**ДвенАдцать часОв**	dvyenAtsat' chasOf

ПОлдень	POldyen'	*Midday*
ПОлночь	POlnoch'	*Midnight*

Час means *hour*. A watch or clock is **часЫ**, literally *hours*. Notice that **час** has different endings depending on which number it follows. After one you use **час**, after two, three and four you use **часА** and after 5–20 you use **часОв**. To complete the 24-hour clock, after 21 you use **час**, and after 22, 23 and 24 you use **часА**.

To ask *At what time?* say **В котОром часУ?**

To say *At five o'clock* say **В пять часОв.**

Telling the time if it is not on the hour can be done in a number of ways, but the easiest is to do it digitally, for example *10.20* is **дЕсять часОв двАдцать минУт** and *4.45* is **четЫре часА сОрок пять минУт.**

ДиалОг 1

когдА	kagdA	*when*
музЕй открывАется	moozyEy atkrivAyetsa	*the museum opens*
выходнОй день	vykhadnOy dyen'	*day off*
втОрник	ftOrneek	*Tuesday*
музЕй-квартИра	moozyEy-kvartEEra	*former flat preserved as museum*
средА	sryidA	*Wednesday*
зоологИческий музЕй	za-alagEEchesky moozyEy	*zoological museum*
пОздно	pOzdna	*late*
пЯтница	pyAtneetsa	*Friday*

ДиалОг 2

концЕрт начинАется	kantsyErt nachinAyetsa	*the concert begins*
четвЕрг	chitvyErk	*Thursday*
рАно	rAna	*early*
кАждый день	kAzhdy dyen'	*every day*

ДиалОг 3

Утром	OOtrum	*in the morning*
я встаЮ	ya fstayOO	*I get up*

я зАвтракаю	ya zAftrakayoo	*I have breakfast*
я идУ	ya eedOO	*I go (on foot in one direction)*
рабОта (на)	rabOta	*work*
я обЕдаю	ya abyEdayoo	*I have dinner*
вЕчером	vyEchirom	*in the evening*
я Ужинаю	ya OOzhinayoo	*I have supper*
я смотрЮ	ya smatryOO	*I watch*
я ложУсь спать	ya lazhOOs' spat'	*I go to bed*

ДиалОг 4		
Где мы встрЕтимся?	Gdye my fstryEtimsa?	*Where shall we meet?*
зАл ФилармОнии	zal FeelarmOnee	*Philharmonic hall*
ВстрЕтимся	FstryEtimsa	*Let's meet*

Dialogues

ДИАЛОГ 1

Steven is visiting his friend CАша in St Petersburg for a week. They are trying to plan their time. There are several museums which Steven wants to visit, but first he must find out which **выходнОй день** *(vykhadnOy dyen') day off each museum has. CАша looks through the phone directory to find out details.*

CD 1, TR 8, 00:54

СтИвен	САша, когдА открывАется рУсский музЕй?
САша	РУсский музЕй открывАется в 10 часОв. ВыходнОй день – втОрник.
СтИвен	И музЕй-квартИра ПУшкина?
САша	ОднУ минУточку. Да, музЕй-квартИра ПУшкина открывАется в 10 часОв. ВыходнОй день – средА.
СтИвен	И когдА открывАется зоологИческий музЕй?
САша	ЗоологИческий музЕй открывАется пОздно, в 11 часОв. ВыходнОй день – пЯтница.

ДИАЛОГ 2

When they have planned their days, they think about the evenings.
They want to go to a concert and see a film.

CD 1, TR 8, 01:52

СтИвен	КогдА начинАется концЕрт?
САша	КонцЕрт в четвЕрг. Он начинАется рАно, в 6 часОв.
СтИвен	И когдА начинАется фильм?
САша	КАждый день фильм начинАется в 4 часА и в 7 часОв.

ДИАЛОГ 3

Steven wants to fit in with Sasha's life, so Sasha tells him about his
daily routine.

CD 1, TR 8, 02:18

| САша | Утром я встаЮ в 8 часОв и зАвтракаю в 9 часОв. ПотОм я идУ на рабОту в библиотЕку. БиблиотЕка открывАется в 10 часОв. Я там обЕдаю, и вЕчером я Ужинаю дОма в 7 часОв. ПотОм я смотрЮ телевИзор и пОздно ложУсь спать. |

ДИАЛОГ 4

Before Sasha leaves for work, Steven asks where they should meet
before going to the concert.

CD 1, TR 8, 02:56

СтИвен	Где мы встрЕтимся, САша?
САша	КонцЕрт начинАется в 6 часОв в зАле ФилармОнии. ВстрЕтимся в 5 часОв в библиотЕке. МОжно, СтИвен?
СтИвен	МОжно.

Mechanics of the language

1 *Days of the week*

🔊 CD 1, TR 8, 03:24

Monday	**понедЕльник**	panidyEl'neek
Tuesday	**втОрник**	ftOrneek
Wednesday	**средА**	sryidA
Thursday	**четвЕрг**	chitvyErk
Friday	**пЯтница**	pyAtneetsa
Saturday	**суббОта**	soobOta
Sunday	**воскресЕнье**	vaskrisyEn'ye

Note that the days of the week and months are written with lower-case letters in Russian.

To ask what day it is, say **КакОй сегОдня день?** (KakOy sivOdnya dyen'?) Notice that the word **сегОдня** *today* is not pronounced as it is spelled, the **г** being pronounced as a **в**. To say what day it is, say **сегОдня суббОта** (sivOdnya soobOta) *today is Saturday*.

If you want to say *on* a day of the week, use **в**. If the day of the week ends in -**а**, change -**а** to -**у**, for example, **в суббОту**.

on Monday	**в понедЕльник**	fpanidyEl'neek
on Tuesday	**во втОрник**	vo vtOrneek
on Wednesday	**в срЕду**	fsryEdoo
on Thursday	**в четвЕрг**	fchitvyErk
on Friday	**в пЯтницу**	fpyAtneetsoo
on Saturday	**в суббОту**	fsoobOtoo
on Sunday	**в воскресЕнье**	v-vaskrisyEn'ye

Notice that when you say **on** *Wednesday* the stress changes from **средА** to **в срЕду**.

2 First, second, third … Ordinal numerals

In the next unit you will be learning the months so that you can say the date in Russian. To prepare for this you need to know the ordinal numerals in Russian, *first, second, third* etc. Once you get past the first few, they are formed quite logically by adding an adjective ending to the numerals you already know. In this unit you will meet the ordinal numerals from first to tenth in their masculine forms, for use with masculine nouns (**десЯтый этАж** disyAty etAsh *tenth floor*).

Insight

When you are in Russia, remember that the ground floor is called **пЕрвый этАж** (pyErvy etAsh), so an English first floor will be **вторОй этАж** (ftarOy etAsh).

1st	**пЕрвый**	pyErvy
2nd	**вторОй**	ftarOy
3rd	**трЕтий**	tryEty
4th	**четвЁртый**	chitvyOrty
5th	**пЯтый**	pyAty
6th	**шестОй**	shestOy
7th	**седьмОй**	syidmOy
8th	**восьмОй**	vas'mOy
9th	**девЯтый**	divyAty
10th	**десЯтый**	disyAty

In the next unit you will need to become familiar with 1st to 31st in order to deal with any date which may arise.

Exercises

1 Listen to the recording and jot down (using numbers) the times that places open and events begin.

◆ CD 1, TR 8, 04:15

a БассЕйн открывАется в . . .
b Опера начинАется в . . .
c БуфЕт открывАется в . . .
d МарафОн начинАется в . . .
e ГалерЕя открывАется в . . .
f КонцЕрт начинАется в . . .
g ЗоопАрк открывАется в . . .
h МоЯ рабОта начинАется в . . .
i Фильм начинАется в . . .

2 КотОрый час? What would you say for these times?

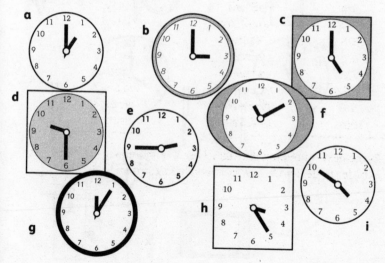

3 Look at the pictures below and fill in the blanks in the captions. If you need to, choose from the verbs below in brackets.

  a В _____ часОв я _____.
  b В _____ часОв я _____.
  c В _____ часОв я _____ на рабОту.
  d В час я _____ на рабОте.
  e В _____ часОв я Ужинаю дОма.
  f В _____ часОв я _____ телевИзор.
  g В _____ часОв я ложУсь спать.

(встаЮ   идУ   обЕдаю   зАвтракаю   смотрЮ)

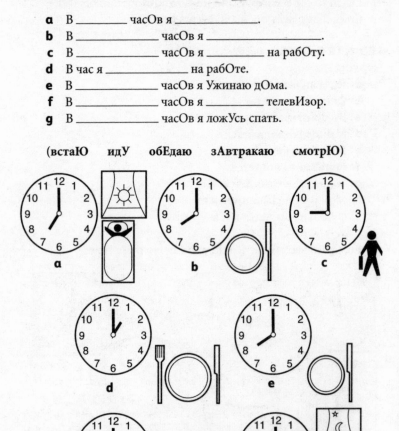

4 Read the details of these St Petersburg museums in your English language guidebook, and tell your Russian friend out loud at what time they open, on which days they are closed, and what their telephone numbers are.

	Time of opening	Day off	Telephone number
a *Museum of Anthropology and Ethnography* МузЕй антрополОгии и этногрАфии	11.00	Sat	218-14-12
b *Museum of Musical Instruments* МузЕй музыкАльных инструмЕнтов	12.00	Tues	314-53-55
c *Museum Apartment of A. A. Blok* МузЕй-квартИра А. А. БлОка	11.00	Wed	113-86-33
d *Museum of the Arctic and Antarctic* МузЕй Арктики и АнтАрктики	10.00	Mon	311-25-49

5 Below is Anna's diary. Note the usual abbreviations for the days of the week. Each day she is seeing someone different and doing a different activity.

Пн.	Вт.	Ср.	Чт.	Пт.	Сб.	Вс.
САша	ТАня	Оля	Юрий	МАша	ДИма	КирИлл
фильм	обЕд	Опера	футбОл	экскУрсия	концЕрт	джаз

In the bottom of her bag she has seven scraps of paper on which her friends wrote down where they would meet her. See if you can match each scrap of paper to the right day.

a ВстрЕтимся на стадиОне в 3 часА.

b ВстрЕтимся в кинотеАтре в 7 часОв.

c ВстрЕтимся дОма в 6 часОв.

d ВстрЕтимся в теАтре Оперы и балЕта в 7 часОв.

e ВстрЕтимся в зАле ФилармОнии в 6 часОв.

f ВстрЕтимся в цЕнтре джАзовой мУзыки в 2 часА.

g ВстрЕтимся в автОбусе в час.

6 Here is a list of departments placed next to the lift in a multi-storey shop.

ШестОй этАж:	Факс.
ПЯтый этАж:	СЕйфы. ЛинОлеум. СувенИры.
Четвёртый этАж:	МР3-плЕеры, нОутбуки, прИнтеры, DVD-тЮунеры, LCD-телевИзоры.
ТрЕтий этАж:	МузыкАльные инструмЕнты. ФОто.
ВторОй этАж:	ПарфюмЕрия. КосмЕтика.
ПЕрвый этАж:	ГомеопатИческая аптЕка. Оптика – контАктные лИнзы.

On which floor would you be likely to find **a** contact lenses **b** perfume **c** a saxophone **d** a matryoshka doll **e** a safe **f** a fax **g** a printer **h** linoleum **i** lipstick?

7 Read the complete meal menus below and decide which one you would be likely to have for **зАвтрак, обЕд** and **Ужин**.

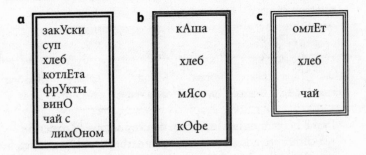

a
закУски
суп
хлеб
котлЕта
фрУкты
винО
чай с
    лимОном

b
кАша

хлеб

мЯсо

кОфе

c
омлЕт

хлеб

чай

8 Remember how the words **в** and **на** may be used in two different ways. The first way you met was in Unit 5 **Как попАсть в галерЕю?** *How do I get to the gallery?* Here **в** means *to*, and it changes the ending of following feminine nouns from **-а** to **-у** and from **-я** to **-ю**. Masculine and neuter nouns do not change. These are called *accusative* endings.

The second way of using **в** and **на** you met in Unit 7: **Я рабОтаю в магазИне в МосквЕ** *I work in a shop in Moscow.* Here **в** means *in* or *at* and it usually changes the ending of following nouns to -**е**. These are called *prepositional* endings.

Choose the correct endings in the following sentences, depending on whether they use **в** and **на** to mean *to* or *in*.

a Я рабОтаю в теАтр / теАтре в НОвгород / НОвгороде.
b Я идУ в библиотЕку / библиотЕке.
c Вы рабОтаете в университЕт / университЕте или в шкОлу / шкОле?
d – КудА вы идёте? – Я идУ в инститУт / инститУте.
e ИзвинИте, пожАлуйста. Как попАсть в поликлИнику / поликлИнике?

9 Listen to the recording. Anna is talking about some of the things she does on each day of the week. Fill in the gaps with the correct day of the week in English, and then say each whole sentence out loud in Russian.

◀) **CD 1, TR 8, 05:08**

a В _____ я рабОтаю в инститУте.
b В _____ я обЕдаю в ресторАне.
c В _____ вЕчером я смотрЮ телевИзор.
d В _____ я встаЮ рАно и слУшаю рАдио.
e В _____ Утром я идУ в библиотЕку. ПотОм в 2 часА я идУ в инститУт.
f В _____ я ложУсь спать Очень пОздно.
g В _____ я встаЮ и зАвтракаю пОздно.

10 This is a notice you might see on a shop door.

МагазИн рабОтает				
Пн	с	9.00	до	19.00
Вт	с	10.00	до	20.00
Ср	с	10.00	до	20.00
Чт	с	10.00	до	20.00
Пт	с	10.00	до	20.00
Сб	с	11.00	до	16.00
Вс	выходнОй день			
ПерерЫв на обЕд 13.00 – 14.00				

a On which day does the shop open early in the morning?
b When is the lunch break?
c On which day does the shop open late in the morning?
d On which day does the shop not open?
e At what time does the shop close on Saturdays?

11 On which day does the museum not open?

КАССА МУЗЕЯ
ВЫХОДНОЙ ДЕНЬ – ПЯТНИЦА

TEST YOURSELF

Now you know how to tell the time, say the days of the week, talk about your daily routine and make arrangements to meet people. Test yourself with these questions to see if you are ready to move on to the next unit.

1 Say the days of the week in the correct order and then in reverse order.

2 Say what time it is now. Keep asking yourself this question throughout the day!

3 How would you ask *When does the bank open?*

4 Ask *When does the film start?*

5 Tell a friend *Let's meet at 7 o'clock at the restaurant.*

6 The breakfast menu says кАша, мЮсли, хлеб, кОфе. What are you being offered?

7 Say that you get up at seven o'clock.

8 Say that you watch television in the evening.

9 Say that you work in Moscow.

10 Say that you are going to the theatre.

Вы лЮбите спорт?
Do you like sport?

In this unit you will learn
- *How to talk about leisure activities*
- *How to say the date*
- *How to talk about likes and dislikes*
- *How to use verbs in different forms*
- *How to use numerals over 1,000*

Before you start

When practising your Russian, do not worry too much about getting the word endings right, as you will still be understood even if you make a mistake. Concentrate on communicating, and with practice you will make fewer errors. Do not let fear of making a mistake stop you from trying to get your message across, as this is how you learn.

Once you make Russian friends you will probably want to express your likes and dislikes and say what you do in your free time. Here are some useful structures:

....

Я **Очень люблЮ** мУзыку	I **really love** music
Я **люблЮ** смотрЕть телевИзор	I **love/like** watching television
Я **не люблЮ** читАть	I **don't like** reading
Я **совсЕм не люблЮ** гулЯть	I **really don't like** walking
Я **игрАю в** бадминтОн	I **play** badminton
Я **игрАю на** гитАре	I **play** the guitar
Я **хожУ в** кинО	I (habitually) **go to the cinema**

....

Insight

ПрАздники Public holidays

Here are just a few of the **прАздники** (prAzdneeky) *public holidays* which are celebrated in Russia.

НОвый год	(NOvy got), 1 январЯ	New Year, 1 January
РождествО	(RazhdyestvO), 7 январЯ	Orthodox Christmas, 7 January
ЖЕнский день	(ZhEnsky dyen'), 8 мАрта	Women's Day, 8 March
День ПобЕды	(Dyen' pabyEdy), 9 мАя	Victory Day, 9 May, end of World War II

The greeting **с прАздником** (s prAzdneekum) means literally (*I congratulate you*) *with the holiday*, and may be applied to any occasion. To wish someone a *Happy New Year* say **с нОвым гОдом** (s nOvym gOdum). On New Year's Eve, Grandfather Frost **Дед МорОз** (Dyet MarOs) with his helper the Snowmaiden **СнегУрочка** (SnyigOOruchka) gives out presents by the tree **ёлка** (yOlka). *Happy Birthday* is rather a mouthful, **с днём рождЕния** (s dnyom razhdyEniya), literally *with the day of birth*.

Months

🔊 **CD 1, TR 9, 00:59**

The names of the months, which are all masculine, are easy to recognize.

January	**янвАрь**	yinvAr'
February	**феврАль**	fyevrAl'
March	**март**	mart
April	**апрЕль**	apryEl'
May	**май**	maee
June	**иЮнь**	eeyOOn'
July	**иЮль**	eeyOOl'
August	**Август**	Avgoost

September	**сентЯбрь**	syentyAbr'
October	**октЯбрь**	aktyAbr'
November	**ноЯбрь**	nayAbr'
December	**декАбрь**	dyekAbr'

....

хОбби	khObbee	hobby
я Очень люблЮ читАть	ya Ochen' lyooblyOO cheetAt'	I really love reading
вы читАете	vy cheetAyetye	you read
я читАю	ya cheetAyoo	I read
газЕта	gazyEta	newspaper
тОже	tOzhe	also
ромАн	ramAn	novel
интерЕсно	intiryEsna	that's interesting
я совсЕм не люблЮ читАть	ya savsyEm nye lyooblyOO cheetAt'	I really don't like reading
я игрАю в бадминтОн	ya eegrAyoo v badmeentOn	I play badminton
гулЯть	goolyAt'	to go for a walk
мУзыка	mOOzyka	music
я игрАю на саксофОне	ya eegrAyoo na saksafOnye	I play the saxophone
ходИть на концЕрты	khadEEt' na kantsyErty	to go (habitually) to concerts
путешЕствовать	pootyishEstvuvat'	to travel
пЯтое октябрЯ	pyAtoye aktyabryA	5th of October
ДИксиленд	DEEkseelend	Dixieland
Вы хотИте пойтИ	Vy khatEEtye paeetEE	Do you want to go?

QUICK VOCAB

Dialogue

ДИАЛОГ

George is introduced to Lyudmila, and they talk about their leisure interests. Listen to the recording or read the dialogue and answer the following questions: What interests does George have? What sports does Lyudmila play? Now listen or read again. What instrument does George play? Where do they decide to go and when?

ЛюдмИла	КакИе у вас хОбби?
Джордж	Я Очень люблЮ читАть.
ЛюдмИла	ЧитАть? КакИе кнИги вы читАете?
Джордж	КАждый день я читАю газЕты, и я тОже люблЮ читАть ромАны.
ЛюдмИла	ИнтерЕсно. Вы лЮбите рУсские ромАны?
Джордж	Да, Очень люблЮ. А вы, у вас есть хОбби?
ЛюдмИла	Да, но я совсЕм не люблЮ читАть! Я люблЮ спорт. Я игрАю в бадминтОн и в тЕннис, и я люблЮ гулЯть.
Джордж	Вы лЮбите мУзыку?
ЛюдмИла	Да, я Очень люблЮ джаз.
Джордж	Я тОже. Я игрАю на саксофОне. В ЛОндоне я Очень люблЮ ходИть на концЕрты.
ЛюдмИла	В ЛОндоне? СкажИте, вы не рУсский?
Джордж	Нет, я англичАнин. Я живУ в ЛОндоне.
ЛюдмИла	Вы хорошО говорИте по-рУсски.
Джордж	СпасИбо. Я говорЮ по-рУсски и по-францУзски, и я Очень люблЮ путешЕствовать.
ЛюдмИла	ИнтерЕсно. Джордж, вы лЮбите джаз и сегОдня пЯтое октябрЯ. СегОдня вЕчером я идУ на концЕрт – ДИксиленд. Вы хотИте пойтИ на концЕрт?
Джордж	Да, конЕчно я хочУ. СпасИбо. КогдА начинАется концЕрт?
ЛюдмИла	В семь часОв. ВстрЕтимся здесь в шесть часОв.
Джордж	ХорошО. СпасИбо, ЛюдмИла.
ЛюдмИла	ПожАлуйста.

126

Numerals 1,000–20,000

◆) CD 1, TR 9, 03:27

1,000	тЫсяча	tYsyacha
2,000	две тЫсячи	dvye tYsyachee
3,000	три тЫсячи	tree tYsyachee
4,000	четЫре тЫсячи	chitYrye tYsyachee
5,000	пять тЫсяч	pyat' tYsyach
6,000	шесть тЫсяч	shest' tYsyach
7,000	семь тЫсяч	syem' tYsyach
8,000	вОсемь тЫсяч	vOsyem' tYsyach
9,000	дЕвять тЫсяч	dyEvyat' tYsyach
10,000	дЕсять тЫсяч	dyEsyat' tYsyach
20,000	двАдцать тЫсяч	dvAtsat' tYsyach

Practise these numbers in whichever way has proved successful for you with lower numbers.

Mechanics of the language

1 КакОе сегОдня числО? *What is the date today?*

In answer to the question **КакОе сегОдня числО?** (KakOye sivOdnya cheeslO?) literally *which today number?*, you need the ordinal numbers which you learned in the previous unit. This time they need their neuter ending **-ое** to agree with the neuter **числО**. This is followed by the month with the ending **-а** or **-я** which gives the meaning *of*.

Ordinal numbers 1st–31st with neuter endings for forming dates:

◀) CD 1, TR 9, 04:11

1st	пЕрвое	pyErvoye	4th	четвёртое	chitvyOrtoye
2nd	вторОе	ftarOye	5th	пЯтое	pyAtoye
3rd	трЕтье	tryEt'ye	6th	шестОе	shestOye
7th	седьмОе	syedmOye	16th	шестнАдцатое	shestnAtsatoye
8th	восьмОе	vas'mOye	17th	семнАдцатое	syemnAtsatoye
9th	девЯтое	dyevyAtoye	18th	восемнАдцатое	vasyemnAtsatoye
10th	десЯтое	dyesyAtoye	19th	девятнАдцатое	dyevitnAtsatoye
11th	одИннадцатое	adEEnatsatoye	20th	двадцАтое	dvatsAtoye
12th	двенАдцатое	dvyenAtsatoye	21st	двАдцать пЕрвое	dvAtsat' pyErvoye
13th	тринАдцатое	treenAtsatoye	22nd	двАдцать вторОе	dvAtsat' ftarOye
14th	четЫрнадцатое	chitirnatsatoye	30th	тридцАтое	treetsAtoye
15th	пятнАдцатое	pitnAtsatoye	31st	трИдцать пЕрвое	trEEtsat' pyErvoye

The months with endings **-a** or **-я** for forming dates:

январЯ, февралЯ, мАрта, апрЕля, мАя, иЮня,
иЮля, Августа, сентябрЯ, октябрЯ, ноябрЯ, декабрЯ

So, **СегОдня пЯтое Августа** means *today is 5th August*.

12 Jan.	**двенАдцатое январЯ**	*2 Dec.*	**вторОе декабрЯ**
7 May	**седьмОе мАя**	*6 Feb.*	**шестОе февралЯ**
30 Sept.	**тридцАтое сентябрЯ**	*19 Mar.*	**девятнАдцатое мАрта**

To say *on* a certain date, the ending of the ordinal numeral should change to **-ого**, pronounced -ovo. An exception to this is **трЕтьего** *on the third*. **ДвенАдцатого Августа** – *on 12th August*.

To say *in* a month, you use **в** and change the ending of the month to **-е**.

в январЕ, в февралЕ, в мАрте, в апрЕле, в мАе,
в иЮне, в иЮле, в Августе, в сентябрЕ, в октябрЕ,
в ноябрЕ, в декабрЕ

in spring	весн**Ой**
in summer	л**Е**том
in autumn	**О**сенью
in winter	зим**Ой**

2 Verbs

Verbs are 'doing words,' for example *run, read, talk, sleep*. You have met some Russian verbs in phrases where they are already in their correct form: Вы **говор**Ите по-р**У**сски? It is hard to say anything without verbs, so to make up sentences yourself you will need to understand how they work. There are two main groups of verbs in Russian, which we will call group 1 and group 2. The infinitive is the form you will find if you look up a verb in the dictionary. It is the form of the verb which in English is expressed as to do, to eat, to sleep, to run.

Look at this English verb.

to work (infinitive)

(singular)		*(plural)*	
I	work	we	work
you	work	you	work
he/she/it	works	they	work

The same verb in Russian **раб**Отать is a group 1 verb, and it changes its endings more than its English equivalent. You have already met the two forms which are underlined in the box below.

раб**О**тать *(infinitive) to work*

(singular)		*(plural)*	
я	раб**О**та**ю**	мы	раб**О**та**ем**
ты	раб**О**та**ешь**	вы	раб**О**та**ете**
он/он**А**/он**О**	раб**О**та**ет**	он**И**	раб**О**та**ют**

To make the different forms of a group 1 verb, remove the -ть from the infinitive and add the endings in bold type. This applies to other group 1 verbs you have met, for example, знать, понимАть, зАвтракать, обЕдать, Ужинать, читАть, игрАть, гулЯть.

You have also met some group 2 verbs, for example говорИть.

говорИть *(infinitive) to speak/talk*

я	говорЮ	мы	говорИм
ты	говорИшь	вы	говорИте
он/онА/онО	говорИт	онИ	говорЯт

To make the different forms of a group 2 verb, remove the last three letters from the infinitive and add the endings. You have also met любИть, which is a group 2 verb. It is slightly unusual in the я form, because it inserts an л before the ending: я люблЮ. In future vocabulary lists you will often see 1 or 2 next to a verb indicating which group it belongs to so that you know what to do with it.

Some verbs are irregular, i.e. they do not follow the patterns given above, like хотЕть (khatyEt') *to want.*

я	хочУ	мы	хотИм
ты	хОчешь	вы	хотИте
он/онА/онО	хОчет	онИ	хотЯт

Another verb which is unusual is the group 1 verb **жить** (zheet') *to live.*

я	живУ	мы	живЁм
ты	живЁшь	вы	живЁте
он/онА/онО	живЁт	онИ	живУт

3 I love to, I want to, I play . . .

- *To say* I love doing something *say* **Я люблЮ** + *verb infinitive:* *e.g.* **Я люблЮ читАть** I love reading.
- *To say* I love something *say* **Я люблЮ** + *noun. Remember that the noun is a direct object, so it needs accusative endings. If it is feminine* **-a** *will change to* **-y** *and* **-я** *to* **-ю:** *e.g.* **Я люблЮ мУзыку** I love music. *If it is masculine or neuter it will not change:* *e.g.* **Я люблЮ спорт** I love sport.
- *To say* I want to do something *say* **Я хочУ** + *verb infinitive:* *e.g.* **Я хочУ говорИть по-рУсски** I want to speak Russian. **Я хочУ есть банАн и пить кОфе** I want to eat a banana and drink some coffee. (**Пить** *is the verb* to drink *and* **есть** *is the verb* to eat – *spelled exactly like* **есть** *in* **у менЯ есть**.)
- *To say* I play a sport *say* **Я игрАю в** + *sport: e.g.* **Я игрАю в бадминтОн/в футбОл/в гольф** I play badminton/football/golf.
- *To say* I play an instrument *say* **Я игрАю на** + *instrument, using the prepositional ending* **-e:** *e.g.* **Я игрАю на гитАре/на балалАйке** I play the guitar/balalaika.
- *To say* I (habitually) go somewhere *say* **Я хожУ в/на** + *place. Remember you are going to the place, so you need to use an accusative ending. If the place is feminine* **-a** *will change to* **-y** *and* **-я** *to* **-ю:** *e.g.* **Я хожУ в больнИцу/на вокзАл** I go to the hospital/station.

Exercises

1 On a visit to Russia you have a programme of cultural events to choose from. Read it out loud, including the dates, and answer the questions. For the first event, you will say:
СуббОта пЕрвое октябрЯ. ПьЕса. ОтЕлло. (**ПьЕса** *is a play*).

сб. 1 октябрЯ	ПьЕса. ОтЕлло
вс. 2 октябрЯ	ПьЕса. Три сестры
пн. 3 октябрЯ	ПьЕса. КлаУстрофобия
вт. 4 октябрЯ	Опера. БорИс ГодунОв
ср. 5 октябрЯ	КонцЕрт. ДИксиленд «МИстер Джаз»
чт. 6 октябрЯ	КонцЕрт. Бах, ШУберт и ШУман
пт. 7 октябрЯ	ПьЕса. Три мушкетёра

a If you liked classical music, which evening would suit you?
b If you liked jazz, which evening would interest you?
c What is the title of the Chekhov play on Sunday?
d On which evening could you see an opera?

2 Volodya is writing an illustrated letter to his little niece saying what he likes to do at different times of year.

ВеснОй я люблЮ путешЕствовать.

ЛЕтом я люблЮ игрАть в тЕннис и читАть на плЯже.

Осенью я люблЮ гулЯть в пАрке.

ЗимОй я люблЮ игрАть в хоккЕй и смотрЕть телевИзор.

Now respond by saying what you like doing at different times of year. You could also add what you like doing at different times of day: **Утром** (OOtrum) *in the morning*, **днём** (dnyom) *in the afternoon*, **вЕчером** (vyEchirom) *in the evening*, **нОчью** (nOch'yoo) *at night*.

3 Listen to the recording, and write down in English which activities the following people like and dislike. You may not catch every word they say, but try to pick out the relevant details.

◆) **CD 1, TR 9, 05:10**

  a БорИс   **b** ЛИза   **c** АндрЕй   **d** НИна

4 КакОе сегОдня числО? Read these dates out loud, and fill in the blanks.

  a 1 Jan. – НОвый год.
  b 7 Jan. – РождествО.
  c 8 March – ЖЕнский день.
  d 9 May – День ПобЕды.
  e СегОдня _____
  f Мой день рождЕния (*birthday*) _____.

For the remaining dates, say *on 13th June* тринАдцатого иЮня and so on.

  g 13 June, 24 December, 31 October
  h 6 September, 3 October, 14 February

Pick some more dates at random from a calendar and practise until you feel confident.

5 Below are 12 jumbled sentences. Match the correct halves together.

a	Я игрАю на	**i**	хОбби?
b	Я игрАю в	**ii**	девЯтое апрЕля.
c	Я хожУ в	**iii**	лимонАд.
d	Я рабОтаю в	**iv**	по-рУсски.
e	Я хочУ есть	**v**	пАрке.
f	Я гулЯю в	**vi**	хоккЕй.
g	Я говорЮ	**vii**	салАт.
h	Я хочУ пить	**viii**	мУзыку.
i	СегОдня	**ix**	саксофОне.
j	Я Очень люблЮ	**x**	магазИне.
k	Я хочУ	**xi**	библиотЕку.
l	КакИе у вас	**xii**	смотрЕть телевИзор.

6 What are these numbers? Write down the answers in figures.

◀)) **CD 1, TR 9, 06:18**

a шесть тЫсяч
b четЫрнадцать тЫсяч пятьсОт
c двАдцать тЫсяч трИста вОсемьдесят
d пять тЫсяч трИста сОрок шесть
e девятнАдцать тЫсяч девятьсОт двАдцать три
f две тЫсячи четЫреста одИннадцать
g тЫсяча двЕсти девянОсто вОсемь.
h дЕсять тЫсяч пятьсОт трИдцать одИн

Now look at your answers and see if you can say the numbers in Russian without looking at the questions! Good luck!

7 Choose the right endings for these verbs.

a Я рабОтаю/рабОтаете в шкОле.
b Вы говорЮ/говорИте по-рУсски?
c Я не понимАете/понимАю.
d Я люблЮ/лЮбите чай с лимОном.
e Вы живУ/живёте в ЛОндоне?

f КАждый день я зАвтракаю/зАвтракаете дОма.

g Осенью я гулЯю/гулЯете в пАрке.

8 НиколАй НиколАевич has agreed to answer some questions for a survey you are conducting. Can you ask him the following questions in Russian?

a What is your name?

b Are you Russian?

c Where do you live?

d What is your profession?

e Where do you work?

f Do you have any hobbies?

g Do you like sport?

How would you answer these questions in Russian if you were asked?

9 КогдА мы встрЕтимся? When shall we meet?
You are making arrangements to meet Russian friends. Read out **a** and **b** and jot down the dates and times in English. Then change **c** and **d** into Russian and say them out loud.

a В суббОту, двАдцать пЯтого мАя, в шесть часОв.

b В четвЕрг, трИдцать пЕрвого иЮля, в дЕвять часОв двАдцать пять минУт.

c On Monday, 8th February, at 7.30.

d On Friday, 16th March, at 5 o' clock.

10 What do you think these people enjoy in their free time?

a Я хожУ в бильЯрдный клуб.

b Я люблЮ смотрЕть спУтниковое ТВ.

c Я люблЮ игрАть в бадминтОн и в америкАнский пул.

d Я люблЮ компьЮтерные Игры.

e Я хожУ в казинО.

f Я Очень люблЮ фен-шУй.

Listen to **АндрЕй** talking about himself. Put ticks in the boxes below to show what he likes and dislikes. If you do not have the recording, work from the text below.

	Я Очень люблЮ	Я люблЮ	Я не люблЮ	Я совсЕм не люблЮ
a Work				
b Sport				
c Music				
d Watching TV				
e Travel				
f Cinema				

ЗдрАвствуйте! МенЯ зовУт АндрЕй. Я живУ в МосквЕ. Я – студЕнт в университЕте и в суббОту и в воскресЕнье я рабОтаю в ресторАне. Я официАнт. Я не люблЮ рабОтать в ресторАне. Я Очень люблЮ спорт, и игрАю в хоккЕй, в футбОл, в тЕннис и в бадминтОн. Я люблЮ мУзыку, игрАю на гитАре и хожУ на концЕрты. Я совсЕм не люблЮ смотрЕть телевИзор. ЛЕтом я Очень люблЮ путешЕствовать и зимОй я люблЮ ходИть в кинО.

Now talk about yourself in Russian, your likes and dislikes. You might like to make a recording. Try to imitate the accent of the people you have heard on the recording.

TEST YOURSELF

You are really doing well and your Russian is now good enough for you to have a genuine conversation in which you can express your own preferences and find out what other people enjoy.

To make sure that you are ready to go on to the next unit, see if you can read this conversation out loud and then write it down in English.

A   КакИе у вас хОбби?

Б   Я Очень люблЮ читАть газЕты и путешЕствовать.

A   ИнтерЕсно.

В   А вы, у вас есть хОбби?

A   Да, но я совсЕм не люблЮ читАть! Я люблЮ спорт. ЗимОй я игрАю в хоккЕй и лЕтом я люблЮ гулЯть.

Б   Вы лЮбите мУзыку?

A   Нет, не Очень. А вы?

Б   Я Очень люблЮ мУзыку и люблЮ ходИть на концЕрты.

Now that you have done that, look at your English answers and see if you can put them back into Russian.

10

ВходИте пожАлуйста!
Do come in!

In this unit you will learn
- *How to talk about home and family (yours and theirs!)*
- *How to be a guest in a Russian home*
- *How to read a public transport route plan*

Before you start

In the last few units you have built up a lot of vocabulary and new structures. In this unit you should aim to consolidate everything you have learned before moving on to the second section of the book. You now know enough to experiment and make up sentences of your own, and you are able to hold a conversation in Russian. If you don't understand what is being said to you, don't panic. Try to guess what is being said, or ask for an explanation of a particular word or phrase. If you can't think how to express yourself, don't give up, but paraphrase or simplify what you want to say. You learn best by trying things out and building up your skills, just as you build up muscles in physical exercise. You will probably find that people are very willing to help you.

Insight

СемьЯ (Sim'yA) *The family*

In many Russian families, three generations share one home. Living space in cities is at a premium, so you may find that the дивАн in the living room is a sofa by day and a bed by night. **БАбушка** *grandmother* may help to bring up the children and run the home while the parents work. Pre-school children may attend **Ясли** (yAsly) *nursery* and **дЕтский сад** (dyEtskee sat) *kindergarten*. If you visit a Russian home, you may be offered slippers **тАпочки** (tApochkee) to wear when you arrive, as outdoor shoes are not generally worn inside. Be prepared for warm hospitality from your Russian hosts.

ДАча (DAcha) *A country house, but much more besides*

A dacha can be anything from a structure like a garden shed to a magnificent lodge in the country. Russian city dwellers fortunate enough to have a **дАча** may use it and its plot of land to grow fruit, vegetables and flowers and to rear chickens and pigs, visiting at weekends to enjoy the fresh air and to bring home-grown produce back to the city. They may house the grandparents and children there in the warmer months, and they gather berries and mushrooms in the woods.

ПрестИжные райОны (PristEEzhneeye rayOny)
Prestige areas

In the 1990s a boom began in creating elite properties for the more affluent Russians. Large buildings in older prestigious areas of cities were converted into **элИтные квартИры** *elite apartments*. New blocks of apartments were also built to high standards, often with a **консьЕрж** *concierge* and a **домофОн** *entry phone* to control access. At the same time, communities of exclusive housing sprang up on the edges of cities, consisting of properties described as **дом** *house* or **кОттедж** *cottage*, but often covering in excess of **сто квадрАтных мЕтров** *100 square metres* and set in secure compounds. When reading adverts for even modest properties in such communities you may come across words such as **комфОрт** *comfort*, **камИн** *a fireplace* and **джакУзи** *a jacuzzi*.

МаршрУты (MarshrOOty) *Transport routes*

When finding your way around a Russian city you may need to consult a plan of bus, trolleybus and tram routes. Major roads on the route will be named. You already know **Улица** *street*, **проспЕкт** *avenue*, **плОщадь** *square* and **мост** *bridge*, but here are two more useful words: **нАбережная** (nAbyiryezhnaya) *embankment* and **шоссЕ** (shossEy) *highway*.

ДиалОг 1

вхо́дИте	vkhadEEtye	come in
садИтесь	sadEEtyes'	sit down
семьЯ	sim'yA	family
Да, есть	Da, yest'	Yes, I have/he has/they have, etc.
посмотрИте	pasmatrEEtye	look (imperative)
у менЯ (есть)	oo minya (yest')	I have
альбОм	al'bOm	album
женА	zhinA	wife
муж	moosh	husband
дЕти	dyEtee	children
вИдите	vEEdeetye	you see
их зовУт	eekh zavOOt	they are called
машИна	mashEEna	car
её зовУт	yiyO zavOOt	she is called
дАча (на)	dAcha	dacha (country house)
мать/отЕц	mat'/atyEts	mother/father
на пЕнсии	na pyEnsee	on a pension (retired)
их	eekh	them
егО зовУт	yivO zavOOt	he is called
энергИчный	inyergEEchnee	energetic
дерЕвня	dyiryEvnya	countryside/village
дЯдя/тётя	dyAdya/tyOtya	uncle/aunt

ДиалОг 2

Улица МИра	OOleetsa MEEra	*street (of) peace*
у нас (есть)	oo nas (yest')	*we have*
гостИная	gastEEnaya	*living room*
спАльня	spAl'nya	*bedroom*
кУхня	kOOkhnya	*kitchen (also cookery)*
нОвый/стАрый	nOvy/stAry	*new/old*
прекрАсный	prikrAsny	*fine*
столОвая	stalOvaya	*dining room*
нАша собАка	nAsha sabAka	*our dog* (**наш** works like **ваш**)
рекА МОйка (на)	ryikA MOika	*River Moika*
кабинЕт	kabeenyEt	*study*
вид	veet	*view*
так приЯтно	tak preeyAtna	*so pleasant*

ДиалОг 3

почемУ?	pachemOO?	*Why?*
потомУ, что	patamOO shta	*because*
магазИн	magazEEn	*shop*
по магазИнам	pa magazEEnam	*round the shops*
наш гОрод	nash gOrat	*our city*
исторИческий	eestarEEcheskee	*historical*
спокОйно	spakOina	*peaceful*
лес, в лесУ	lyes, vlyesOO	*forest, in the forest*
ПриезжАйте к нам в гОсти	PreeyezhAitye k nam v gOstee	*Come and visit us* (literally *Come to us as guest*)

Insight

Russians are extremely well educated but they also have some superstitious practices which are quite deep rooted in their culture. For example, you should never shake hands or greet someone over the threshold. This is considered to be very bad luck. Instead you should step inside first.

Dialogues

ДИАЛОГ 1

Sally goes with НатАша to visit НиколАй. Once the introductions are over, she asks him if he has any family. He gets out his photos. How many children does he have, and where do his parents live in the summer?

♦ CD 2, TR 1

НиколАй	ВходИте, САлли! МенЯ зовУт НиколАй.
САлли	Очень приЯтно, НиколАй.
НиколАй	Очень приЯтно, САлли. СадИтесь, пожАлуйста.
САлли	*(sitting down on toy car)* ИзвинИте! СкажИте, у вас есть семьЯ?
НиколАй	Да, есть. ПосмотрИте, у менЯ здесь альбОм. Это моЯ женА, и вот дЕти, вИдите? У менЯ сын и дочь. Их зовУт АлЁша и ЛИза. АлЁша Очень лЮбит машИны и ЛИза лЮбит спорт. ЖенА – учИтельница. ЕЁ зовУт ГАля. ЖенА и дЕти сейчАс на дАче.
САлли	На дАче? Как хорошО. *(looking at next photo)* А кто Это? Мать и отЕц?
НиколАй	Да, Это мАма и пАпа. ОнИ на пЕнсии, и лЕтом онИ живУт на дАче. Я их Очень люблЮ. А вот мой брат. ЕгО зовУт ВИктор. Он студЕнт, хорошО говорИт по-немЕцки и по-англИйски и хОчет путешЕствовать.
САлли	ИнтерЕсно…
НиколАй	И вот моЯ сестрА. ЕЁ зовУт Ира. ОнА Очень энергИчная дЕвушка, игрАет в баскетбОл и лЮбит гулЯть в дерЕвне. И вот дЯдя и тЁтя. ОнИ инженЕры, рабОтают на фАбрике в НовосибИрске.

ДИАЛОГ 2

СерЁжа, Tim and БЕлла are comparing photos of their homes. Match their descriptions to the pictures.

◈ CD 2, TR 1, 01:42

СерЁжа	Я живУ в квартИре на Улице МИра. У нас в квартИре гостИная, спАльня, кУхня, вАнная и балкОн. КвартИра нОвая, и у нас есть лифт и телефОн. А где вы живЁте, Тим?
Тим	Я живУ в дОме в ЛиверпУле. Это стАрый, большОй дом. У нас большАя гостИная, прекрАсная столОвая, мАленькая кУхня, три спАльни и вАнная.
СерЁжа	У вас есть сад?
Тим	Да, у нас большОй сад. НАша собАка, ТрИкси, лЮбит там игрАть.
БЕлла	У менЯ стАрая квартИра в дОме на рекЕ МОйке. ОнА красИвая. У менЯ в квартИре гостИная, кабинЕт, кУхня и вАнная. У менЯ прекрАсный вид на рЕку МОйку. Там так приЯтно!

ДИАЛОГ 3

You are conducting interviews. This time you are asking why people have chosen to live in the city or in the country. Where do Anna and Sasha prefer to live, and why?

Вы	ПочемУ вы лЮбите жить в гОроде?
Анна	Я люблЮ жить в гОроде потомУ, что мОжно ходИть на концЕрты, в теАтр, в кинО, по магазИнам. Наш гОрод исторИческий, красИвый. Мы живЁм в цЕнтре и у нас есть стАнция метрО недалекО.
Вы	САша, почемУ вы лЮбите жить в дерЕвне?
САша	Я люблЮ жить в дерЕвне потомУ, что там спокОйно и мОжно гулЯть в лесУ. ПриезжАйте к нам в гОсти. В дерЕвне Очень приЯтно.

Mechanics of the language

1 У вас есть...? *Do you have...?*

You have already met this question, which means literally *by you is there?* Yes, there is to say the answer is **Да, есть** (Da, yest'). Or in full it may be **Да, у менЯ есть. . .** (Da, oo minyA yest'. . .) *Yes, by me there is . . .* If you want to make a statement rather than ask a question, simply omit the question mark: **У вас есть брат** *You have a brother.* **У вас есть** does not function like a verb, but is simply a phrase which is used in place of the verb *to have.* To ask or say that different people have something, use these forms:

я	**У менЯ**	oo minyA	*I have*		мы	**У нас**	oo nas	*we have*
ты	**У тебЯ**	oo tibyA	*you have*		вы	**У вас**	oo vas	*you have*
он/онО	**У негО**	oo nyivO	*he/it has*		они	**У них**	oo neekh	*they have*
онА	**У неЁ**	oo nyiyO	*she has*					
кто	**У когО?**	oo kavO	*who has?*					

You may choose whether or not to include the word **есть** in your statements. **Есть** adds emphasis: **У менЯ есть газЕта** *I do have a newspaper.*

У менЯ, у тебЯ etc. may also mean *at my home, at your home,* or even *in my country.* This is a very useful phrase for making comparisons between cultures: **У вас рождествО седьмОго январЯ, но у нас рождествО двАдцать пЯтого декабрЯ.** *In your country Christmas is on 7 January, but in our country Christmas is on 25 December.*

2 More about verbs

You already know that **я хожУ** is used to say *I go somewhere habitually,* and **я идУ** is usually used to say *I am going somewhere now.* Here are the verbs **ходИть** and **идтИ** in full. They both refer to going on foot, not by transport.

....

ходИть *to go habitually*		**идтИ** *to go on one occasion*	
я хожУ	мы хОдим	я идУ	мы идём
ты хОдишь	вы хОдите	ты идёшь	вы идёте
он хОдит	онИ хОдят	он идёт	онИ идУт

....

КудА вы хОдите кАждый день в 7 часОв?	*Where do you go every day at 7 o'clock?*
КудА вы идЁте?	*Where are you going now?*

3 Points of the compass

You may wish to say in which part of the country your town or city is. The points of the compass are: **сЕвер** (syEvyir) *north,* **юг** (yook) *south,* **зАпад** (zApat) *west,* **востОк** (vastOk) *east.* To say *in the north* etc., use **на** with the prepositional endings, adding **-e** to the end of the following word.

на сЕвере	
на зАпаде	АвстрАлии, АмЕрики, Англии, ИрлАндии,
на востОке	РоссИи, УЭльса, ШотлАндии
на Юге	**of** *Australia, America, England, Ireland, Russia,*
в цЕнтре	*Wales, Scotland*

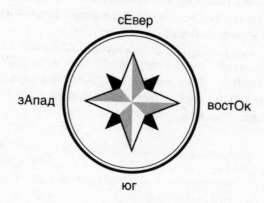

4 Whose is it?

You have already met **мой** and **ваш**, *my* and *your*. Here are the words meaning *your* (if you address someone as **ты**) and *our*. They are **твой** (tvoy) *your* and **наш** (nash) *our*. Remember that **мой** and **ваш** have different forms to agree with the gender of the nouns to which they refer (see Unit 6). The same is true of **твой** and **наш**.

Masculine	Feminine	Neuter	Plural
твой пАспорт	**твоЯ** балалАйка	**твоЁ** пианИно	**твоИ** кнИги
your passport	*your balalaika*	*your piano*	*your books*
наш пАспорт	**нАша** балалАйка	**нАше** пианИно	**нАши** кнИги
our passport	*our balalaika*	*our piano*	*our books*

The words **егО** (yivO) *his*, **еЁ** (yiyO) *her* and **их** (eekh) *their* are easier to use as they do not change at all. So, **егО** can be used with any noun to mean *his*: **егО** пАспорт, **егО** балалАйка, **егО** пианИно, **егО** кнИги. **ЕЁ** *her* is just as simple, as is **их** *their*.

5 Him, her, them: Direct object pronouns

As well as meaning *his, her* and *their*, the words **егО**, **её** and **их** have another meaning: *him, her* and *them* in phrases where people are the direct object of the verb. To fill in a few gaps, here is the full range of *me, you, him, her, us, you, them*. You have met many of these forms before, for example in the phrase **Как вас зовУт?** literally '*How you do they call?*'

ты лЮбишь **менЯ**	*you love **me***	вы лЮбите **нас**	*you love **us***
я люблЮ **тебЯ**	*I love **you***	онИ лЮбят **вас**	*they love **you***
онА лЮбит **егО**	*she loves **him***	мы лЮбим **их**	*we love **them***
он лЮбит **её**	*he loves **her***		

Exercises

1 Look at these route plans below for St Petersburg public transport. What should you catch to go to the following places?

a Finland station **b** Arsenal Embankment **c** Revolution Highway **d** Moscow Avenue **e** Gor'kovskaya metro station **f** Tuchkov Bridge **g** Kazan Square **h** Industrial Avenue

СемнАдцатый троллЕйбус: КазАнская плОщадь – ГорОховая Улица – ВитЕбский вокзАл – ЗАгородный проспЕкт – МоскОвский проспЕкт

ШестьдесЯт трЕтий трамвАй: ФинлЯндский вокзАл – СампсониЕвский мост – стАнция метрО «ГОрьковская» – ТУчков мост

ДвАдцать восьмОй автОбус: ФинлЯндский вокзАл – АрсенАльная нАбережная – шоссЕ РеволЮции – ИндустриАльный проспЕкт

2 Listen to these descriptions of people. Each description mentions where they live, where they work, their family, their hobbies, and something they want to do. Listen and try to note down something in English in each category for each person.

🔊 CD 2, TR 1, 04:17

	Аня	ПИтер	ЛеонИд	ЗОя
живёт				
рабОтает				
семьЯ				
хОбби				
хОчет				

3 Fill in the blanks in this description of Nadyezhda's home and life, using the words in brackets below. Listen to the recording to check your answers.

🔊 CD 2, TR 1, 05:32

НадЕжда _____ в квартИре в АрхАнгельске, на сЕвере РоссИи. У неЁ нОвая квартИра, не Очень красИвая, но НадЕжда лЮбит там жить потомУ, что _____ недалекО. В квартИре, у неЁ большАя гостИная и мАленькая спАльня, _____ и вАнная. ЕЁ муж рабОтает в МосквЕ. В квартИре живУт НадЕжда, её мАма и _____ дочь. Их зовУт ГалИна и МАша. У них кот. ЕгО зовУт ГОрби. МАша егО Очень _____. КАждый _____ НадЕжда хОдит на фАбрику, где онА рабОтает. МАша хОдит в шкОлу, и бАбушка _____ по магазИнам.

(лЮбит живЁт еЁ день магазИны хОдит кУхня)

4 Look at this map of Russia and say where these cities are:

a МагадАн на _____ РоссИи.   **i** сЕвере

b МосквА на _____ РоссИи.   **ii** Юге

c ИркУтск на _____ РоссИи.   **iii** востОке

d НорИльск на _____ РоссИи.   **iv** зАпаде

5 Listen to the recording to find out what these people have. Put a tick in the correct columns when you have understood. When you have finished, you could construct an imaginary interview with each person, asking **У вас есть машИна?** etc. and improvising answers based on your chart and on what you can remember from the recording.

◀) CD 2, TR 1, 06:53

	МашИна	Брат	Кот	КвартИра	ДАча
БорИс					
НАстя					
ЛИза					

6 Choose the correct form of the verb to complete each of these sentences.

a – СкажИте, пожАлуйста. Где здесь банк?
– ИзвинИте, я не знАете/знАю/знАем.

b – КудА вы идУ/идЁшь/идЁте?
– Я идУ/идёшь/идЁте в музЕй.

c Я хотИм/хОчешь/хочУ купИть сувенИры.

d Он хорошО говорЮ/говорИт/говорЯт по-рУсски.

e Где ты рабОтаем/рабОтают/рабОтаешь?

f Утром я зАвтракаю/зАвтракает/зАвтракаете в 7 часОв.

g – У вас есть хОбби? – Да, я Очень лЮбит/люблЮ/лЮбят читАть.

h Мы играЮ/игрАет/игрАем в хоккЕй.

i ОнИ Ужинает/Ужинают/Ужинаем пОздно вЕчером.

7 Read this property advert and list its features.

ЭлИтный кОттедж. ПрестИжный райОн. ЭлектрИчество, водА, газ. ДжакУзи и сАуна. КамИн. СпУтниковое ТВ. 250кв.м. БольшОй гарАж.

TEST YOURSELF

You are halfway through this course now so, before you go on to learn how to write in Russian, why don't you check to see how much you remember about Russian life and language?

1 What would you do with a папирОса? **i** eat it **ii** smoke it **iii** put it in a letter box?

2 In which city would you find ГУМ? **i** St Petersburg **ii** Magadan **iii** Moscow?

3 If you were at a вокзАл would you catch **i** a train **ii** a plane **iii** a cold?

4 If you were speaking to an официАнт would you be **i** showing your passport **ii** ordering a drink **iii** paying a fine?

5 Is кАша **i** porridge **ii** someone's name **iii** a cash desk?

6 Is прАздник **i** a day of the week **ii** a shop assistant **iii** a holiday?

7 If you are walking along a нАбережная should you look out for **i** a runway **ii** a river **iii** a hospital?

8 If someone asked you СкОлько сейчАс врЕмени? would you tell them **i** your name **ii** the time **iii** how much something costs?

9 If someone told you that the date today was девятнАдцатое Августа would you think that it was **i** 20th August **ii** 9th August **iii** 19th August?

10 If someone said to you ВстрЕтимся в пЯтницу would you expect to meet them on **i** Friday **ii** Sunday **iii** Monday?

11

....

НапишИте, пожАлуйста!
Write it down, please!

In this unit you will learn
- *How to read Russian script*
- *How to write in Russian*

Before you start

Before moving on to the second part of the book you have the chance to meet the handwritten form of the language. At some time you may need to read Russian in script rather than the printed form. You may also want to write some Russian yourself, and if you learn some basic writing skills at this stage, it will help you to monitor your progress as you work through the rest of the book. The exercises in the second half of the book will still require you to read, speak and listen to Russian, but some of them will also give you the opportunity to write a little. However, if you choose not to learn to write in script, you can always print your answers or find alternative ways of answering.

Here are the letters of the Russian alphabet in their handwritten forms. Get used to their appearance, and then try copying them down in pencil until you feel confident with them. Carry on to a blank sheet of paper if necessary.

As in any language, the style of handwriting varies from person to person and from generation to generation. The writing in this book is in a traditional style, produced by someone brought up in the Soviet education system. Younger people may write in a less elaborate style but, if you can read this writing, you should be able to cope with most styles.

А	а	*A*	*a*
Б	б	*Б*	*б*
В	в	*В*	*в*
Г	г	*Г*	*г*
Д	д	*Д*	*д*
Е	е	*Е*	*е*
Ё	ё	*Ё*	*ё*
Ж	ж	*ж*	*ж*
З	з	*З*	*з*
И	и	*И*	*и*
Й	й	*Й*	*й*
К	к	*К*	*к*
Л	л	*л*	*л*
М	м	*М*	*м*
Н	н	*Н*	*н*
О	о	*О*	*о*
П	п	*П*	*п*

Р	р	*Р р*
С	с	*С с*
Т	т	*Т т*
У	у	*У у*
Ф	ф	*Ф ф*
Х	х	*Х х*
Ц	ц	*Ц ц*
Ч	ч	*Ч ч*
Ш	ш	*Ш ш*
Щ	щ	*Щ щ*
	ъ	*ъ*
	ы	*ы*
	ь	*ь*
Э	э	*Э э*
Ю	ю	*Ю ю*
Я	я	*Я я*

When you are happy with the individual letters, move on to
looking at some words in handwritten form. Notice that the letters

л *л*
м *м*
and я *я*

must always begin with a little hook, so you cannot join them onto a preceding о σ.

The letter т $\bar{m}$

is often written with a line above it and

the letter ш $\underline{uu}$

with a line beneath it so that they can easily be distinguished from surrounding letters. Sometimes you will see the letter т written just as it is printed. You do not show which syllable is stressed when writing Russian so of course you will not use capital letters within words to show the stress.

First read the words out loud to make sure you recognize them and then try writing them yourself on a blank sheet for more practice.

А	а	Атом	*Атом*	Atom
Б	б	Борщ	*Борщ*	Beetroot soup
В	в	ВходИте	*Входите*	Come in
Г	г	Горбачёв	*Горбачёв*	Gorbachev
Д	д	ДиАгноз	*Диагноз*	Diagnosis
Е	е	Ельцин	*Ельцин*	Yeltsin
Ё	ё	Ёлка	*Ёлка*	Fir tree
Ж	ж	ЖенА	*жена*	Wife
З	з	ЗдрАвствуйте	*Здравствуйте*	Hello
И	и	ИнститУт	*Институт*	Institute

Й	й	МузЕй	*Музей*		Museum
к	к	Ключ	*Ключ*		Key
Л	л	ЛЕтом	*Летом*		In summer
М	м	МашИна	*Машина*		Car
Н	н	НапрАво	*Направо*		On the right
О	о	ОфициАнт	*Официант*		Waiter
П	п	ПоЭт	*Поэт*		Poet
Р	р	РоссИя	*Россия*		Russia
С	с	Сын	*Сын*		Son
Т	т	ТрАнспорт	*Транспорт*		Transport
У	у	Ужин	*Ужин*		Supper
Ф	ф	ФАбрика	*Фабрика*		Factory
Х	х	ХорошО	*Хорошо*		Good
Ц	ц	Царь	*Царь*		Tsar
Ч	ч	Чай	*Чай*		Tea
Ш	ш	Шесть	*Шесть*		Six
Щ	щ	Щи	*Щи*		Cabbage soup
	ъ	ОбъЕкт	*Объект*		Object
	ы	РЫнок	*Рынок*		Market
	ь	ИЮнь	*Июнь*		June

Э	э	ЭтАж	*Этаж*	Floor
Ю	ю	Юг	*Юг*	South
Я	я	ЯпОния	*Япония*	Japan

You have now written all the letters of the Russian alphabet in both their lower case and capital forms where possible. For further practice you could try converting words and phrases from elsewhere in the book into handwriting.

Exercises

In the following exercises you will be asked to read and write Russian script. If you decide that writing will not be useful to you, then find another way of responding to the exercises. You may be able to say the answers aloud, or print the words asked for, or group them using numbers or symbols.

1 To test your new skills, see if you can read all the handwritten words in this box. Now sort them into three categories: sport, food and members of the family. If you are going to practise your writing skills, write out the three lists.

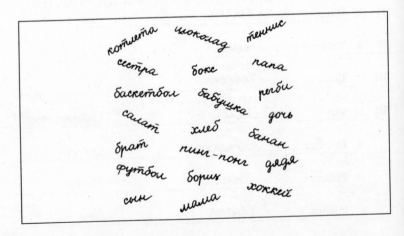

2 Write down or indicate the odd one out in each of these groups.

Город
парк
библиотека
музей
гитара
гастроном

Музыка
балалайка
оркестр
саксофон
инженер
опера

Профессия
врач
больница
учитель
футболист
дипломат

For further practice you could copy out the rest of the words in the boxes.

3 Can you complete the words in the grid using the clues in English given below?

1) Plays are performed here.
2) He studies at the university.
3) Underground train system.
4) You come here to eat out.
5) This dish is made of eggs.
6) General weather conditions.
7) Document for foreign travel.
8) Do come in!
9) Farm vehicle.
10) City in the Netherlands.

11) Tenth month of the year.
12) Day after Monday.
13) A means of talking to distant friends.

1	*m̄*								
2		*m̄*							
3			*m̄*						
4				*m̄*					
5					*m̄*				
6						*m̄*			
7							*m̄*		
8							*m̄*		
9						*m̄*			
10					*m̄*				
11				*m̄*					
12		*m̄*							
13	*m̄*								

4 Write out the following words, not forgetting the little hooks at the start of *л*, *м* and *я*.

кассета _____

водка _____

администратор _____

ресторан _____

телевизор _____

институт _____

рекорд _____

атом _____

Now take the first letter of each word to make another word. What is it? Can you write it?

5 Identify at least five words from this menu and write them out. A translation is provided in the **Answers** at the back of the book.

МЕНЮ

ХОЛОДНЫЕ ЗАКУСКИ
Салат
Грибы
Икра
Колбаса
Сыр

ПЕРВЫЕ БЛЮДА
Борщ
Щи

ВТОРЫЕ БЛЮДА
Рыба
Котлеты
Курица
Омлет
Пицца
Сосиски

СЛАДКИЕ БЛЮДА
Фрукты
Мороженое
Конфеты

НАПИТКИ
Минеральная вода
Фруктовый сок
Пиво
Вино
Водка

---

6 Read these words and write down or say the missing word in each sequence.

a Север, юг, запад и _____ .

b Брат и сестра, тётя и дядя, бабушка и _____ .

c Май, июнь, июль, _____ , сентябрь, октябрь

d Десять, двадцать, _____ , сорок, пятьдесят

e Англия, англичанин.
Франция, француз.
_____ , русский.

Continue to practise your writing little and often, and refer back to this unit frequently to make sure that you are not learning any bad habits!

12

В аэропортУ
At the airport

In this unit you will learn
- **What to do and say on the plane**
- **What to do and say at the airport**

Before you start
Revise
- greetings, Unit 3
- times, dates and numbers, Units 8 and 9 and the Numbers section at the back of the book
- *my* and *your*, Unit 6, and *whose is it?* Unit 10
- how to use the verb **хотЕть**, Unit 9

Now that you have reached the second half of the book, you should need less help with reading Russian, so the transliteration of words will no longer be shown. There will still be lots of listening and speaking, and in many exercises you can choose whether to write in Russian or not. To test your reading skills, there will be exercises and anecdotes both in print and script. The Russian anecdote has a long tradition, and by reading anecdotes from the Soviet era and the modern day you can learn a lot about the history, culture and humour of the Russian people. Some of the anecdotes appear on the recording.

Insight

ПАспорт, вИза и декларАция *Passport, visa and declaration*

When you arrive in Russia you will have to show your **пАспорт, вИза** and **декларАция**. The declaration is a form declaring any foreign currency and valuables you are taking into Russia. This is stamped on entry, and you may be asked to show it again on exit, declaring what you are taking out and showing receipts for goods purchased and money exchanged.

В самолЁте *In the aeroplane*

If you travel on a Russian plane, you will feel that you are on Russian territory from the moment you board, and you may want to try out your Russian immediately. Here are some signs that you may see:

Не курИть *No smoking*
ЗастегнИте рЕмни *Fasten your seat belts*

Learn the key words, some of which you already know, and then listen to or read the dialogue.

самолЁт	*aeroplane*
стюардЕсса	*stewardess*
стюАрд	*steward*
мЕсто	*seat/place*
обЕдать	*to have dinner*
пИво	*beer*
журнАлы	*magazines*
грАдус	*degree* (temperature)

QUICK VOCAB

ДИАЛОГ 1 ГДЕ МОЁ МЕСТО? *Where's my seat?*

CD 2, TR 2, 00:13

Вы	Где моЁ мЕсто?
СтюардЕсса	ПокажИте, пожАлуйста, билЕт.
Вы	Вот он.
СтюардЕсса	СпасИбо. ШестнАдцатое «а». НапрАво, пожАлуйста.

(Once you are in the air, the stewardess asks you a question.)

СтюардЕсса	Вы хотИте обЕдать?
Вы	ОбЕдать? Да, конЕчно, Очень хочУ.
СтюардЕсса	И что вы хотИте пить? У нас минерАльная водА, винО, пИво, кОфе и чай.
Вы	ДАйте, пожАлуйста, бЕлое винО.
СтюардЕсса	ХотИте журнАлы, газЕты?
Вы	Да, пожАлуйста. У вас есть англИйские газЕты?
СтюардЕсса	Да, англИйские и америкАнские.

(Just before landing, the pilot gives you some information.)

ПилОт	В МосквЕ сейчАс восемнАдцать часОв трИдцать пять минУт, температУра – пятнАдцать грАдусов.

Exercise 1

Say in English and Russian:

a your seat number **б** what you chose to drink **в** the time using the 24-hour clock, and the temperature in Moscow.

Exercise 2

Read through the dialogue aloud, altering the information as follows:

a Your seat number is now 9 «б» on the left. **б** The stewardess offers you lemonade, fruit juice, and coffee with milk. **в** You choose fruit juice. **г** You ask for a Russian magazine.

Exercise 3

Listen to the recording and note down, using a numeral and a Russian letter, the seat numbers as the stewardess reads them out:

🔊 **CD 2, TR 2, 01:36**

    a
    б
    в
    г

and the time and temperature in these cities:

    д В КраснодАре
    е В АрхАнгельске
    ж В ПетербУрге

Insight

If you have the chance to go to Russia, just walking around will give you lots of practice in the passive skills of reading and listening to Russian. Signs on streets, on buildings and in the airport and metro will help you to practise reading the alphabet, as will advertisements, packaging and tickets. You will overhear people talking, you will hear announcements and you will gradually pick out words and phrases.

АэропОрт *The airport*

Once you arrive at the airport in Russia, you may see these signs. The first group you will already recognize.

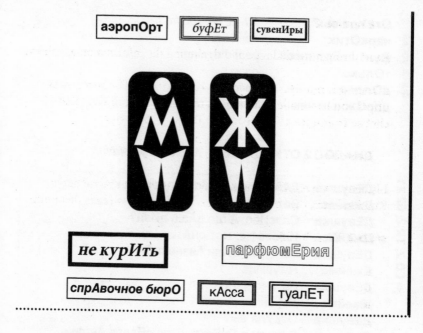

aэропОрт буфЕт сувенИры

не курИть парфюмЕрия

спрАвочное бюрО кАсса туалЕт

Exercise 4

The following groups of words you have not seen before. Work out what they mean.

a вЫход   вЫхода нет   вЫход на посАдку

б тамОженный контрОль   вЫдача багажА   транзИт
пАспортный контрОль   № рЕйса

в регистрАция   крАсный коридОр   зал ожидАния   вход
*exit / boarding gate (exit to embarkation) / no exit / luggage
reclaim / passport control / flight number / customs control /
transit / red channel / check-in / entrance / waiting room*

Insight

ПАспортный контрОль *Passport control*

Upon arrival at the airport, you will first go through passport control, and then on to customs – **тамОженный контрОль**.

ОткУда вы?	*Where are you from?*
наркОтик	*narcotics*
фунт стЕрлингов	*pound sterling*
тОлько	*only*
дОллар	*dollar*
дорОжный чек	*traveller's cheque*

ДИАЛОГ 2 ОТКУДА ВЫ? *Where are you from?*

ДЕвушка	ДАйте, пожАлуйста, пАспорт.
Джеймс	Вот он.
ДЕвушка	СпасИбо. А где вАша вИза?
Джеймс	ИзвинИте. Вот онА.
ДЕвушка	Вы турИст Или бизнесмЕн?
Джеймс	Я турИст.
ДЕвушка	Вы англичАнин?
Джеймс	Да, англичАнин.
ДЕвушка	ОткУда вы?
Джеймс	Я живУ в ПрЕстоне, на сЕвере Англии.
ДЕвушка	ХорошО. Вот ваш пАспорт.
Джеймс	СпасИбо.

James moves on to customs.

МолодОй человЕк	Это ваш багАж?
Джеймс	Да, Это мой чемодАн и моЯ сУмка. И вот моЯ декларАция.
МолодОй человЕк	СпасИбо. У вас в багажЕ есть наркОтики?
Джеймс	Нет.
МолодОй человЕк	У вас есть фУнты стЕрлингов?
Джеймс	Нет, тОлько дОллары и дорОжные чЕки.
МолодОй человЕк	ХорошО. Вот вАша декларАция. До свидАния.

Listen to the dialogue several times, then work on it by covering up James's lines and answering the questions yourself, altering information as you choose.

Exercise 5

In the **декларАция** you are asked to declare large amounts of foreign currency and, of course, weapons, drugs and valuables. Underline the items in this handwritten list which you think you should declare.

доллары   книга
план   фунты стерлингов
компьютер

пистолет   дорожные чеки
виза   камера
минеральная вода   газета

Exercise 6

Last week you rang your friend, **ВалентИн**, to tell him when you would be arriving in Moscow. Read through what he says first, and familiarize yourself with the new words. Then complete your side of the conversation.

здрАвствуй	*hello*
ты бУдешь	*you will be*
Анна бУдет	*Anna will be*
понЯтно	*understood*
так	*so*

QUICK VOCAB

а	**You**	*Hello. Valentin?*
	ВалентИн	АллО! Это ты?
б	**You**	*Yes. How are you?*
	ВалентИн	ХорошО, спасИбо. КогдА ты бУдешь в Москве?
в	**You**	*On Friday.*
	ВалентИн	ШестОго иЮля?
г	**You**	*Yes, on the 6th of July.*
	ВалентИн	В котОром часУ?
д	**You**	*At 18:40.*
	ВалентИн	А Анна тОже бУдет на самолёте.
е	**You**	*Yes, of course.*
	ВалентИн	И какОй нОмер рЕйса?
ж	**You**	*The flight number is SU242.*
	ВалентИн	SU двЕсти сОрок два. ПонЯтно. Так, мы встрЕтимся в аэропортУ шестОго иЮля в восемнАдцать часОв сОрок минУт. До свидАния.
з	**You**	*Goodbye, Valentin.*

Well done! Did you notice the unusual ending on **аэропОрт** when Valentin says *at the airport?* You would expect to see -е, but instead you see -у. This happens with a few masculine nouns, including **сад** *garden*, and **лес** *forest:* **в садУ** *in the garden*, **в лесУ** *in the forest.*

The verb **быть** *to be* in the future tense (i.e. not what is happening now, but what *will* happen in the future), which you also met in this dialogue, is very useful when making arrangements, so here it is:

я бУду	*I will be*	мы бУдем	*we will be*
ты бУдешь	*you will be*	вы бУдете	*you will be*
он/онА бУдет	*he/she will be*	онИ бУдут	*they will be*

Exercise 7

You are flying to St Petersburg, and you need to ring your Russian friend with the details. Prepare what you will say on the phone.

Flight no. BA 878
Arrival in St Petersburg: 19.40
Date of travel: Thursday 26 Jan.

наконЕц	*at last*
Как долетЕли?	*How was (your flight)?*
прекрАсно	*fine*
Как вы поживАете?	*How are you (getting on)?*
поживАть [1]	*to get on*
немнОжко	*a little*
устАл/устАла/устАли	*tired (m/f/pl)*
как всегдА	*as always*
ждать [1] (я жду, ты ждёшь, онИ ждут)	*to wait*
скОро	*soon*

QUICK VOCAB

At last you have completed the formalities, and you see ВалентИн waiting for you.

ДИАЛОГ 3 ЗДРАВСТВУЙ, ВАЛЕНТИН! *Hello, Valentin!*

ВалентИн	ЗдрАвствуй, Стив! ЗдрАвствуй, Анна! НаконЕц!
Анна	ЗдрАвствуй, ВалентИн! Как приЯтно тебЯ вИдеть!
ВалентИн	Как долетЕли?
Стив	ПрекрАсно, спасИбо.
ВалентИн	Как вы поживАете? ХотИте есть, пить?
Анна	СпасИбо нет, ВалентИн. Я немнОжко устАла.
Стив	Я тожЕ немнОжко устАл. Но я, как всегдА, Очень хочУ есть и пить.
ВалентИн	ХорошО, мы скОро бУдем дОма. ИрИна там ждёт.

CD 2, TR 2, 05:19

Exercise 8

Listen to the dialogue or read it and find the Russian for:

а *How lovely to see you!*
б *How are you?*
в *I am a little tired.*
г *as always*
д *We will soon be at home.*

Exercise 9

Read out loud the arrival dates and times of these travellers. Listen to the recording to check your pronunciation.

◄) **CD 2, TR 2, 06:05**

а САлли бУдет в СОчи   *16/Авг.*, в *22,30*.
б СтанислАв бУдет в МУрманске *5/ноя.*, в *10,15*.
в ЛЮба бУдет в МосквЕ *29/мАя*, в *13,50*.
г Алла бУдет в ИркУтске *10/фев.*, в *15,20*.

Insight
ОбмЕн валЮты *Currency exchange*

Now that you are through passport control and customs, you may need to change some money into roubles. To do this you need to find a bank or a sign saying **обмЕн валЮты** *exchange of currency*. It is generally more secure and you get a better rate if you change money in a bank. Check the exchange rate **курс**, ask if commission is charged – **есть ли коммИсия?** – and don't forget to get your **декларАция** stamped and keep your receipt.

Exercise 10

Look at these numerals 1–10 written by hand, and copy them until you can write them authentically without looking at the original.

$$1 \quad 6$$
$$2 \quad 7$$
$$3 \quad 8$$
$$4 \quad 9$$
$$5 \quad 10$$

Exercise 11

🔊 **CD 2, TR 2, 06:48**

At the information office **спрАвочное бюрО** of the airport you overhear people asking where the check-in **регистрАция** is for various flights **рЕйсы:** СкажИте, пожАлуйста, где регистрАция, рейс вОсемьсот сЕмьдесят дЕвять (879) в ЛОндон?

For practice, you decide to note down the flight numbers. Listen to the recording and fill in the numbers as a Russian would write them.

а	Рейс	_____	в ДЕли.
б	Рейс	_____	в АмстердАм.
в	Рейс	_____	в ЦЮрих.
г	Рейс	_____	в ПарИж.
д	Рейс	_____	в Нью-ЙОрк.

Exercise 12

Rearrange the words in these questions so that they make sense.
You could choose to say the sentences out loud, number the words,
or write them.

а пить вы что хотИте?
б вАша как фамИлия?
в мЕсто моЁ где?
г вас фУнты есть стЕрлингов у?
д вАша чемодАн Это и сУмка ваш?

Exercise 13

Match up the questions and answers.

а) Где моё место?
б) Где ваша виза?
в) Вы бизнесмен?
г) Это ваш багаж?
д) У вас есть доллары?
е) Что вы хотите пить?
ж) У вас есть русские газеты?

1) Нет, я турист.
2) Нет, это не мой багаж.
3) Нет, у меня есть фунты.
4) Чай, пожалуйста.
5) Пятое "г", налево.
6) Да, русские и английские.
7) Вот она.

АНЕКДОТ *Anecdote*

◀) **CD 2, TR 2, 07:45**

This anecdote from pre-glasnost days is about a Russian emigré in America recalling life in the Soviet Union. He explains why he chose to emigrate. There is one key phrase you need before you begin: **НельзЯ пожАловаться** *Mustn't grumble*.

ИнтервьюЕр	ПродУкты есть в МосквЕ?
РУсский эмигрАнт	НельзЯ пожАловаться.
ИнтервьюЕр	И как трАнспорт в МосквЕ?
РУсский эмигрАнт	НельзЯ пожАловаться.
ИнтервьюЕр	Как там больнИцы?
РУсский эмигрАнт	НельзЯ пожАловаться.
ИнтервьюЕр	И как там шкОлы?
РУсский эмигрАнт	НельзЯ пожАловаться.
ИнтервьюЕр	ПочемУ вы сейчАс живЁте в АмЕрике?
РУсский эмигрАнт	ПотомУ, что здесь мОжно пожАловаться.

1 Which four aspects of Soviet life was the emigré questioned about?

2 What was his reason for emigrating?

Congratulations on successfully negotiating the airport!

Now it's time for a quick revision test before you move on to look at other situations in which you might find yourself if visiting Russia or entertaining Russian guests at home.

TEST YOURSELF

1 You are on a plane about to land in Samara and you hear the pilot say В СамАре сейчАс двАдцать два часА восемнАдцать минУт. What time is it?

2 *You* are at the airport and you see a sign saying ВЫход. Where will it take you?

3 You are at the theatre and you want to ask the usher where your seat is. What will you say?

4 At customs you are asked Это ваш чемодАн? It is, so what will you say?

5 Your Russian friend tells you Я бУду в ВашингтОне четвЁртого иЮля. What is he telling you?

6 How do you say *We are a bit tired?*

7 Your Russian friends have just arrived at your house. How will you ask them *What would you like to eat and drink?*

8 You call your Russian friend and ask her what the weather is like as you are going to visit her in Moscow the next day. She tells you ТемператУра – трИдцать грАдусов. Will you take your winter coat or your shorts?

9 How will you ask the Russian kiosk holder if they have any English newspapers?

10 Someone asks you ОткУда вы? What do they want to know?

13

··

Как попАсть на МоскОвский вокзАл?
How do I get to Moscow station?

In this unit you will learn
- *How to use public transport*
- *How to ask for further directions*

Before you start
Revise
- directions, Unit 5
- numbers and telling the time, Unit 8
- how to say *to Moscow* and *in Moscow*, Units 5 and 7

Russian distinguishes between going somewhere on foot and by some means of transport, so two verbs which will be useful to you are **идтИ** *to go on foot* and **Ехать** *to go by transport*.

идтИ *to go on foot*		**Ехать** *to go by transport*	
я идУ	мы идЁм	я Еду	мы Едем
ты идЁшь	вы идЁте	ты Едешь	вы Едете
он/онА идЁт	онИ идУт	он/онА Едет	онИ Едут

Insight
ГОРОДСКОЙ ТРАНСПОРТ *Public Transport*

To find the stop for a bus, trolleybus or tram, look out for these signs.

A for a bus **автОбус** is written in black letters on a yellow background.

Т or **Тб** for a trolleybus **троллЕйбус** is written in black letters on a white background.

Т or **Тм** for a tram **трамвАй** is written in black letters on a white background. The signs for buses and trolleybuses are usually attached to a wall, but tram signs are suspended from cables over the road.

To travel on any of these vehicles you need a ticket **талОн** which may be for single or multiple trips. These may be bought from kiosks or sometimes from the bus driver, and they should be validated when you get on. Plain clothes inspectors fine people travelling without a ticket. Some people prefer to buy a season ticket **едИный билЕт** or **проезднОй**. In some cities, when you get on you should get your ticket punched at one of the little contraptions mounted in the vehicle. If it is too crowded to reach one, ask someone to do it for you: **ПробЕйте талОн, пожАлуйста.** If someone is trying to get off when the vehicle is crowded they will say: **Вы сейчАс выхОдите?** *Are you getting off now?* If you are not, you should try to let them past.

автОбус	*bus*
троллЕйбус	*trolleybus*
трамвАй	*tram*
останОвка (на)	*stop*
останОвка автОбуса	*bus stop*
останОвка троллЕйбуса	*trolleybus stop*

останОвка трамвАя	tram stop
талОн	ticket (bus, trolleybus and tram)
едИный (билЕт)	season ticket
пешкОм	on foot
минУта	minute
Как попАсть в...?	How do I get to ...?
СадИтесь на пЯтый автОбус	Get on bus no. five
ПробЕйте талОн, пожАлуйста	Punch my ticket, please
КогдА мне вЫходить?	When do I need to get off?
ЧЕрез три останОвки	After three stops

ДИАЛОГ 1 КАК ПОПАСТЬ В ЦИРК? *How do I get to the circus?*

Robert has arranged to meet Slava at the circus, but he doesn't know how to get there.

◆ CD 2, TR 3

РОберт	ДЕвушка, извинИте, пожАлуйста, как попАсть в цирк?
ДЕвушка	В цирк? СадИтесь на четЫрнадцатый трамвАй.
РОберт	Где останОвка?
ДЕвушка	Там, напрАво. ВИдите?
РОберт	Да. А мОжно пешкОм?
ДЕвушка	МОжно.
РОберт	СкОлько минУт пешкОм, и скОлько на трамвАе?
ДЕвушка	ПешкОм двАдцать – трИдцать минУт. А на трамвАе дЕсять.

On the tram

РОберт	ИзвинИте, я Еду в цирк. КогдА мне выходИть?
БАбушка	ЧЕрез три останОвки.
РОберт	ПробЕйте талОн, пожАлуйста.

Exercise 1

Listen to the dialogue above, and say **a** which tram Robert has to catch **б** where the tram stop is **в** how long it would take on foot **г** how long it would take by tram **д** how many stops he has to travel.

Now work through the dialogue playing the parts of дЕвушка and бАбушка, and altering these details: **e** Robert needs bus no. eight **ж** the bus stop is straight ahead **з** it will take 30–40 minutes on foot and 15 on the bus **и** he needs to get off after four stops.

Exercise 2

You see this sign on a bus. What must you not do?

В АВТОБУСЕ НЕЛЬЗЯ КУРИТЬ!

Insight
МЕТРО *The Metro*

To spot a metro station **стАнция метрО** look out for a big red letter **M** in Moscow and a big blue letter **M** in St Petersburg. To enter the metro, you buy a ticket **билЕт** from the window at the station, pass through the turnstile and you are free to travel as far as you want for a certain number of journeys until you exit the metro system. The metro generally runs from at least six a.m. to midnight. At each station an announcement is made. The order varies, but it will usually include the name of the station you are at, **СтАнция «ЛубЯнка»,** the name of the next station, **СлЕдующая стАнция – «КитАй ГОрод»,** and a warning to be careful because the doors are shutting, **ОсторОжно. ДвЕри закрывАются.**

стАнция метрО	*metro station*
билЕт	*ticket*
автомАт	*slot*
турникЕт	*turnstile*
пересАдка	*change*
без пересАдки	*without a change*
с пересАдкой	*with a change*
дЕлать пересАдку	*to make a change*
доЕдете до стАнции ...	*go as far as station ...*

Look out for these signs:

ВХОД	*entrance*
ВЫХОД	*exit*
НЕТ ВХОДА	*no entrance*
НЕТ ВЫХОДА	*no exit*
К ПОЕЗДАМ	*to the trains*
ПЕРЕХОД НА СТАНЦИЮ	*Transfer to station 'Theatre*
«ТЕАТРАЛЬНАЯ ПЛОЩАДЬ»	*Square'*

ДИАЛОГ 2 НА МЕТРО *On the metro*

Martin has heard that the view over Moscow from the University is worth seeing. He has left his plan of the metro at the hotel so he stops Valya and asks her the way.

МАртин	СкажИте пожАлуйста, как попАсть в университЕт?
ВАля	На метрО?
МАртин	Да, на метрО.
ВАля	ХорошО. Там налЕво стАнция метрО «Парк КультУры».
МАртин	ПонЯтно.
ВАля	На метрО доЕдете до стАнции «УниверситЕт».
МАртин	Это далекО?
ВАля	Нет, четЫре останОвки.
МАртин	СпасИбо.

♦ CD 2, TR 3, 01:03

Exercise 3

а In the dialogue above, which station does Martin go from?
б Which station must he go to?
в How many stops does he have to go?

Exercise 4

You are staying with Lydia in Moscow, but she has to work today. She writes you out a list of places you could visit and how to get there.

станция метро

Кремль	Александровский сад
Ботанический сад	Ботанический сад
Рынок	Пушкинская
Дом книги	Арбатская
ГУМ	Площадь Революции

Which metro station do you need for **а** the Kremlin **б** the market **в** the bookshop **г** the Botanical Gardens **д** the department store GUM?

Another friend wants to meet you later. Arrange which metro station to meet at and write it down so you don't forget. (You choose which one!)

Now make up questions and answers based on the information above, for example – СкажИте, пожАлуйста, как попАсть в Кремль?   – ДоЕдете до стАнции «АлексАндровский сад».

Train journeys in Russia are often long as cities are far apart. Russian trains offer differing degrees of comfort: **мЯгкий** *soft* (seated), **купЕ** shared sleeping compartment, **плацкАрт** reserved place with bunks or reclining seats in a carriage and **Общий вагОн,** which is the same as **плацкАрт** but without a guaranteed berth. Each train has a **проводнИк** or **проводнИца** *conductor*, who checks tickets and supplies bedding and tea on long journeys. The names of main-line stations refer to the places to and from which trains travel, so **КИевский вокзАл** in Moscow is where you would catch a train to Kiev, and **МоскОвский вокзАл** in St Petersburg is where you would catch a train to Moscow. If Russian friends are going to see you off on a long journey, you may find that before leaving home, everyone sits down for a moment in silence. This is a tradition meant to bring the traveller safely back home.

вокзАл (на)	*station*
пОезд (pl поездА)	*train(s)*
скОрый пОезд	*express train*
электрИчка	*suburban electric train*
вагОн	*carriage*
купЕ	*compartment*
мЕсто	*seat*
вагОн-ресторАн	*dining car*
расписАние	*timetable*
отправлЕние	*departure*
платфОрма	*platform*
обрАтный билЕт	*return ticket*
билЕт в одИн конЕц	*single ticket*
мЯгкий вагОн	*soft (seated) carriage*
купЕ	*shared sleeping compartment*
плацкАрт	*reserved seat or bunk in coach*
Общий вагОн	*general coach without a reserved place*
пОезд отхОдит в 7 часОв	*The train leaves at 7 o'clock*

QUICK VOCAB

проводнИк, проводнИца	conductor
кассИр	ticket office cashier
пассажИр	passenger
для курЯщих	for smokers
для некурЯщих	for non-smokers

Look out for these notices:

ВЫХОД В ГОРОД	exit to the town
ЗАЛ ОЖИДАНИЯ	waiting room
БУФЕТ	snack bar
КАССА	ticket office

ДИАЛОГ 3 КОГДА ОТХОДИТ ПОЕЗД? When does the train leave?

Trevor wants to travel to Moscow by train to see Konstantina. First, he goes to the кАсса to get a ticket.

ТрЕвор	ДАйте, пожАлуйста, одИн обрАтный билЕт в МосквУ на шестОе Августа.
КассИр	ОднУ минУточку... ХорошО. ПОезд семь, вагОн тринАдцать.
ТрЕвор	КогдА отхОдит пОезд?
КассИр	Утром, в дЕсять часОв трИдцать минУт.

ШестОго Августа. На платфОрме:

ТрЕвор	Это тринАдцатый вагОн?
ПроводнИца	Да. Ваш билЕт, пожАлуйста.
ТрЕвор	Вот он.
ПроводнИца	ВторОе мЕсто. ИдИте в пЕрвое купЕ, пожАлуйста.
ТрЕвор	СкажИте, в пОезде есть вагОн-ресторАн?
ПроводнИца	Есть.
ТрЕвор	КогдА он открывАется?
ПроводнИца	В одИннадцать часОв.

Exercise 5

Reread the dialogue above and find out **a** on which date Trevor wants to travel **б** the number of his train and carriage **в** the departure time **г** the seat number **д** the opening time of the dining car.

– МЯгкий вагОн ищУ.

Exercise 6

ищУ   *I am looking for*

Read this timetable and give out information about it, for example, **ПОезд нОмер пятьсОт одИннадцать в ПетербУрг отхОдит в дЕвять часОв трИдцать шесть.**

РАСПИСАНИЕ		
ПОЕЗД		**ОТПРАВЛЕНИЕ**
– 511	ПЕТЕРБУРГ	9.36
– 96	НОВГОРОД	12.55
– 716	ИВАНОВО	20.47
– 82	ТУЛА	23.05

Now look back to Trevor's dialogue at the ticket office and substitute the St Petersburg train for Trevor's train, altering the dialogue accordingly. Perhaps you could change other details as well, or write down part of the conversation in English or Russian.

> **Insight**
> **ТАКСИ** *Taxi*
>
> Taxis come in all shapes and sizes, but they generally have a black and yellow chequered sign on the roof. Some Russians prefer to hitch a lift with a passing vehicle and negotiate a fare but this is not a good idea for tourists.

QUICK VOCAB

таксИ	*taxi*
маршрУтка	*fixed-route minibus taxi*
машИна	*car*
автомобИль (*m*)	*car*
стоЯнка таксИ (на)	*taxi rank*
ТаксИ! СвобОдно?	*Taxi! Are you free?*
КудА поЕдем?	*Where are we going?*
Не волнУйтесь	*Don't worry!*

ДИАЛОГ 4 ТАКСИ! *Taxi!*

Lorna is in a hurry to catch a train at **МоскОвский вокзАл** *so she flags down a taxi.*

CD 2, TR 3, 02:52

ЛОрна	ТаксИ! СвобОдно?
ТаксИст	СадИтесь. КудА поЕдем?
ЛОрна	На МоскОвский вокзАл, пожАлуйста.
ТаксИст	КогдА отхОдит ваш пОезд?
ЛОрна	В дЕвять часОв сОрок минУт.
ТаксИст	Не волнУйтесь. Мы скОро бУдем на вокзАле.

Exercise 7

а At what time does her train leave?

б Will she be in time to catch it?

в Now put yourself in Lorna's position. You are going to Kiev, so you need to go to **КиЕвский вокзАл** and your train leaves at ten o'clock. What will you say to the taxi driver?

Now that you know all the forms of transport, here is a summary of how to say *I am going to the university on the bus* etc. **Я Еду в университЕт на автОбусе:**

автОбус		автОбусе
троллЕйбус		троллЕйбусе
трамвАй		трамвАе
таксИ	на	таксИ
метрО		метрО
машИна		машИне
автомобИль		автомобИле
пОезд		пОезде

Exercise 8

Would you understand these instructions and signs?

а **СадИтесь на пЯтый троллЕйбус** means
  i Get on trolleybus no. 15
  ii Get on trolleybus no. 5
  iii Get on trolleybus no. 50

б **ВЫХОД В ГОРОД** means
  i To the trains   **ii** No exit   **iii** Exit to the town

в **ДАйте, пожАлуйста, обрАтный билЕт** means
  i Please give me a return ticket.
  ii Please give me a single ticket.
  iii Please give me a metro ticket.

Exercise 9

How would you say:

a How do I get to the Kremlin?
б Where is the bus stop?
в Are you getting off now?
г I am going to the Botanical Gardens on the metro.
д What time does the train leave?

АНЕКДОТ 1 *Anecdote 1*

🔊 **CD 2, TR 3, 03:21**

This anecdote is about a man and a little boy on a bus. The words below will help you to understand it, but you need only learn **Если** *if* for active use. Notice that the man is addressed as **дЯдя** *uncle*, meaning that he is probably too old to be called **молодОй человЕк**.

вхОдит	*(he) gets on*
пробивАет (талОн)	*punches (a ticket)*
мАльчик	*boy*
Если я терЯю	*if I lose*
Если вы терЯете	*if you lose*
дурАк	*fool*

ЧеловЕк вхОдит в автОбус и пробивАет три талОна.

МАльчик	ДЯдя, почемУ у вас три талОна?
ЧеловЕк	Если я терЯю пЕрвый талОн, у менЯ вторОй есть.
МАльчик	А Если вы терЯете вторОй талОн?
ЧеловЕк	У менЯ трЕтий есть.
МАльчик	А Если вы терЯете трЕтий талОн?
ЧеловЕк	Я не дурАк! У менЯ едИный билЕт.

1 Why does the man punch the third талОн *ticket*?

2 Why does he not need any талОны *tickets* at all?

АНЕКДОТ 2 *Anecdote 2*

This anecdote is set in a train and is about someone who can't find his way back to his carriage from the dining car. Again, you do not need to learn the vocabulary for active use, although **Что вы!**, or **Что ты!**, *What?!* is excellent for expressing amazement!

я не пОмню	*I can't remember*
что вы!	*What on earth?!*
за окнОм	*through the window*
был	*there was*

В пОезде Едет дурАк. Он обЕдает в вагОн-ресторАне.

ДурАк	ИзвинИте, дЕвушка, я не пОмню, где мой вагОн.
ПроводнИца	Что вы! Вы не знАете, где ваш вагОн?
ДурАк	Нет, не знАю. Но за окнОм лес был.

1 Who does he ask to solve his problem?

2 What does he remember seeing through his carriage window?

TEST YOURSELF

Now it's time to try out ten quick questions before your next unit.

1 You call your friend on her mobile. She says to you Я идУ на вокзАл. Where is she going and is she on foot or travelling by transport?

2 You are on a bus and someone says to you Вы сейчАс выхОдите? Should you a) let them past b) validate their ticket for them c) tell them the time?

3 You ask someone how you can get to the botanical gardens. They say to you СадИтесь на восьмОй трамвАй. What will you do?

4 You want to travel in a non-smoking compartment. Which one do you choose? a) ДЛЯ КУРЯЩИХ b) ДЛЯ НЕКУРЯЩИХ

5 At the station someone asks you КогдА отхОдит пОезд? What do they want to know?

6 You are in St Petersburg and you want to catch a train to Moscow. Which station will you go to? a) КИевский вокзАл b) ЛенингрАдский вокзАл c) МоскОвский вокзАл

7 You are looking for the ticket office in the train station. Which sign will you look for? a) ВЫХОД b) КАССА c) БУФЕТ

8 You hear an announcement. What is it telling you? ПОезд нОмер сто дЕвять в КИев отходит в пять часОв одИннадцать.

9 You are with two Russian friends who are worried they will be late for a plane. How do you tell them not to worry?

10 Your friend calls you and asks you what you are doing. Tell him you are going to the theatre on the bus.

14

Где мОжно купИть самовАр?
Where can I buy a samovar?

In this unit you will learn
- ***More about shopping***
- ***What to buy and where***

Before you start
Revise
- shopping vocabulary from Unit 6
- numbers, at the back of the book; times, Unit 8; directions, Unit 5; days of the week, Unit 8.

Insight
ГДЕ ПЛАТИТЬ? *Where do I pay?*

As mentioned before, the system of shopping in a few remaining old-fashioned shops involves quite a bit of queueing. The word for a queue is **Очередь**. First, you queue to find out the availability and price of what you want, then queue a second time at the **кАсса** to pay for the goods and collect the **чек**. At the cash desk you will need to say the number of the department **отдЕл** for which you need the receipt. Finally you queue for a third time to hand over the receipt and collect the goods. This system can make shopping a long process. However, for the language learner the queues and transactions are an opportunity not to be missed and this is why you will find this almost obsolete system used in this unit! In reality in most shops now you simply take your goods to the till.

СУВЕНИРЫ *Souvenirs*

A samovar **самовАр** is an urn, usually powered by charcoal or electricity, in which water is heated. Very strong tea is made in a tiny tea pot which stands on top of the samovar to keep warm. A little strong tea is poured into a glass and topped up with water from the samovar. Tea may be taken with sugar **сАхар,** lemon **лимОн** or fruit preserves **варЕнье.**

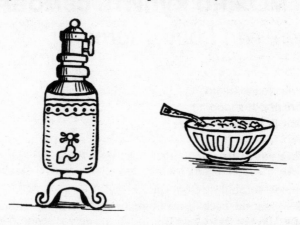

Other popular souvenirs which you have encountered in earlier units include the balalaika **балалАйка,** which is a triangular stringed musical instrument used for playing Russian folk music, and the *matryoshka* doll **матрёшка.** These dolls are made of wood, brightly painted, and when they are opened they reveal a whole series of smaller dolls hidden inside each other.

Bear in mind that changes in the Russian economy mean that any prices quoted in this book may be out of date.

In this unit there are inevitably a lot of key words, but some of them you already know, and some you will not need to learn for active use. When you have learned as many of them as possible, test yourself by covering up first the English side and then the Russian, saying out loud the words which are hidden.

What you say

МОжно посмотрЕть?	May I have a look?
ПокажИте, дАйте . . .	Show me, give me . . .
СкОлько стОит? СкОлько стОят?	How much is it? How much are they?
НапишИте, пожАлуйста, скОлько стОит	Please write down how much it is
ПовторИте, пожАлуйста, мЕдленнее	Repeat that more slowly please
У вас есть/есть ли у вас кнИги о спОрте?	Do you have any books about sport?
ПожАлуйста, да!	Yes please,
СпасИбо, нет!	No thank you,
СкОлько с менЯ?	How much do I owe?
ДОрого/недОрого	That's expensive/not expensive
Всё? Да, всё	Is that all? Yes, that's all
Где платИть? В кАссу?	Where do I pay? At the cash desk?
Где кАсса?	Where is the cash desk?
НапрОтив	Opposite
Сто двАдцать рублЕй на вторОй отдЕл	120 roubles for department 2
МагазИн открЫт/закрЫт	The shop is open/closed
Я хочУ купИть . . .	I want to buy . . .
КудА мне пойтИ?	Where should I go?
Где продаЮтся газЕты?	Where are newspapers sold?

What the shop assistant says

СлУшаю вас	I'm listening (May I help?)
Вам помОчь?	May I help you?
Что вы хотИте?	What do you want?
СкОлько вы хотИте?	How much do you want?
Сыр стОит 200 рублЕй килогрАмм	Cheese costs 200 roubles a kilo

Exercise 1

What does this shop sell?

ГДЕ МОЖНО КУПИТЬ ПРОДУКТЫ? *Where can you buy food?*

УниверсАм	*Supermarket*
супермАркет	*supermarket*
гастронОм	*grocer's*
Здесь продаЮтся . . .	*Here you can buy . . .*
продУкты	*provisions*
мЯсо	*meat*
рЫба	*fish*
колбасА	*sausage (salami)*
сосИска	*sausage (frankfurter)*
кОфе, чай, сАхар	*coffee, tea, sugar*
конфЕты	*sweets*
торт	*cake*
винО, пИво, вОдка	*wine, beer, vodka*
МолОчные продУкты	*Dairy produce*
молокО	*milk*
сметАна	*sour cream*
сыр	*cheese*
мАсло	*butter*

БУлочная   *Bakery*

чёрный/бЕлый хлеб	*black/white bread*
батОн	*long loaf*
бУлка	*sweet bread roll*
сУшка	*dry ring-shaped biscuit*

РЫнок   *Market*

свЕжие фрУкты/Овощи/цветЫ	*fresh fruit/vegetables/flowers*
яблоко (pl Яблоки)	*apple(s)*
грУша	*pear*
апельсИн	*orange*
картОшка	*potato*
помидОр	*tomato*
огурЕц (pl огурцЫ)	*cucumber(s)*

СКОЛЬКО ВЫ ХОТИТЕ?   *How much do you want?*

You will find that after any expression of quantity (kilo, litre, packet, etc.) the next word will change its ending: **килО банАнов** *a kilo of bananas*. This is called the *genitive case*. It is not essential for you at this stage to know how this works. Not knowing the endings will not prevent you from understanding or being understood.

килО	*kilo*
грамм	*gram*
литр	*litre*
метр	*metre*
бАнка	*jar, tin*
бутЫлка	*bottle*
пАчка	*packet*
сто грамм/пятьсОт грамм	*100 grams/500 grams*

Insight

When speaking Russian out loud, don't worry about getting things wrong. Just speak clearly and ask people to correct your pronunciation and your mistakes as you go along. This is how you will learn and improve. Russians will generally be very happy to help you, unless they want to practise their English instead!

ДИАЛОГ 1 В ГАСТРОНОМЕ *In the delicatessen*

Nick is looking for some cheese. Read the dialogue and answer the questions in Exercise 2.

CD 2, TR 4, 01:14

ПродавщИца	СлУшаю вас.
Ник	У вас есть сыр?
ПродавщИца	Есть ли у нас сыр? Да, конЕчно. Вот он.
Ник	КакОй Это сыр? МОжно посмотрЕть, пожАлуйста?
ПродавщИца	МОжно. Это эстОнский сыр. СтОит двЕсти рублЕй килО.
Ник	ПовторИте, пожАлуйста, мЕдленнее.
ПродавщИца	ДвЕсти рублЕй.
Ник	Это дОрого?
ПродавщИца	Нет, недОрого. СкОлько вы хотИте?
Ник	ПятьсОт грамм. СкОлько с меня́?
ПродавщИца	Сто рублЕй. Всё?
Ник	Да, всё. Где платИть?
ПродавщИца	В кАссу.
Ник	А где кАсса?
ПродавщИца	НапрОтив. ВИдите?
Ник	Да. СпасИбо. КакОй здесь отдЕл?
ПродавщИца	ЧетвЁртый.

Exercise 2

a Where do you think the cheese is from, and how much does it cost? Find the Russian for **б** Could I have a look? **в** How much do you want? **г** Is that all? **д** Opposite.

Now put yourself in Nick's place and work through the dialogue covering up his lines and saying his part.

Exercise 3

The following is a list of products from a supermarket's advertising brochure. Read this list, identify the products, and answer the questions.

МайонЕз
Сыр ЭдАмский, ГоллАндия
КивИ, ГрЕция
ЛимОны, ИспАния
МандарИны, ИспАния
КЕтчуп, БолгАрия
Чай индИйский
КОфе, БразИлия
ШоколАд, ГермАния
ВОдка, «СтолИчная», «Смирнофф», «Абсолют»

а Which two fruits from Spain can you buy?
б What sort of cheese is there?
в What has been imported from Bulgaria?
г What sort of tea can you buy?
д Which brands of vodka are listed?

Exercise 4

🔊 CD 2, TR 4, 02:17

You are in a **гастронОм**. Listen to people asking for things.
Underline the items which you hear requested on the list below. For
further practice, you could copy the list.

чай   сахар
огурец   колбаса
сосиски   конфеты
банка кофе   торт
кило помидоров   мясо
рыба   бутылка пива

Exercise 5

Find five drinks and six types of food below.

кофе
ФРУКТОВАЯ ВОДА
ВОДКА
СОУСЫ И КЕТЧУПЫ
конфеты
шоколад
КАРАМЕЛЬ
шампанское
ЛАНЧЕН МИТ
чай фруктовый

Exercise 6

Ask in the **гастронОм** if they have:

a salami sausage **б** tea **в** cake **г** fish **д** milk **e** oranges **ж** cucumbers

ХОДИТЬ ПО МАГАЗИНАМ *Going round the shops*

УнивермАг *Department store*	
подАрок (pl подАрки)	*present(s)*
одЕжда	*clothes*
джИнсы	*jeans*
шАпка	*fur hat*

СувенИры *Souvenirs*
матрЁшка — *stacking matryoshka doll*
электрИческий самовАр — *electric samovar*
платОк (pl платкИ) — *shawl(s)*
деревЯнная игрУшка — *wooden toy*

КиОск *Kiosk*
газЕта, журнАл, план — *newspaper, magazine, plan*
открЫтка — *postcard*
морОженое — *ice cream*

АптЕка *Chemist's*
аспирИн — *aspirin*
лекАрство — *medicine*

ДИАЛОГ 2 РУССКИЕ СУВЕНИРЫ *Russian souvenirs*

Chris is asking Oleg to help organize her day. Read the dialogue several times and then go on to the exercises.

Крис	Я сегОдня хочУ ходИть по магазИнам.
ОлЕг	Что ты хОчешь купИть?
Крис	ПодАрки и сувенИры. Я хочУ купИть кнИги, деревЯнные игрУшки, открЫтки и самовАр. Я Очень люблЮ рУсский чай с лимОном.
ОлЕг	ПонЯтно. КнИги и открЫтки продаЮтся в магазИне «Дом КнИги». Это недалекО.
Крис	А где продаЮтся самовАры и игрУшки?
ОлЕг	В магазИне «РУсский сувенИр». КотОрый сейчАс час?
Крис	ДЕвять часОв.

CD 2, TR 4, 02:55

ОлЕг	ХорошО. «Дом КнИги» открывАется в дЕвять часОв.
Крис	Как попАсть в «Дом КнИги»?
ОлЕг	Три останОвки на автОбусе. ОстанОвка там, напрОтив.

Later, in «РУсский сувенИр»

ДЕвушка	Вам помОчь?
Крис	ПожАлуйста, да! ПокажИте, пожАлуйста, Этот самовАр. Нет, вот Этот. ОлЕг, какОй Это красИвый самовАр! ДЕвушка, Это электрИческий самовАр?
ДЕвушка	Да, электрИческий. ОткУда вы?
Крис	Я англичАнка, живУ в ЛОндоне.
ДЕвушка	Не волнУйтесь. МоЯ тётя живёт в ЛОндоне, и онА говорИт, что нАши самовАры хорошО там рабОтают.
Крис	ПонЯтно. ПокажИте, пожАлуйста, Эти деревЯнные игрУшки. Да, крАсные и зелёные. И вот Эти жёлтые.
ДЕвушка	Вот Эти?
Крис	Да. СпасИбо. НапишИте, пожАлуйста, скОлько онИ стОят.

Exercise 7

Read the shopping list in the left-hand column and match up the items with an appropriate shop from the right-hand column. You could then rewrite the list correctly.

аспирин   киоск
масло   сувениры
сахар   рынок
вино   молочные продукты
мороженое   универсам
цветы   аптека
хлеб   универмаг
самовар   булочная
шапка   гастроном

Exercise 8

а What does Chris want to do today?
б What four things does she want to buy?
в Is it far to the bookshop?
г Where is the bus stop?
д What is the Russian for she says that?
е How does Chris know that the samovar will work in England?
ж What colours are the toys she wants to look at?

Now you could make up your own dialogue, buying things which you would particularly like.

Exercise 9

◀ CD 2, TR 4, 05:06

Listen to the three conversations. Note down in Russian or English what Sasha wants to buy, the shop he needs and the directions he is given.

СAша хOчет купИть ...	МагазИн	КудA?

а

б

в

Exercise 10

Here is an alphabetical list of the types of shops you could find in a major Russian city, and of items to buy. You have met many of the words, and the rest you can probably work out.

АвтомобИли

АнтиквариАт

Аудио-ВидеотЕхника

БУлочная

ГастронОм

ДиетИческие продУкты

ДизАйн-стУдия

КнИги

КолбасА

КосмЕтика

МолОчные продУкты

МузыкАльные инструмЕнты

МЯсо

Овощи-фрУкты

Оптика

ПодАрки

РЫба

СпортИвные товАры

СувенИры

ТабАк

ЦветЫ

ЧасЫ

Read the list and underline where you think you could buy **а** spectacles **б** a watch **в** a bread roll **г** antiques **д** food for a special diet **е** a herring **ж** a trombone **з** a video player **и** a car.

АУДИО
ВИДЕО
ФОТО
Мойка, 56 ◀▥

Exercise 11

How would you say:

а I want to buy bread, cheese, tomatoes and tea.
б Where can I buy a newspaper?
в That's all.
г Repeat that, please.
д Do you have any white wine?
е How much is it?

АНЕКДОТ *Anecdote*

This anecdote from the times of food shortages in the Soviet era is set in an empty butcher's shop opposite an empty fish shop. How would you say the punchline in English?

БАбушка	У вас есть мЯсо?
ПродавЕц	Нет.
БАбушка	У вас есть колбасА?
ПродавЕц	Нет.
БАбушка	У вас есть сосИски?
ПродавЕц	Нет.
БАбушка	У вас есть рЫба?
ПродавЕц	Нет. РЫбы нет в магазИне напрОтив.

And finally, here is a tongue twister for you to learn by heart to practise the letters с and ш. It means *Sasha walked along the road and sucked a biscuit* (literally, *walked Sasha along road and sucked biscuit*).

◀)) CD 2, TR 4, 05:51

Шла САша по шоссЕ и сосАла сУшку.

TEST YOURSELF

Now you can go shopping, which is a great opportunity to have conversations. Try these ten questions to make sure you have remembered everything.

How do you say the following things?

1 Can I have a look?

2 Show me

3 How much is it?

4 Do you have sweets?

5 That's expensive

6 Repeat that please

What does the shop assistant mean by the following phrases?

7 СлУшаю вас

8 Вам помОчь?

9 СкОлько вы хотИте?

10 Вот Эти?

15

В чём дЕло?
What's the matter?

In this unit you will learn
- *How to book a hotel room*
- *How to complain*
- *How to sort out problems*

Before you start
Revise
- vocabulary and structures from Unit 7
- у вас есть . .? Unit 10

When learning new vocabulary, decide which words it will be most useful to learn actively and which you only need to recognize. Test yourself by covering up the English words first and then the Russian words, and see how many you can remember.

Insight
В ГОСТИНИЦЕ *At the hotel*

Like hotels the world over, you will find that Russian hotels vary, but many will provide these facilities: a restaurant **ресторАн**, bar **бар**, café **кафЕ**, shops **магазИны**, post office **пОчта**, service desk **бюрО обслУживания**, bureau de change **обмЕн валЮты**, lost property office **бюрО нахОдок**, cloakroom **гардерОб**, lifts **лИфты** and hairdresser's **парикмАхерская**.

ОТ СЕБЯ/К СЕБЕ *Push/Pull*

От себЯ and **к себЕ** mean literally *away from yourself* and *towards yourself*. This is what you will see on doors in public buildings to tell you when to push and when to pull.

заказАть нОмер	*Booking a room*
У вас есть свобОдный нОмер/свобОдная кОмната?	*Do you have a free room?*
нОмер на одногО с вАнной	*a room for one with a bath*
нОмер на двоИх с дУшем	*a room for two with a shower*
нОмер на день	*a room for a day*
нОмер на 2, 3, 4 дня	*a room for 2, 3, 4 days*
нОмер на 5, 6 дней	*a room for 5, 6 days*
нОмер на недЕлю	*a room for a week*
день, недЕля, мЕсяц, год	*day, week, month, year*
СкОлько стОит нОмер в день?	*How much is a room per day?*
МОжно заказАть нОмер?	*Could I book a room?*
нОмер на одногО на четЫрнадцатое мАя	*a room for one for 14 May*
к сожалЕнию	*unfortunately*
к счАстью	*fortunately*
зАвтрак начинАется/ кончАется в . . .	*breakfast starts/ finishes at . . .*
КогдА нАдо заплатИть?	*When do I have to pay?*
вчерА, сегОдня, зАвтра	*yesterday, today, tomorrow*
счёт	*the bill*
прАвильно/непрАвильно	*that's right/that's not right*

ДИАЛОГ 1 У ВАС ЕСТЬ СВОБОДНЫЙ НОМЕР?
Do you have a free room?

Steve has just arrived at a hotel without having made a reservation. Listen to or read the dialogue. When you have got the gist of the conversation, look at the questions below and answer them. You will notice that, in this dialogue, Steve is given a price in dollars. At times in recent years it has been usual to express prices in dollars or euros, even if payment has to be made in roubles.

Стив	У вас есть свобОдный нОмер на сегОдня?
АдминистрАтор	Да, есть. КакОй нОмер вы хотИте?
Стив	НОмер на одногО с вАнной, пожАлуйста.
АдминистрАтор	К сожалЕнию, у нас тОлько большОй нОмер на двоИх с дУшем.
Стив	СкажИте, пожАлуйста, скОлько стОит нОмер на двоИх?
АдминистрАтор	Сто двАдцать дОлларов в день.
Стив	Это дОрого. КогдА нАдо заплатИть?
АдминистрАтор	ЗАвтра.
Стив	В котОром часУ начинАется зАвтрак?
АдминистрАтор	В семь часОв. И кончАется в дЕвять часОв.
Стив	МОжно обЕдать в гостИнице?
АдминистрАтор	КонЕчно, мОжно. В гостИнице Очень хорОший ресторАн. Вот ваш ключ. Ваш нОмер – 104.
Стив	СпасИбо. А как попАсть в нОмер 104? У менЯ чемодАн и большАя сУмка.
АдминистрАтор	Лифт прЯмо и напрАво.

Exercise 1

a What sort of room does Steve want? **б** What is he offered? **в** How much does it cost per day? **г** When does he have to pay? **д** What is the earliest he may have breakfast? And the latest? **е** Can he have dinner in the hotel? **ж** What luggage does he have? **з** Where is the lift?

Exercise 2

Steve decides to go out and explore the town, but first he must give his key to the woman on duty on his landing.

ДежУрная	МолодОй человЕк, где ваш ключ?
Стив	Вот он. СкажИте, в котОром часУ нОчью закрывАется вход?
ДежУрная	В пОлночь.
Стив	СпасИбо. А где здесь бар?
ДежУрная	ВнизУ. НалЕво.

a At what time does the entrance to the hotel close?
б Where is the bar?

Exercise 3

◀) CD 2, TR 5, 01:13

Listen to these customers. What sort of rooms do they want, and for how long?

a
б
в

Exercise 4

◀) CD 2, TR 5, 01:36

Complete your part of this dialogue.

a	**You**	*Do you have a free room?*
	АдминистрАтор	Да. КакОй нОмер вы хотИте?
b	**You**	*A double room with a bath, please.*
	АдминистрАтор	ОднУ минУточку. Да, у нас есть нОмер на двоИх с вАнной. СтОит сто дОлларов в день.

208

c	**You**	*Good. What time is dinner?*
	АдминистрАтор	ОбЕд начинАется в шесть часОв.
d	**You**	*Is there a lift here? I have a big suitcase.*
	АдминистрАтор	Да, лифт прЯмо, вИдите?
e	**You**	*Yes, I see.*
	АдминистрАтор	Вот ваш ключ. Ваш нОмер – 34.
f	**You**	*Thank you. Room number 34. Is that right?*
	АдминистрАтор	Да. прАвильно. НОмер 34.
g	**You**	*Thank you very much. Goodbye.*

В НОМЕРЕ *In the hotel room*

окнО	*window*	**вАнная**	*bathroom*
дверь *(f)*	*door*	**туалЕт**	*toilet*
стол	*table*	**душ**	*shower*
стул	*chair*	**вАнна**	*bath*
крЕсло	*armchair*	**кран**	*tap*
шкаф	*cupbord*	**одеЯло**	*blanket*
кровАть *(f)*	*bed*	**подУшка**	*pillow*
лАмпа	*lamp*	**полотЕнце**	*towel*
телефОн	*telephone*	**мЫло**	*soap*
телевИзор	*television*	**шампУнь** *(m)*	*shampoo*
часЫ	*clock*	**зЕркало**	*mirror*

To help you learn this vocabulary you could make labels for your furniture at home.

Exercise 5

The vocabulary list above is a checklist of things which should be in each hotel room. Look at the pictures overleaf and make a list in Russian (written or spoken) of those things which Simon has in his room. Or you could underline the items in the vocabulary list. Make another list of what is missing from his room.

В нОмере хОлодно	*It's cold in my room*
жАрко	*it's hot*
тИхо	*it's quiet*
теплО	*it's warm*
грЯзно	*it's dirty*
хОлодно	*it's cold*
мне хОлодно	*I'm cold*
шУмно	*it's noisy*
мне плОхо	*I feel bad*

Exercise 6

Choose appropriate words from the list above to describe what it is like in these places.

а	На плЯже	_____ и _____.
б	В АнтАрктике	_____ и _____.
в	На концЕрте	_____ и _____.
г	В больнИце	_____ и _____.
д	В бассЕйне	_____ и _____.

ЧЕМ Я МОГУ ВАМ ПОМОЧЬ? *How may I help you?*

МОжно ещЁ одеЯло, пожАлуйста	*Could I have another blanket, please?*
Я хочУ заказАть билЕт в теАтр на зАвтра	*I want to book a theatre ticket for tomorrow*
Я хочУ заказАть таксИ на зАвтра на 10 часОв	*I want to book a taxi for tomorrow at ten*
КудА вы поЕдете?	*Where are you going?*
Я хочУ позвонИть домОй в АвстрАлию	*I want to call home to Australia*
код в АвстрАлию	*the code for Australia*
МОжно принестИ зАвтрак в нОмер?	*Could you bring breakfast to my room?*

ДИАЛОГ 2 АЛЛО! *Hello!*

Your friend Katya is a hotel administrator. You go to work with her one day, and overhear the following conversations at her desk and while she is on the phone. To say hello on the phone you say **АллО!**

Клайв	ИзвинИте, я хочУ позвонИть домОй в АвстрАлию. МОжно?
КАтя	МОжно. Код в АвстрАлию 61.
Анна	АллО, Это ресторАн?
КАтя	Нет, Это администрАтор.
Анна	МОжно принестИ зАвтрак в нОмер, пожАлуйста? Мне плОхо.
КАтя	МОжно. Что вы хотИте?
Анна	Чай с лимОном и фрУкты, пожАлуйста.
ТрЕвор	АллО, администрАтор?
КАтя	Да, слУшаю.
ТрЕвор	Я хочУ заказАть таксИ на зАвтра на 10 часОв.
КАтя	КудА вы поЕдете?
ТрЕвор	На вокзАл.
КАтя	У вас есть багАж?
ТрЕвор	Да, чемодАн.

Exercise 7

a Where does Clive want to phone, and what code does he need?

б What does Anna want the restaurant to send to her room, and why?

в Where does Trevor want to go, and when?

To practise your writing, you could pretend to be the administrator and jot down notes in English or Russian to remind you what your customers wanted.

ПРОБЛЕМЫ! *Problems!*

Всё хорошО?	*Is everything all right?*
В чём дЕло?	*What's the matter?*
кАжется, мы потерЯли ключ	*It seems we have lost the key*
горЯчая/холОдная водА не идёт	*The hot/cold water is not running*
окнО выхОдит на плОщадь	*The window looks out onto the square*
окнО не открывАется/ закрывАется	*The window won't open/shut*
телефОн не рабОтает	*The telephone doesn't work*
Как это мОжет быть?	*How can that be?*
У менЯ пропАл бумАжник/ фотоаппарАт/кошелЁк (m)	*I have lost my wallet/camera/ purse*
У менЯ пропАла сУмка (f)	*I have lost my bag*
У менЯ пропАло пальтО (n)	*I have lost my coat*
У менЯ пропАли дЕньги/ докумЕнты (pl)	*I have lost my money/documents*
я, ты, он не/довОлен (m)	*I am, you are, he is un/happy*
я, ты, онА не/довОльна (f)	*I am, you are, she is un/happy*
мы, вы, онИ не/довОльны (pl)	*We, you, they are un/happy*
СпасИбо большОе	*Thank you very much*

ДИАЛОГ 3 ИЗВИНИТЕ *Excuse me*

Read these dialogues, imagining you are the administrator.

а

Эдна	ИзвинИте, в нОмере жАрко.
КАтя	ОкнО открЫто?
Эдна	Нет, закрЫто. ОкнО выхОдит на плОщадь, и там Очень шУмно.

б

Марк	ИзвинИте, мне хОлодно. МОжно ещё одеЯло, пожАлуйста?
КАтя	МОжно. КакОй ваш нОмер?
Марк	НОмер 73. Там хОлодно, кран не закрывАется и телевИзор плОхо рабОтает.

в

ВанЕсса	ИзвинИте, кАжется, мы потерЯли ключ.
КАтя	КакОй ваш нОмер?
ВанЕсса	ШестнАдцать.
КАтя	Вот ваш ключ.
ВанЕсса	Здесь? У вас? Как это мОжет быть? СпасИбо большОе.

г

Билл	ДАйте, пожАлуйста, счёт.
КАтя	Вот счёт. НОмер на двоИх на недЕлю. ПрАвильно?
Билл	Да, прАвильно.
КАтя	Всё хорошО?
Билл	Да, здесь Очень приЯтно. В нОмере теплО и тИхо. СпасИбо большОе. Мы Очень довОльны.

д

КАтя	В чём дЕло? Вы недовОльны?
ГАри	Мы Очень недовОльны. ГорЯчая водА не идЁт, телефОн не рабОтает и в нОмере грЯзно.

Exercise 8

Make brief notes in English of the conversations above.

Exercise 9

Here is a list of repair work that needs to be done in a hotel. What needs putting right in these rooms? Read the list out loud including the numbers, before summarizing the problems in English.

номер 9, телевизор не работает
номер 14, телефон плохо работает
номер 23, кран не закрывается
номер 31, холодно, окно не закрывается
номер 35, жарко, окно не открывается
номер 40, шумно
номер 52, грязно
номер 55, радио не работает

Exercise 10

You have been put in a room which is cold, dirty and noisy. The television doesn't work, the tap won't turn off and the window looks out onto the station. Bad luck! What will you say to the hotel administrator?

Exercise 11

◀)) CD 2, TR 5, 06:13

Listen to the recording, and describe what these four people have lost.

а
б
в
г

214

Exercise 12

Here is a page from a hotel brochure. What facilities are there in this hotel, on which floor are they and when are they open? Where telephone numbers are provided, read them out in Russian. Don't forget that the first floor in Russian is the ground floor in English!

ПЕрвый этАж
ГардерОб   (перерЫв на обЕд* 14.00–15.00)
БюрО нахОдок   10.00–16.00
РесторАн   8.00–23.00 тел. 229-02-31

ВторОй этАж
ДирЕктор   тел. 229-569-28
АдминистрАтор   тел. 229-899-57
БюрО обслУживания   8.00–22.00 тел. 229-08-46
ГазЕтный киОск   8.00–16.00
БуфЕт   8.00–22.00

ТрЕтий этАж
ПОчта   8.00–20.00 тел. 229-33-13
ПарикмАхерская   8.00–20.00 тел. 229-29-09
Бар   14.00–24.00
*lunch break

And finally, remembering that the word **гостИница** comes from **гость** *a guest,* here is a proverb – the equivalent of *there's no place like home* (literally, *Being a guest is good, but being at home is better*):

В гостЯх хорошО, а дОма лУчше.

TEST YOURSELF

You have just learned lots of new words and phrases which will help you to get by in Russian. You can now complain and explain and ask for help if you need to.

1 If you see a door with a notice on it saying к себE, will you push or pull?

2 Does к сожалЕнию mean fortunately or unfortunately?

3 It's cold, dirty and noisy in your room. What will you say to the hotel administrator?

How do you say the following phrases in Russian?

4 I want to order a taxi.

5 I don't feel well.

6 Thank you very much

7 What's the matter?

8 We are very unhappy.

9 The telephone isn't working.

10 Do you have a free room?

16

ПриЯтного аппетИта!
Bon appétit! Enjoy your meal!

In this unit you will learn
- *How to read a menu and order a meal*
- *How to buy a snack, ice creams or drinks*
- *What to say if you are eating at a friend's home*

Before you start
Revise
- likes and dislikes, Unit 9
- prices, Unit 6, particularly Dialogue 3

Insight
ХОЧУ ЕСТЬ И ПИТЬ *I'm hungry and thirsty*

As a visitor to Russia, you will find a variety of options if you want to eat out, varying from high-class restaurants to bars and kiosks selling food and drinks on the street. Many museums, train stations and department stores may have a stand-up snack bar **буфЕт.** If you are opting for a full meal you will start with appetizers **закУски,** followed by a soup, or first course **пЕрвое блЮдо,** which might be beetroot soup **борщ** or cabbage soup **щи.** Then will come a main, or second, course **вторОе блЮдо,** usually based on meat or fish with side dishes **гарнИр**, and finally dessert **слАдкое**. Much Russian cuisine contains meat, but if you are a vegetarian then salads and dishes with mushrooms **грибЫ** can usually be found, and are very good. If it is a special occasion, the meal may be accompanied by vodka **вОдка**, wine **винО** and champagne **шампАнское**.

The verbs 'to eat' **есть** and 'to drink' **пить**

есть (irregular) to eat		**пить** (1) to drink	
я ем	I eat	**я пью**	I drink
ты ешь	you eat	**ты пьёшь**	you drink
он ест	he eats	**он пьёт**	he drinks
мы едИм	we eat	**мы пьём**	we drink
вы едИте	you eat	**вы пьЕте**	you drink
онИ едЯт	they eat	**онИ пьют**	they drink

В РЕСТОРАНЕ At the restaurant

Я Очень хочУ есть/пить!	I'm really hungry/thirsty
Мы хотИм стол на пять/ шесть человЕк	We want a table for five/six people
ОфициАнт/ка, идИте сюдА, пожАлуйста	Waiter/waitress, come here please
Дайте, пожАлуйста, менЮ	Please give me/us the menu
СлУшаю вас	Can I help you? (I'm listening)
Что вы хотИте заказАть?	What do you want to order?
Что вы хотИте есть/пить	What do you want to eat/drink?
Что вам?	What would you like?
Что вы рекомендУете?	What would you recommend?
На закУску, на пЕрвое, на вторОе, на слАдкое	For a starter, for 1st/2nd course, for dessert

Я хочУ заказАть шашлЫк	I want to order kebab (shashlik)
ДАйте мне, пожАлуйста, хлеб с колбасОй	Please give me bread with salami sausage
Вот вам бутербрОд	Here's your sandwich
чай с лимОном, с сАхаром, с молокОм	tea with lemon, sugar, milk
чай без лимОна, без сАхара, без молокА	tea without lemon, sugar, milk
ПриЯтного аппетИта! (PriyAtnuva appitEEta!)	Bon appétit!
Дайте, пожАлуйста, счёт	Please give me the bill
СкОлько с меня?	How much do I owe?
С вас ...	You owe ...

Bear in mind that any prices quoted in this book may be out of date.

ДИАЛОГ 1 В КАФЕ *In the café*

Henry visits a small café for a snack.

ХЕнри	ОфициАнтка! ДАйте, пожАлуйста, менЮ.
ОфициАнтка	ЗдрАвствуйте. Вот менЮ. СлУшаю вас. Что вы хотИте?
ХЕнри	Чай, пожАлуйста.
ОфициАнтка	С лимОном?
ХЕнри	Да, с лимОном и с сАхаром.
ОфициАнтка	Это всё?
ХЕнри	Нет. У вас есть бутербрОды?
ОфициАнтка	Есть.
ХЕнри	ДАйте, пожАлуйста, хлеб с колбасОй.
ОфициАнтка	Вот вам чай с лимОном и с сАхаром, и хлеб с колбасОй.
ХЕнри	СкОлько с меня?
ОфициАнтка	С вас девянОсто рублЕй.

Exercise 1

Listen to the dialogue above. **a** How does Henry like his tea?
б What does he want to eat?

Exercise 2

🔊 **CD 2, TR 6, 00:56**

Now complete your part of a dialogue in the café.

а	**You**	*You would like to see the menu.*
	ОфициАнт	Вот вам менЮ. Что вы хотИте?
б	**You**	*You ask for coffee and ice cream.*
	ОфициАнт	КОфе без молокА?
в	**You**	*No, you want your coffee with milk and sugar.*
	ОфициАнт	Вы хотИте шоколАдное морОженое или ванИльное?
г	**You**	*You don't understand. Ask the waiter to repeat it.*
	ОфициАнт	Что хотИте? ШоколАдное морОженое Или ванИльное?
д	**You**	*You understand now. Ask for vanilla ice cream.*
	ОфициАнт	Вот вам кОфе и ванИльное морОженое. ПриЯтного аппетИта!
е	**You**	*Thank the waiter. Ask him how much it all costs.*
	ОфициАнт	С вас сто сОрок рублЕй.

Opposite is a dinner menu from the Hotel Ukraine. Study the headings, and see how many dishes you can work out. Find those which you don't know from the vocabulary list opposite and learn them, testing yourself by covering up first the English words and then the Russian. You could then see how many dishes you can remember from each category.

ГостИница «УкраИна»

МенЮ

ЗакУски
СалАт москОвский
ГрибЫ в сметАне
ИкрА чЁрная
ИкрА крАсная
Сыр голлАндский

ПЕрвые БлЮда
Щи
Борщ украИнский
Суп с грибАми

ВторЫе блЮда
ШашлЫк
Беф-стрОганов
КУрица

ГарнИр
Рис
ГрибЫ

СлАдкие блЮда
КомпОт
ШоколАдное морОженое
ФрУкты
Торт НаполеОн

НапИтки
КрАсное винО
БЕлое винО
КОфе
Чай индИйский
Чай с лимОном
ТомАтный сок
ГазирОванная водА
МинерАльная водА
ВОдка
КоньЯк

Using the menu above as a guide, write out a meal which you would like to order, or underline the dishes which you would select.

Now make up a conversation with a waiter, ordering what you have chosen. The waiter begins: **СлУшаю вас. Что вы хотИте заказАть?**

Exercise 3

In a hotel you see a notice telling you at what time and on which floor you may get your meals. A Russian standing next to you is trying to read the notice as well, but he has just broken his spectacles. Explain the details to him.

На пЕрвом этажЕ рабОтает ресторАн.

ЗАвтрак	— с 8.00 до 10.00
ОбЕд	— с 13.00 до 15.00
Ужин	— с 18.00 до 20.00

На вторОм этажЕ рабОтает гриль-бАр. Здесь мОжно заказАть кОфе и бутербрОды.

ЗА СТОЛОМ *At the table*

QUICK VOCAB

стол	*table*	**хлеб**	*bread*
стул	*chair*	**мАсло**	*butter*
блЮдо	*dish*	**нож**	*knife*
тарЕлка	*plate*	**вИлка**	*fork*
чАшка	*cup*	**лОжка**	*spoon*
стакАн	*glass*	**соль** *(f)*	*salt*
рЮмка	*wine glass*	**пЕрец**	*pepper*
салфЕтка	*serviette*		

ДИАЛОГ 2 В РЕСТОРАНЕ *In the restaurant*

Victoria is ordering a meal in a restaurant. Read the dialogue before answering the questions below.

CD 2, TR 6, 02:34

ВиктОрия	МолодОй человЕк! Я хочУ заказАть, пожАлуйста.
ОфициАнт	СлУшаю вас.
ВиктОрия	На закУски у вас есть салАт москОвский?
ОфициАнт	ИзвинИте, нет.
ВиктОрия	Жаль. Что вы рекомендУете?
ОфициАнт	Я рекомендУю грибЫ в сметАне.
ВиктОрия	ХорошО, на закУски – грибЫ в сметАне. На пЕрвое, у вас есть борщ?
ОфициАнт	Нет, сегОдня у нас есть тОлько щи.
ВиктОрия	Так, на пЕрвое – щи, на вторОе – шашлЫк с рИсом, и на слАдкое – фрУкты.
ОфициАнт	ПонЯтно, на закУски – грибЫ в сметАне, на пЕрвое – щи, на вторОе – шашлЫк с рИсом, и на слАдкое – фрУкты. А что вы хотИте пить?
ВиктОрия	У вас есть винО?
ОфициАнт	Да, какОе винО вы хотИте?
ВиктОрия	ДАйте бЕлое винО, и чай, пожАлуйста.
ОфициАнт	Чай с сАхаром?
ВиктОрия	Нет, чай с лимОном без сАхара.
ОфициАнт	Это всё?
ВиктОрия	Да, Это всё, спасИбо. Нет! Вот идЁт мой брат! ДАйте, пожАлуйста, ещЁ рЮмку и тарЕлку. ЗдрАвствуй, НиколАй. Что ты хОчешь есть и пить?

Exercise 4

a What two things are not available today?

б What does Victoria order, and how does she like her tea?

в She sees someone come into the restaurant. Who is it, and what does Victoria ask for on his behalf?

Exercise 5

Did you notice how Victoria asked for *another* **ещЁ** glass and plate? – **Дайте, пожАлуйста, ещЁ рЮмку и тарЕлку**. Don't forget to change **-a** to **-y** and **-я** to **-ю** if you are asking for a feminine object. How would you ask for an extra cup, spoon, knife and chair?

Exercise 6

◀) **CD 2, TR 6, 04:04**

Now imagine you are a bilingual waiter in the КафЕ «ТбилИси» taking down a Russian customer's order. Listen to the recording and jot down in English or Russian what the customer wants.

Exercise 7

Look at this picture. Make sure that you know how to say everything on the table in Russian. Then cover the picture and try to remember everything. You could try writing a list in Russian.

Exercise 8

How would you ask for: Moscow salad, mushroom soup, beef stroganoff, rice, chocolate ice cream, white wine and coffee with milk? Now ask for the bill.

Exercise 9

◀ CD 2, TR 6, 04:36

See if you can unscramble the dialogue below. It is set in a **буфЕт**. The first sentence is in bold type. Listen to the recording to check your answer.

а ДАйте, пожАлуйста, хлеб, сыр и кОфе.
б Что у вас есть сегОдня?
в С вас пятдесЯт рублей.
г Да, дАйте чай без сАхара.
д ИзвинИте, у нас нет кОфе. Вы хотИте чай?
е СпасИбо. СкОлько с меня?
ж **СлУшаю вас.**
з У нас сегОдня хлеб, сыр, колбасА, шоколАд и фрУкты.
и Вот вам хлеб, сыр и чай.

Exercise 10

Imagine that you are running a restaurant in Russia. Fill out the menu below, putting at least two items in each column, and don't forget the date at the top.

МЕНЮ

_____ 201_____ гОда

ЗакУски	ПЕрвое блЮдо	ВторОе блЮдо	СлАдкое	НапИтки

Exercise 11

КАша is any sort of porridge dish cooked with grains and liquid. There is a Russian saying: **Щи да кАша – пИща нАша** *Cabbage soup and porridge are our food*. What ingredients do you need to make a milky rice pudding? See if you can read them out loud from the recipe below, including the numerals.

Каша рисовая молочная
рис   100 грамм
масло   25 грамм
сахар   20 грамм
соль   5 грамм
молоко   260 миллилитров
вода   200 миллилитров

У ДРУЗЕЙ *With friends at their home*

You can now cope with anything which is likely to occur in a restaurant, but what about visiting friends at their home? Here are some phrases which may help.

ВходИте, раздевАйтесь!	*Come in, take your coat off!*
рОзы	*roses*
нормАльно	*fine, OK*
УгощАйтесь!	*Help yourself!*
вкУсно	*It's tasty*
За вАше здорОвье!	*Cheers! Your health!*
БерИте ещЁ . . .	*Take some more . . .*
СпасИбо большОе за всё	*Thanks very much for everything*
УжЕ пОздно	*It's late already*
ПорА идтИ	*It's time to go*
СпокОйной нОчи	*Good night*
До зАвтра	*Until tomorrow*

....

Insight

Russians do not smile much in formal settings, unless there is really something to smile about. Too much smiling is seen as being insincere. Think about the faces of Russian politicians you have seen on TV. They have very serious expressions and rarely smile even when they are talking about positive things. However, at home and at social events, Russians really know how to have fun!

....

ДИАЛОГ 3 В КВАРТИРЕ *In the flat*

Exercise 12

You have been invited to Yulia and Volodya's for supper. Read the dialogue, and say: **a** what you take as a gift, **б** how Volodya is feeling, **в** what is for starters, **г** whether you like it, **д** what you have to drink and **е** why you have to leave.

Юлия	ДОбрый вЕчер. ВходИте, раздевАйтесь!
Вы	ДОбрый вЕчер. Вот вам мАленький подАрок – шампАнское и цветЫ.
Юлия	СпасИбо большОе. Я так люблЮ рОзы. Вот идёт ВолОдя.
Вы	ЗдрАвствуйте, ВолОдя. Как делА?
ВолОдя	НормАльно, спасИбо. Всё хорошО. СадИтесь, пожАлуйста.
Вы	СпасИбо. Ой, какИе прекрАсные закУски. Я Очень люблЮ грибЫ в сметАне и икрУ.
Юлия	Вот вам тарЕлка. УгощАйтесь!
Вы	Мм! Всё Очень вкУсно, Юлия.
ВолОдя	И вот вам вОдка. За вАше здорОвье!
Вы	За вАше здорОвье!
Юлия	БерИте ещЁ закУски.
Вы	СпасИбо большОе.

Later that evening, in the entrance hall.

Вы	УжЕ пОздно. ПорА идтИ.
ВолОдя	СпокОйной нОчи. До зАвтра.
Вы	СпасИбо за всё. СпокОйной нОчи.

Exercise 13

How would you say:

a I really love champagne.
б Cheers.
в What lovely wine glasses!
г How are you?

АНЕКДОТ *Anecdote*

To finish off the unit, here is an anecdote set in a bar. Why does the waiter tell the customer it is now all right to drink beer?

ОфициАнт	Что вам? Вы хотИте пИво?
БорИс	Нет, я на велосипЕде. ДАйте, пожАлуйста, сок.
ЧЕрез минУту ...	
ОфициАнт	Вы мОжете сейчАс пить пИво. Ваш велосипЕд ктО-то укрАл.

| **велосипЕд** | *bicycle* |
| **ктО-то укрАл** | *someone has stolen* |

TEST YOURSELF

A country's cuisine says a lot about its culture, and eating with people helps you to really get to know them and to practise your language. Here are ten questions on the theme of food and drink to show how much you know about the subject.

What do the following phrases mean?

1 ПриЯтного аппетИта!

2 Что вам?

3 Что вы рекомендУете?

4 СкОлько с менЯ?

5 Всё Очень вкУсно.

How will you say the following in Russian?

6 *Knife, fork, spoon*

7 *Your health!*

8 *Can I have the menu please?*

9 *Dessert*

10 *Champagne*

17

На пОчте
At the post office

In this unit you will learn
- *How to send a letter, postcard, parcel, telegram*
- *How to make a phone call*

Before you start
Revise
- numerals, at the back of the book
- telling the time, Unit 8
- filling in forms, Unit 15

Insight
ТЕЛЕФОННАЯ И АДРЕСНАЯ КНИГА
Telephone directory

Until the 1990s, there was no system of public telephone directories in Russia and you had to ask at an enquiry office **спрАвочное бюрО** if you wanted to find a telephone number. These still exist but are not widespread. Instead there are now complete directories available, giving private numbers as well as administrative and commercial numbers. They also offer tourist information, and many have foreign language sections. There are business Yellow Pages **ЖЁлтые странИцы** and of course there is the Internet. You can also dial 09 for a free directory enquiries service or 099 for a paid service.

If there is an emergency you dial 01 for all the emergency services. Words you might need include *fire* **пожАр**, *police* **милИция**, *ambulance* **скОрая медицИнская пОмощь** and *gas* **газ**.

If you want to know the exact time in Moscow dial 100.

Learning the Russian alphabet in the correct order will save a lot of time when using a directory. Remember too that Russian directories will boast that they provide everything you need to know not from A to Z, but from **А** to **Я «от А до Я»**.

Я ХОЧУ ПОЗВОНИТЬ ДОМОЙ *I want to call home*

Many Russians use the phone a lot, making long, late calls from the comfort of an armchair. Local calls are free to and from landlines. If you want to use the phone, you have several choices. The easiest and cheapest way to make a call is by private telephone, but if this is not possible, you will need to use a pay phone **телефОн-автомАт** or **таксофОн** for local calls, using a pre-payment card or credit card. If the number you want to call is abroad, you may be able to call direct from your hotel or book a call through hotel reception. A less expensive option is to book a call at the telephone section of a main post office **пОчта**, or at the special telephone and telegraph offices **ТелефОн – телеграАф**. Don't forget the time difference with the country you are calling. If you choose the post office, you book a call at the counter for a certain number of minutes at a certain time and wait for the staff to call out your booth number over the public address system. Then you dash to the right booth (practise your numerals beforehand) and start your call, which is counted from the moment of the announcement. The whole thing can be a little flustering! Some major post offices offer a bookable Internet service available in little computer booths, and they also sell pre-payment cards for home Internet connection on behalf of Internet providers **ИнтернЕт провАйдеры.** You can also buy Internet cards,

SIM cards and mobile phone top-ups in shops and kiosks called a salon of connection **салОн свЯзи**. Of course many visitors prefer to use their mobile phones to make calls. A mobile phone is called **мобИльный телефОн,** or more casually **мобИльник.** Of course there are Internet cafes and wi-fi provision as well, so you need not be out of touch. However, a visit to the post office enables you to have a conversation with the staff and to practise your numbers!

ПО ТЕЛЕФОНУ *On the phone*

Я хочУ позвонИть в Англию/в АвстрАлию	*I want to call England/Australia*
МОжно заказАть разговОр на зАвтра на 3 минУты?	*Can I book a 3-minute call for tomorrow?*
КакОй нОмер телефОна?	*What's the phone number?*
КакОй код?	*What's the code?*
СкОлько минУт вы хотИте заказАть?	*How many minutes do you want to book?*
2, 3, 4 минУты, 5, 6, 7, 8, 9, 10, минУт	*2, 3, 4 minutes, 5–10 minutes*
КогдА вы хотИте говорИть?	*When do you want to talk?*
разговОр	*conversation*
чек	*bill, chit*

ДИАЛОГ 1 МОЖНО ЗАКАЗАТЬ РАЗГОВОР?
May I book a call?

Wendy has a call to make, so she goes to the post office to make a booking.

УЭнди	ИзвинИте, пожАлуйста. Я хочУ позвонИть в Англию.	**CD 2, TR 7**
ДЕвушка	Да. КакОй нОмер телефОна?	
УЭнди	987–25–55.	
ДЕвушка	И какОй код?	

УЭнди	0115.
ДЕвушка	СкОлько минУт вы хотИте заказАть?
УЭнди	ЧетЫре минУты, пожАлуйста.
ДЕвушка	КогдА вы хотИте говорИть?
УЭнди	МОжно заказАть разговОр на сегОдня на восемнАдцать часОв?
ДЕвушка	Нет, ужЕ пОздно на сегОдня.
УЭнди	МОжно на зАвтра, Утром?
ДЕвушка	ОднУ минУточку ... Да, мОжно заказАть разговор на зАвтра на дЕвять часОв. Вот вам чек. Всё понЯтно?
УЭнди	Да, понЯтно.

Exercise 1

Choose the correct phrase to complete each sentence.

а УЭнди хОчет позвонИть
  i в МосквУ.
  ii в больнИцу.
  iii в Англию.

б УЭнди хОчет заказАть разговОр
  i на восемнАдцать минУт.
  ii на сегОдня на восемнАдцать часОв.
  iii пОздно вЕчером.

в УЭнди не мОжет заказАть разговОр на сегОдня потомУ, что
  i пОчта закрЫта.
  ii дЕвушка не понимАет.
  iii ужЕ пОздно.

Exercise 2

You have to fill in a form at the post office to request a call to another city. You guess that the title of the form **ЗаЯвка на**

междугорОдный разговОр probably means *Request for intercity conversation.* **МЕжду** means *between,* so **междугорОдный** means *intercity* and **междунарОдный** means *international* (between nations). Now you have to decide where to put the rest of the details which you assume are being asked for.

ЗаЯвка на междугорОдный разговОр

а	**С гОродом**	**i**	*How many minutes*
б	**ТелефОн и Адрес**	**ii**	*Which city*
в	**ДАта и врЕмя вЫзова**	**iii**	*Telephone number and address*
г	**КолИчество минУт**	**iv**	*Signature*
д	**ПОдпись**	**v**	*Date and time of call*

Exercise 3

◀ **CD 2, TR 7, 01:05**

Listen to the recording and jot down details of where and when people are calling.

	To which city	Phone no.	At what time	For how many minutes
а				
б				
в				

Exercise 4

An independent telecommunications company is advertising its products and services. What is it offering to its customers? Cover up the right-hand column while you try to work it out.

а	24 часА междунарОдная телефОнная связь	**i**	*email*
б	МеждунарОдные бИзнес-лИнии	**ii**	*fax, telex*
в	КАрточные таксофОны	**iii**	*mobile phones*
г	ЭлектрОнная пОчта	**iv**	*tele-conferences*
д	ТелеконферЕнции	**v**	*24-hour international phone link*
е	МобИльные телефОны	**vi**	*telephone modems*
ж	ТелефОнные мОдемы	**vii**	*five-year guarantee*
з	Факс, тЕлекс	**viii**	*web design*
и	ГарАнтия – 5 лет	**ix**	*international business lines*
к	Веб дизАйн	**x**	*public card phones*

Insight
НА ПОЧТЕ *At the Post Office*

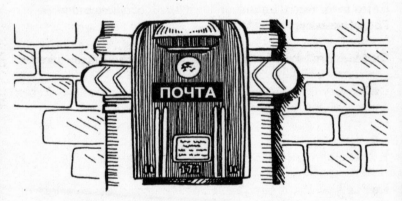

If you want to send something by post **по пОчте** you will need to visit the post office again, unless you already have the stamps and can use a letter box **почтОвый Ящик.** The post office is usually open from Monday to Saturday from 9.00 till 21.00 and on Sunday from 10.00 till 20.00. If you only need a stamp **мАрка** then it may be quicker to buy it from your hotel. At the post office, as well as buying stamps, you may buy an envelope **конвЕрт**, and send parcels **посЫлки** and telegrams. Residents can also pay bills there. Some post offices now also deal with faxes, as do telephone and telegraph offices and hotels. To send a parcel, take the contents only to the post office, where they will be inspected, weighed and wrapped for you. There is usually a long list on the wall of items which may not be sent by post, such as liquids and perishable goods.

....

письмО	*letter*
открЫтка	*postcard*
посЫлка	*parcel*
междунарОдная телегрАмма	*international telegram*
конвЕрт	*envelope*
мАрка	*stamp*
авиаписьмО	*airmail letter*
почтОвый Ящик	*letter box*
Что нАдо дЕлать?	*What do I need to do?*
НАдо запОлнить бланк	*You need to fill in a form*
Где мОжно купИть мАрки, конвЕрты, открЫтки?	*Where can I buy stamps, envelopes, postcards?*
СкОлько стОит послАть письмО в ВеликобритАнию?	*How much is it to send a letter to the UK?*
СкОлько стОит мАрка на письмО в ГермАнию?	*How much is a stamp for a letter to Germany?*
три мАрки по 500 (пятьсОт) рублЕй	*three stamps at 500 roubles each*
Я хочУ послАть посЫлку в Англию	*I want to send a parcel to England*
НапишИте Адрес вот здесь	*Write the address right here*
КУда, комУ, Адрес отправИтеля, вес	*Where to, to whom, address of sender, weight*
Я хочУ послАть телеграмму в Англию	*I want send a telegram to England*
НапишИте здесь текст	*Write the text here*
15 рублЕй за слОво	*15 roubles per word*

ДИАЛОГ 2 Я ХОЧУ ПОСЛАТЬ ПИСЬМО В ВЕЛИКОБРИТАНИЮ *I want to send a letter to Great Britain*

Dan has a lot of things to do at the post office. He goes to a small branch so that everything can be done at one counter, instead of queueing at different windows in the main post office.

CD 2, TR 7, 02:19

Дэн	ИзвинИте, дЕвушка, где мОжно купИть мАрки?
ДЕвушка	Здесь у менЯ мОжно всё купИть: мАрки, конвЕрты, открЫтки. КакИе мАрки вы хотИте?
Дэн	Я хочУ послАть Это письмО в ВеликобритАнию. СкОлько стОит мАрка на письмО?
ДЕвушка	ШестнАдцать рублЕй. Вот четЫре мАрки по четЫре рублЯ.
Дэн	СпасИбо. И я хочУ послАть телегрАмму домОй. СкОлько стОит?
ДЕвушка	ПятнАдцать рублЕй за слОво.
Дэн	Что нАдо дЕлать?
ДЕвушка	НАдо запОлнить бланк. НапишИте здесь текст.
Дэн	СпасИбо. И мОжно тОже послАть Эти кнИги и игрУшки в Англию?
ДЕвушка	КонЕчно мОжно. НАдо запОлнить бланк. НапишИте Адрес вот здесь.
Дэн	Адрес в ВеликобритАнии?
ДЕвушка	Да, прАвильно. И напишИте ваш Адрес в МосквЕ здесь.
Дэн	ПонЯтно. СпасИбо.
ДЕвушка	Это всё?
Дэн	Да, всё. СпасИбо вам большОе. До свидАния.

Exercise 5

a What does the girl sell at her counter? **б** What stamps does Dan buy, and what for? **в** What does he have to do to send a telegram? **г** What does he want to send home in a parcel?

Exercise 6

Without looking at the dialogue above, can you remember how to say the following phrases in Russian?

a Three stamps at ten roubles. **б** What do I need to do? **в** Of course you can. **г** That's right. **д** Thanks very much.

And can you fill in these blanks? Write or say your answers.

e Где _____ купИть мАрки?
ж КакИе мАрки вы _____?
з НАдо _____ бланк.
и _____ всё? Да, всё.
к До _____.

Exercise 7

Choose a suitable question word to fill in the blanks. Question words which you already know are кто? что? где? когдА? кудА? как? почемУ? скОлько?

a _____ попАсть на пОчту?
б _____ здесь почтОвый Ящик?
в _____ мне пойтИ?
г _____ вы по профЕссии?
д _____ сейчАс врЕмени?
e _____ вас зовУт?
ж _____ у вас есть?
з _____ открывАется пОчта?

Exercise 8

You have just arrived in Moscow and are staying in Room 331
at the hotel РоссИя on Улица ВарвАрка. You can't find Andrei
Ivanov's phone number, so you decide to send him a telegram
to tell him where you are. His address is Flat 9, Block 26 on
ПроспЕкт МИра. (Don't forget that Russian addresses begin with
the name of the city and work down to the number of the flat and
the person's name.) Fill in this form at the post office.

ТелегрАмма

КудА, комУ _____

_____

Текст_____

_____

_____

_____

ФамИлия и Адрес отправИтеля _____

_____

_____

Exercise 9

Match up the words which go together.

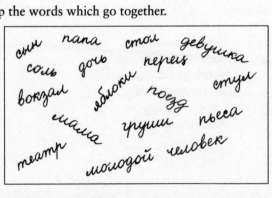

сын   папа   стол   девушка
соль   дочь   перец
вокзал   яблоки   стул
поезд
мама   груши   пьеса
театр   молодой человек

Exercise 10

Your friend has received an unexpected letter from Russia, but is unable to read the name and address on the envelope in order to reply. Look at the envelope and find out who has sent it.

Куда England
Bristol
Green Lane, 39,

Кому Macintosh, H.

Индекс предприятия связи	и адрес отправителя
194358	Россия

Санкт - Петербург
Проспект Энгельса
121 - 2 - 69
Кузнецова, Т. И.

Пишите индекс предприятия связи места назначения

АНЕКДОТ _Anecdote_

Finally, here is an anecdote set in a doctor's office in a busy hospital. The phone rings. It's an enquiry about a patient.

- ДОктор, скажИте, как поживАет ИвАн ИвАнович ИванОв?
- ХорошО.
- А когдА он пойдЁт домОй?
- Если всё пойдЁт хорошО, он пойдЁт домОй зАвтра.
- Очень интерЕсно. СпасИбо.
- ПожАлуйста. А кто говорИт?
- ИвАн ИвАнович ИванОв.

CD 2, TR 7, 03:55

TEST YOURSELF

Of course you may never need to use a Russian post office, but it's good to know how to just in case. Answer these ten quick questions to be sure you have the right words and phrases if you need them.

What do these words and phrases mean?

1 письмО, открЫтка, мАрка, конвЕрт

2 СкОлько стОит мАрка на письмО в ВеликобритАнию?

3 Как попАсть на пОчту?

4 междунарОдный разговОр

5 КакОй нОмер телефОна?

How would you say these words and phrases in Russian? They will be useful for all sorts of situations, not just at the post office.

6 Excuse me, please

7 Yes, that's understood

8 enquiry office

9 police

10 Who is speaking?

18

КакАя сегОдня погОда?
What's the weather like today?

In this unit you will learn
- *How to talk about the weather*
- *How to talk about your holidays*
- *How to use a tourist brochure*
- *How to book an excursion*

Before you start
Revise
- free time, Unit 9
- finding your way around town, Unit 5

Insight
ЗИМНИЙ СПОРТ *Winter sports*

From west to east, Russia stretches around 10,000 kilometres, taking in 11 time zones, and its climatic zones from north to south include arctic tundra, forest, steppe and southern deserts, so no generalizations may be made about the climate or weather. This means that whatever you learn to say about the weather will be useful somewhere at some time! However, it would be true to say that in those parts of Russia where the climate permits, many Russians love to participate in winter sports. From a young age they enjoy doing downhill skiing **катАться на гОрных лЫжах**, cross-country skiing

катАться на лЫжах, skating **катАться на конькАх**, snowboarding **катАться на сноубОрде**, playing ice hockey **игрАть в хоккЕй**, sledging **катАться на сАнках** and throwing snowballs **игрАть в снежкИ**.

ОТПУСК *Holidays*

In the past it was difficult for Russians to visit non-Communist countries, but now travel agents offer holidays anywhere in the world. Popular destinations include Bulgaria **БолгАрия,** the Canary Islands **КанАрские островА,** Croatia **ХорвАтия,** Cyprus **Кипр,** Egypt **ЕгИпет,** Greece **ГрЕция,** Montenegro **ЧерногОрия,** Thailand **ТаилАнд,** Tunisia **ТунИс,** Turkey **ТУрция** and the UAE **ОАЭ.**

You may hear a different word for holidays if you are talking to schoolchildren and students: **канИкулы.**

Below is a typical advert for a holiday. Read it and check anything you don't understand in the Answers section at the back of the book.

Кипр

Рейсы «Аэрофлота»

Отель *** : 2-местные номера, бар, кафе, дискотеки, теннис, бассейн, шоп-тур, казино, экскурсии и дайвинг. Персонал говорит по-русски.

ПОГОДА *The weather*

КакАя сегОдня погОда?	*What's the weather like today (sivOdnya)?*
СегОдня хОлодно	*Today it's cold*
прохлАдно	*It's cool*
теплО	*It's warm*
слИшком жАрко	*It's too hot*
дУшно	*It's close*
вЕтрено	*It's windy*
тумАнно	*It's foggy*
пАсмурно	*It's overcast*
идЁт дождь	*It's raining*
идЁт снег	*It's snowing*
сОлнце свЕтит	*The sun is shining*
морОз	*It's frosty*
температУра вОздуха	*air temperature*
температУра водЫ	*water temperature*
плюс 5 грАдусов теплА	*+ 5 degrees of warmth (5 above)*
мИнус одИн грАдус морОза	*– 1 degree of frost (1 below)*
вЕтер Юго-зАпадный	*The wind is south-westerly*
КакОй прогнОз погОды на зАвтра?	*What is the weather forecast for tomorrow?*
ЗАвтра бУдет хОлодно, теплО	*Tomorrow it will be cold, warm*
ЗАвтра бУдет дождь, снег	*Tomorrow there will be rain, snow*
веснОй, лЕтом, Осенью, зимОй	*in spring, in summer, in autumn, in winter*
веснА, лЕто, Осень, зимА	*spring, summer, autumn, winter*
зИмний спорт	*winter sport*
КакОй твой любИмый сезОн?	*Which is your favourite season?*
Мой любИмый сезОн – веснА	*My favourite season is spring*
Что дЕлать?	*What is to be done?*

ДИАЛОГ 1 СЕГОДНЯ ХОЛОДНО *It's cold today*

Rosemary is spending her first winter in Russia and is determined to make the most of the snow. But her friend Maxim is not so keen.

РОузмэри	МаксИм, ты хОчешь сегОдня катАться на лЫжах в лесУ?
МаксИм	Нет, не Очень хочУ. СегОдня хОлодно.
РОузмэри	КонЕчно хОлодно! ЗимА! Но сегОдня так прекрАсно. МорОз и сОлнце свЕтит.
МаксИм	Да, но по рАдио говорЯт, что температУра вОздуха сегОдня мИнус дЕсять грАдусов. СлИшком хОлодно. Я хочУ смотрЕть телевИзор и читАть дОма, где теплО.
РОузмэри	СмотрЕть телевИзор? МаксИм, что ты! Как Это мОжет быть? Ты совсЕм не лЮбишь зИму?
МаксИм	Нет, я люблЮ лЕто, когдА жАрко. МОжно гулЯть на плЯже и есть морОженое.
РОузмэри	ПонЯтно. Я тОже Очень люблЮ лЕто. Но я так хочУ сегОдня катАться на лЫжах. Жаль. Что дЕлать?
МаксИм	МОжно позвонИть Андрю. Он Очень лЮбит зИмний спорт.
РОузмэри	ПрАвильно. НАдо позвонИть Андрю. КакОй у него нОмер телефОна?
МаксИм	СемьсОт трИдцать дЕвять, пятнАдцать, сОрок два.

Exercise 1

a What does Rosemary want to do? **б** What is the weather like? **в** What does Maxim want to do? **г** What is his favourite season and why? **д** What does Rosemary decide to do? **е** What is Andrew's phone number?

Exercise 2

Match up the captions with the pictures.

а идЁт дождь
б тумАнно
в идЁт снег
г вЕтрено
д сОлнце свЕтит

Exercise 3

Listen to the weather forecast and tick the features of the weather which you hear mentioned.

◀)) **CD 2, TR 8, 01:43**

а Rain
б Snow
в Warm
г Cold
д Northerly wind

е Temperature –7°
ж Frost
з Sun
и Temperature –17°

Exercise 4

Look at the weather map overleaf and play the part of the weather forecaster on television. You could try writing down your script, and check it with the suggested script in the back of the book. Don't forget the points of the compass: *in the north* **на сЕвере**, *in the south* **на Юге**, *in the west* **на зАпаде**, *in the east* **на востОке**.

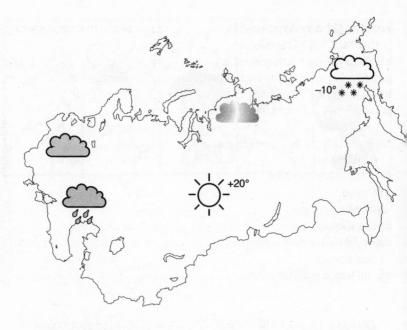

ЧТО ТЫ ДЕЛАЕШЬ В СВОБОДНОЕ ВРЕМЯ? *What do you do in your free time?*

дЕлать [1]	*to do*
свобОдное врЕмя	*free time*
ловИть [2] рЫбу (я ловлЮ, ты лОвишь)	*to go fishing*
собирАть [1] мАрки, грибЫ	*to collect stamps, mushrooms*
готОвить [2] (я готОвлю, ты готОвишь)	*to cook*
катАться на лЫжах, на конькАх, на сАнках	*to ski, skate, sledge*
катАться на велосипЕде, на лОшади, на лОдке	*to cycle, ride a horse, go boating*
отдыхАть [1] за гранИцей, на берегУ мОря	*to holiday abroad, at the seaside*
купАться в мОре	*to swim in the sea*
загорАть [1] на плЯже	*to sunbathe on the beach*
гулЯть [1] в лесУ	*to walk in the woods*

QUICK VOCAB

ходИть [2] в теАтр, кинО (я хожУ, ты хОдишь)	*to go to the theatre, cinema*
ходИть [2] по магазИнам	*to go shopping*
игрАть [1] в футбОл, в шАхматы	*to play football, chess*
игрАть [1] на гитАре	*to play the guitar*
рисовАть [1] (я рисУю, ты рисУешь)	*to draw*
танцевАть [1] (я танцУю, ты танцУешь)	*to dance*
актИвный человЕк	*active person*
обЫчно	*usually*
чАсто	*often*
с удовОльствием	*with pleasure*
идЁт балЕт, Опера, фильм, пьЕса	*There is a ballet, opera, film, play on*
ты хОчешь пойтИ в/на . . .?	*Do you want to go to . . .?*

QUICK VOCAB

ДИАЛОГ 2 КАКИЕ У ТЕБЯ ХОББИ? *What are your hobbies?*

ХЕлен	КакИе у тебЯ хОбби?
Юра	Я Очень актИвный человЕк. ЗимОй я люблЮ игрАть в хоккЕй и катАться на лЫжах, а лЕтом я чАсто гулЯю в дерЕвне и игрАю в тЕннис. Я тОже люблЮ купАться в мОре. Осенью я собирАю грибЫ в лесУ. А у тебЯ есть хОбби?
ХЕлен	Да, но я не Очень актИвный человЕк. Я люблЮ слУшать рАдио, игрАть в шАхматы, читАть кнИги, смотрЕть фИльмы и ходИть на концЕрты.
Юра	В ЛанкАстре есть теАтр?
ХЕлен	КонЕчно есть. Но я не Очень чАсто хожУ в театр в ЛанкАстре потомУ, что дОрого стОит.
Юра	Да, понЯтно. Здесь в КраснодАре у нас хорОшие теАтры. Ты хОчешь пойтИ в теАтр зАвтра вЕчером?
ХЕлен	Да, с удовОльствием!

CD 2, TR 8, 02:02

Exercise 5

From the dialogue above, find out where Helen and Yura are from and what their interests are.

Exercise 6

You are working at a sports complex in a resort on the shores of the Black Sea **Чёрное мОре**. You answer an enquiry about what is available for the active holidaymaker. You consult your list of symbols for help and begin: **Здесь мОжно . . .**

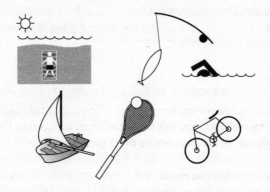

Exercise 7

Opposite are three mini-dialogues. Read or listen to them and match them up with their titles: (i) At the kiosk (ii) An invitation to the theatre (iii) At the theatre.

а	**ДЕвушка**	ВАши билЕты, пожАлуйста.
	ВАня	ОднУ минУточку. Вот онИ.
	ДЕвушка	ХотИте прогрАмму?
	ВАня	Да. ДАйте, пожАлуйста, три прогрАммы.
б	**ЛАра**	СкажИте, пожАлуйста, когдА идЁт балЕт «ЖизЕль»?
	Киоскёр	ВосьмОго, девЯтого и десЯтого апрЕля.
в	**ГАля**	У менЯ есть билЕты в БольшОй теАтр. Вы свобОдны?
	Чарльс	КонЕчно. Как хорошО! БилЕты на сегОдня?
	ГАля	Да, на сегОдня на вЕчер.
	Чарльс	Где мы встрЕтимся?
	ГАля	У менЯ в квАртире в шЕсть часОв.

Exercise 8

You are a very uncooperative person. Whatever Liza suggests, whatever the season, you use the weather as an excuse. Find a suitable phrase to get you out of these activities.

а ХОчешь пойтИ на пляж?
б ХОчешь катАться на велосипЕде?
в ХОчешь пойтИ на концЕрт?
г ХОчешь пойтИ в лес собирАть грибЫ?
д ХОчешь катАться на конькАх?
е ХОчешь купАться в мОре?
ж ХОчешь пойтИ на стадиОн на футбОл?

i Нет, сегОдня идЁт дождь.
ii Нет, сегОдня слИшком хОлодно.
iii Нет, сегОдня слИшком жАрко.
iv Нет, сегОдня тумАнно.
v Нет, сегОдня вЕтрено.
vi Нет, сегОдня дУшно.
vii Нет, сегОдня сОлнце свЕтит.

Exercise 9

You want to book an excursion to Novgorod.

a When do you want to go?

б How many are there in your group?

в When does the tour guide **экскурсовОд** tell you to be ready to set off?

CD 2, TR 8, 04:13

Вы	МОжно заказАть экскУрсию на зАвтра в НОвгород?
ЭкскурсовОд	МОжно. СкОлько вас человЕк?
Вы	ВОсемь.
ЭкскурсовОд	ХорошО. В автОбусе есть свобОдные местА. ВстрЕтимся здесь зАвтра Утром в вОсемь часОв.

Exercise 10

Now you are in Novgorod, you have lost the tour guide and you are the only one who speaks any Russian. Help your friends out with this list of facilities in the Russian guidebook. You may not understand every word but you should be able to work out most things. The only word you have to look up is **пАмятник** *a monument*.

1	СпрАвочное бюрО
2	ТурИстский кОмплекс
3	ГостИница
4	КЕмпинг
5	ПАмятник архитектУры
6	МузЕй
7	АрхеологИческий пАмятник
8	ТеАтр, концЕртный зал

9	СтадиОн
10	РесторАн, кафЕ, бар
11	УниверсАльный магазИн
12	РЫнок
13	СтоЯнка таксИ
14	АвтозапрАвочная стАнция
15	ЖелезнодорОжный вокзАл
16	Пляж
17	Сад, парк

Exercise 11

Read this postcard from Sveta to Lena.

а Where is she staying?
б What is the weather like?
в What does she do every day?

Здравствуй, Лена.
Мы отдыхаем в Сочи и живём
в гостинице на берегу моря.
Солнце светит и жарко.
Каждый день я ем
мороженое и играю в
волейбол на пляже.

Света.

Why not write a postcard describing your ideal holiday?

Exercise 12

Browse through this TV programme listing and use all your powers of deduction to say at what time you would watch television if you were interested in **a** sport **б** politics **в** children's programmes **г** games of chance **д** news.

ТЕЛЕВИДЕНИЕ

6.00	Телеутро	14.30	Наш сад
8.30	Олимпийское утро	16.30	Кенгуру
9.20	Новости Эй-би-си	16.55	Чемпионат России по футболу.
			Полуфинал.
9.55	Парламентская неделя		ЦСКА - «КамАЗ»
10.10	Утренний концерт	18.00	Астрология
10.25	Утренняя почта	18.20	Лотто «Миллион»
10.45	«Санта-Барбара»	19.20	Гандбол. Чемпионат мира.
11.10	Русское лото	20.00	Новости
11.30	«Живём и любим»	20.40	Спокойной ночи, малыши!
12.05	Милицейская хроника	21.00	Спортивный карусель
12.30	Футбол «Динамо» -	21.40	Москва - Кремль
	«Спартак»	22.00	Кинотеатр «Си-би-эс»
14.00	Новости и погода	22.50	Что? Где? Когда?
14.20	Винни-Пух	23.50	Футбол «Ювентус» - «Парма»

Exercise 13

a Как попАсть на зИмний стадиОн?
б Как попАсть в цирк?

ИдИте **i** напрАво **ii** налЕво **iii** прЯмо.

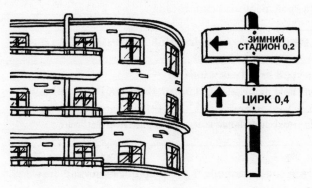

Exercise 14

Answer these questions about your favourite things.

КакОй твой любИмый сезОн? Мой любИмый сезОн _____
_____

КакОй твой любимый спорт? Мой_____
_____

КакАя твоЯ любИмая кнИга? МоЯ любИмая кнИга_____
_____

КакАя твоЯ любИмая машИна?_____
КакИе твоИ любИмые фИльмы? МоИ любИмые фИльмы_____
_____

КакИе твоИ любИмые композИторы/спортсмЕны? _____
_____

Now you could continue making up questions and answers.

АНЕКДОТ *Anecdote*

На Улице, пОздно вЕчером.
– КудА ты идЁшь так пОздно?
– ПорА идтИ домОй.
– ПочемУ так рАно?

And finally, a Russian proverb about making the most of your time. **ЛенИвцы** means *lazy people*.

◄) CD 2, TR 8, 04:43

ЗАвтра, зАвтра, не сегОдня – так ленИвцы говорЯт.

TEST YOURSELF

You can talk about so many things now that you can have really interesting conversations. Answer these ten questions to try out some of the things you can say.

What do these phrases mean?

1 КакАя сегОдня погОда?

2 КакОй твой любИмый сезОн?

3 Что ты дЕлаешь в свобОдное врЕмя?

4 ИдЁт дОждь.

5 Ты хОчешь пойтИ в кинО?

How do you say the following phrases in Russian?

6 *With pleasure*

7 *I like watching films*

8 *Today it's too hot*

9 *Can I book an excursion?*

10 *No, I don't really want to.*

19

У менЯ болИт головА
I've got a headache

In this unit you will learn
- *What to do if you feel ill*
- *How to say what is hurting*
- *How to say someone's age*

Before you start
Revise
- how to say *I have* у менЯ, etc., Unit 10

Insight
БАНЯ *The Bath House*

The Russian health service provides free emergency medical care for everyone, and there are also many private clinics using state-of-the-art equipment. Many Russians prefer to use natural cures involving herbs and often vodka. Suggested remedies for a cold may include taking a cold shower, chewing garlic, using nose drops made from the juice of an onion, and going to bed warmly dressed with extra blankets and a restorative tumbler of pepper vodka and frequent glasses of tea. All of these treatments are sure to leaving you feeling 'as fresh as a little gherkin' **свЕжий как огУрчик** the next morning! Another favourite cure is a visit to the bath house **бАня**. Many bath houses operate on a single sex system, and offer a cold pool, a wet steam room, bunches of birch twigs to help the circulation, tea and a massage. A Finnish dry sauna **сАуна** is also available and very popular. Whichever type of sauna you choose, a visit may take the best part of a day and is extraordinarily relaxing and convivial. Even if you are no better by the end of it, you will hardly care!

···

ЧТО С ВАМИ? *What's the matter with you?*

мне плОхо	*I'm ill*
Я чУвствую себЯ хорошО/ невАжно/плОхо	*I feel good/not so good/bad*
я плОхо сплю	*I'm sleeping badly*
у менЯ температУра	*I've got a temperature*
менЯ тошнИт	*I feel sick/nauseous*
мне то жАрко, то хОлодно	*I'm feeling hot and cold*
у менЯ грипп	*I've got flu*
Что у вас болИт?	*What's hurting?*
у менЯ болИт головА/ Ухо/зуб/живОт	*my head/ear/tooth/ stomach aches*
у менЯ болИт гОрло/ глаз/нос	*my throat/eye/nose hurts*
у менЯ болИт рукА/ногА/ спинА/сЕрдце	*my arm/leg/back/heart hurts*
у менЯ болЯт зУбы/ Уши/глазА	*my teeth/ears/eyes hurt*

Exercise 1

◀) CD 2, TR 9

Listen to Vadim, Tanya and Anton describing their symptoms. Decide which of them has just run a marathon, has flu or has food poisoning.

Exercise 2

Look at the picture below and number the words correctly.

[ ] головА [ ] глаз [ ] Ухо [ ] нос [ ] зУбы
[ ] гОрло [ ] рукА [ ] ногА [ ] спинА [ ] живОт
[ ] сЕрдце

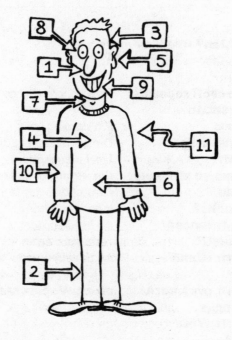

В КАБИНЕТЕ *In the consulting room*

кабинЕт	*consulting room*
поликлИника	*health centre*
больнИца	*hospital*
аптЕка	*pharmacy*
скОрая пОмощь	*ambulance*
врач, дОктор	*doctor*
медсестрА	*nurse*
консультАция	*consultation*

симптОм	symptom
диАгноз	diagnosis
рецЕпт	prescription
идтИ к врачУ	to go to the doctor's
принимАть [1] лекАрство	to take medicine
таблЕтка	tablet
раз, 3 рАза в день	once, 3 times a day
открОйте рот	open your mouth
я сломАл/а рУку	I've (m/f) broken my arm
лЕвый, прАвый	left, right
серьЁзно, несерьЁзно	it's serious, not serious
дУмать [1]	to think
вЫзвать скОрую пОмощь	to send for an ambulance
Не беспокОйтесь!	Don't worry

QUICK VOCAB

ДИАЛОГ 1 СКАЖИТЕ *А-А-А-!* Say 'Aah'!

Listen to this conversation in a doctor's surgery and answer the questions overleaf.

Врач	ВходИте. СадИтесь. Как вас зовУт?
БрАйан	МенЯ зовУт БрАйан УИлкинсон.
Врач	Что у вас болИт? КакИе у вас симптОмы?
БрАйан	У менЯ болИт головА. Мне то жАрко, то хОлодно, и у менЯ температУра.
Врач	У вас болИт гОрло?
БрАйан	Да, немнОжко.
Врач	ПожАлуйста, открОйте рот и скажИте а-а-а.
БрАйан	А-а-а-а-а.
Врач	Вы кУрите?
БрАйан	Нет.
Врач	Я дУмаю, что у вас начинАется грипп. Это не Очень серьЁзно. НАдо отдыхАть дОма и принимАть лекАрство три рАза в день. ПонЯтно?

● CD 2, TR 9, 00:54

БрАйан	Да, понЯтно.
Врач	Вот рецЕпт.
БрАйан	СпасИбо. До свидАния.

Exercise 3

а What is the patient's name?
б What are his symptoms?
в Does he smoke?
г What does the doctor advise?

ДИАЛОГ 2 ЭТО СЕРЬЁЗНО! *That's serious!*

Leaving the surgery, poor Brian falls down the stairs. He is in some pain, but he still manages to speak Russian!

CD 2, TR 9, 01:47

Врач	Что с вАми?
БрАйан	Ой, мне плОхо. У менЯ болИт ногА.
Врач	КакАя ногА? ЛЕвая Или прАвая?
БрАйан	ПрАвая.
Врач	ПокажИте, пожАлуйста. МОжно посмотрЕть?
БрАйан	Да, мОжно. Ой, я дУмаю, что я сломАл нОгу.
Врач	Да, прАвильно. Это серьЁзно! НАдо вЫзвать скОрую пОмощь.
БрАйан	ДАйте, пожАлуйста, аспирИн.
Врач	Нет, нельзЯ. Не беспокОйтесь. СкОрая пОмощь скОро бУдет здесь.

Exercise 4

а What has Brian done? **б** What does the doctor send for? **в** What will he not let Brian do?

ДИАЛОГ 3 СКОРАЯ ПОМОЩЬ *First aid*

Meanwhile, back at the hotel, Caroline has found the administrator collapsed on the floor. She phones for an ambulance.

КЭролайн	АллО, «СкОрая пОмощь»?	
ТелефонИст	Да, слУшаю вас. В чём дЕло?	
КЭролайн	Я не знАю, но администрАтор чУвствует себЯ плОхо.	
ТелефонИст	КакОй у вас Адрес?	
КЭролайн	Адрес? ИзвинИте, я не пОмню.	
ТелефонИст	Вы в гостИнице?	
КЭролайн	Да, в гостИнице «ИзмАйлово».	
ТелефонИст	ХорошО. Я знАю Адрес. Так, администрАтор чУвствует себЯ плОхо. А что у негО болИт?	
КЭролайн	Не знАю, но я дУмаю, что у негО болИт сЕрдце.	
ТелефонИст	Не беспокОйтесь. Мы скОро бУдем у вас. ЧЕрез три минУты.	

CD 2, TR 9, 02:47

Exercise 5

Caroline is in a bit of a panic, but she is able to tell the switchboard operator everything he needs to know. **a** Where is she staying? **б** What is the matter with the administrator? **в** When will the ambulance be there?

Exercise 6

Read what people say is wrong with them, and underline the most advisable course of action.

a У менЯ болИт головА.   Я принимАю таблЕтку/я читАю газЕту/я идУ к врачУ.

б У менЯ грипп.   Я идУ на рабОту/я идУ в бассЕйн/ я идУ к врачУ.

в Я сломАла нОгу.	Я игрАю в футбОл/я Еду в больнИцу/я пью чай.
г МенЯ тошнИт.	Я ем котлЕты с рИсом/я принимАю лекАрство/я игрАю в волейбОл.

Exercise 7

Many private hospitals advertise their specialist services in the telephone directories. Which heading would you look under if you wanted:

- **а** a diagnostic service
- **б** specialized laboratories
- **в** Tibetan medicine
- **г** express analysis
- **д** advice on preventive medicine
- **е** physiotherapy
- **ж** advice on your infectious disease?

- **i** ТибЕтская медицИна
- **ii** центр превентИвной медицИны
- **iii** инфекциОнная больнИца
- **iv** специализирОванные лаборатОрии
- **v** экспрЕсс-анАлизы
- **vi** физиотерапевтИческая больнИца
- **vii** диагнОстика

Exercise 8

Your medical expertise is called for again! Study the chart opposite, and fill in the blanks with ticks or crosses to show whether you think certain activities are advisable for your patients. Then tell them what they may and may not do. For example, you might say to Leonid: **НельзЯ игрАть в тЕннис, но мОжно читАть газЕту**. *You must not play tennis, but you may read the paper.*

	(a) игрАть в тЕннис	(б) читАть газЕту	(в) пить винО	(г) купАться в мОре

ЛеонИд (сломАл нОгу)

ИрИна (болЯт глазА)

АркАдий (тошнИт]

МариАнна (болИт сЕрдце)

СКОЛЬКО ВАМ ЛЕТ? *How old are you?*

QUICK VOCAB

вОзраст	*age*
СкОлько вам/емУ/ей лет?	*How old are you/is he/is she?*
мне двАдцать одИн год	*I am 21 years old*
емУ трИдцать три гОда	*he is 33 years old*
ей сОрок шесть лет	*she is 46 years old*

In Russian, you choose a different word for year depending on the number.

1 – одИн **год**

2, 3, 4 – два, три, четЫре **гОда**

5, 6, 7 etc., up to 20 – пять, шесть, семь, двАдцать **лет**

For numbers over 20, look at the last digit, and if it is 1 use **год**, if it is 2–4, use **гОда**, and if it is 5, 6, 7, 8, 9, or a multiple of 10, use **лет**.

Exercise 9

Choose the correct word for year to complete these phrases. Don't forget to read the numbers out loud!

а Мне 53 _____ .
б ЕмУ 18 _____ .
в Ей 2 _____ .
г ЕмУ 85 _____ .
д Ей 61 _____ .

Exercise 10

◀) **CD 2, TR 9, 03:49**

Listen to the recording and make a note of these patients' names, ages and symptoms.

	Имя	Отчество	ВОзраст	СимптОмы
а				
б				
в				

Exercise 11

Look at the family portrait opposite, invent names and relationships for the people in it and say how old they are. For example, you might say **Это мой дЕдушка. ЕгО зовУт СтанислАв и ему девянОсто дЕвять лет. От Это моЯ дочь. ЕЁ зовУт ЛЮда и ей три гОда.**

Exercise 12

Find these words in Russian in the wordsearch grid. Words may be written in any direction, vertically, horizontally or diagonally.

flu
arm
head
mouth

leg
prescription
throat

doctor (врач)
back
heart
stomach

eye
ears
tooth

р	щ	ф	я	н	г	т	г
е	ю	й	о	л	р	о	г
щ	е	с	а	п	л	в	в
е	ц	з	п	о	э	и	г
п	д	и	в	з	ш	ж	а
т	р	а	к	у	р	г	ч
г	е	ж	ы	б	о	о	б
ч	с	п	и	н	а	х	т

АНЕКДОТ *Anecdote*

Why is this elderly patient unimpressed by the doctor's advice?

QUICK VOCAB

вы проживЁте до . . .   *You will live to . . .*

CD 2, TR 9, 04:20

Врач	Если вы не кУрите и не пьЁте, вы проживЁте до девянОста лет.
БАбушка	Э, дОктор, ужЕ пОздно!
Врач	ПочемУ?
БАбушка	Мне ужЕ девянОсто три гОда!

Read this Russian proverb and see if you can work out what the first line means.

Кто не кУрит и не пьёт,
Тот здорОвеньким умрЁт.

The whole saying could be translated as *Whoever neither smokes nor drinks will die healthy.*

TEST YOURSELF

Let's hope you never have to visit the doctor or go to the hospital in Russia, but just in case you do, try these ten questions to make sure you would know what to say.

What is the doctor saying to you?

1 Что у вас болИт?

2 КакИе у вас симптОмы?

3 СкОлько вам лет?

4 Вы кУрите?

5 ОткрОйте рот.

How would you say these phrases to the doctor?

6 I feel bad.

7 I have a temperature.

8 My back hurts.

9 Is it serious?

10 I feel sick.

20

КакОй он?
What's he like?

In this unit you will learn
- *How to say what people are wearing*
- *How to say what people look like*
- *How to describe someone's character*
- *How to express your opinions and preferences*

Before you start
Revise
- how to say *my, your, his, her* etc., Unit 10
- singular adjective endings, Unit 4

Insight
ОДЕЖДА И ОБУВЬ *Clothes and footwear*

In the Soviet era, fashionable clothes and footwear were often in short supply in the shops. There was a joke at the time that Adam and Eve must have been Soviet citizens because in the garden of Eden they were naked, barefoot, with one apple between them, and they believed they were living in paradise! Nowadays, a wide range of Russian and imported clothes are available in the shops, including many international designer labels. The image of the country **бАбушка** dressed in padded coat, shawl **платОк** and felt boots **вАленки** has never applied to the younger generation, who have always been as fashion-conscious as young people anywhere.

Compared with some cultures, Russians may seem quite emotional. Their body language is expressive and they may stand closer, talk more loudly and be more tactile than you are used to. Whether you meet them socially or in business, they will probably want to know all about you. They may take a long time getting to know you but, once you have a Russian friend, they will be a friend for life.

Expressing your opinion

Showing your pleasure, surprise, agreement or regret is something you will want to do as you talk to Russian friends. Don't forget the verbs **любИть** to love, and **хотЕть** to want. And here is another useful verb, **мочь** to be able.

любИть [2]		хотЕть [irregular]		мочь [1]	
я люблЮ	мы лЮбим	я хочУ	мы хотИм	я могУ	мы мОжем
ты лЮбишь	вы лЮбите	ты хОчешь	вы хотИте	ты мОжешь	вы мОжете
он лЮбит	онИ лЮбят	он хОчет	онИ хотЯт	он мОжет	онИ мОгут

ОН В КОСТЮМЕ *He's wearing a suit*

Как он одЕт? Как онА одЕта?	*How is he/she dressed?*
брЮки/он в брЮках	*trousers/he's wearing trousers*
джИнсы/онА в джИнсах	*jeans/she's wearing jeans*
Юбка/онА в Юбке	*skirt/she's wearing a skirt*
рубАшка/он в рубАшке	*shirt/he's wearing a shirt*
блУза/онА в блУзе	*blouse/she's wearing a blouse*
свИтер/он в свИтере	*sweater/he's wearing a sweater*
костЮм/он в костЮме	*suit/he's wearing a suit*
гАлстук/он в гАлстуке	*tie/he's wearing a tie*

QUICK VOCAB

плАтье/онА в плАтье	dress/she's wearing a dress
пальтО/он в пальтО	coat/he's wearing a coat
шАпка/он в шАпке	hat (fur)/he's wearing a hat
тУфли/онА в тУфлях	shoes/she's wearing shoes
ботИнки/онА в ботИнках	ankle boots/she's wearing ankle boots
очкИ/он нОсит очкИ	glasses/he wears glasses
он бУдет в шАпке	he will be wearing a hat

Exercise 1

Listen to or read the dialogues below.

a Where do you think Nikita and Alan are? **б** Describe Nikita's sister. **в** Where and when are Monica and Victor meeting? **г** How will Monica recognize him?

ДИАЛОГ 1 КАК ОНА ОДЕТА? *What is she wearing?*

НикИта	Алан, вот моЯ сестрА МАша на платфОрме. ОнА нас ждёт.
Алан	А я её не знАю. Как онА одЕта?
НикИта	ОнА нОсит очкИ, и онА в пальтО, в ботИнках и шАпке.
Алан	Да, вИжу. ОнА красИвая. СкОлько ей лет?
НикИта	ДвАдцать три гОда.

ДИАЛОГ 2 Я БУДУ В КОСТЮМЕ *I'll be wearing a suit*

МОника	Где мы встрЕтимся?
ВИктор	В ресторАне «ВостОк», в семь часОв.
МОника	ХорошО. Я бУду в плАтье, а вы?
ВИктор	Я бУду в костЮме и в гАлстуке. Мне сОрок лет и я курЮ сигАры.

КАК ОНА ВЫГЛЯДИТ? *What does she look like?*

мужчИна/жЕнщина	*man/woman*
брюнЕт(ка)/блондИн(ка)	*person with dark brown/blond hair (m/f)*
высОкий/невысОкий	*tall/short*
пОлный/стрОйный	*chubby/slim*
тОлстый/худОй	*fat/thin*
красИвый/некрасИвый	*good looking/not good looking*
молодОй/пожилОй	*young/elderly*
свЕтлые, рЫжие, тЁмные вОлосы	*light/red/dark hair*
длИнные, корОткие вОлосы	*long/short hair*
голубЫе, кАрие, сЕрые, зелЁные глазА	*blue/brown/grey/green eyes*
с бородОй	*bearded*
лЫсый	*bald*

Exercise 2

Tick the correct statements overleaf.

ВАня

ГАля

а	ВАня невысОкий.
б	Он худОй.
в	Он пожилОй.
г	Он красИвый.
д	Он лЫсый.
е	Он в костЮме.
ж	Он в джИнсах.
з	У негО длИнные вОлосы.
и	У негО свЕтлые вОлосы.
к	Он нОсит очкИ.

а	ГАля невысОкая.
б	ОнА стрОйная.
в	ОнА молодАя.
г	ОнА некрасИвая.
д	ОнА блондИнка.
е	ОнА в Юбке и блУзе.
ж	ОнА в пальтО.
з	У неЁ корОткие вОлосы.
и	У неЁ тЁмные вОлосы.
к	ОнА нОсит очкИ.

Exercise 3

You see someone behaving suspiciously, so you ring the police and give them a description. Fill in your half of the conversation. To give the suspect's approximate age, change the order of the words: **емУ лет двАдцать** *he's about 20* instead of **емУ двАдцать лет** *he's 20*.

CD 2, TR 10, 01:13

МилиционЕр	Как он вЫглядит?
Вы	*It's a young man.*
МилиционЕр	СкОлько емУ лет?
Вы	*He's about 19.*
МилиционЕр	КакОй он? ВысОкий?
Вы	*Yes, he's tall and thin.*
МилиционЕр	КакИе у негО вОлосы?
Вы	*He has short, dark hair.*
МилиционЕр	Как он одЕт?
Вы	*He's wearing jeans and a shirt.*
МилиционЕр	СпасИбо.

КАКОЙ У НЕГО ХАРАКТЕР? *What is his personality like?*

симпатИчный	*nice*
интерЕсный	*interesting*
энергИчный	*energetic*
весЁлый	*cheerful*
дОбрый	*good*
мИлый	*sweet*
талАнтливый	*talented*
Умный	*clever*
глУпый	*stupid*
ленИвый	*lazy*
скУчный	*boring*
неприЯтный	*unpleasant*
протИвный	*revolting*
Он не человЕк,	*He is not a man, but a wet hen*
а мОкрая кУрица	*(i.e. a wimp)*

Exercise 4

Kostya and Kolya are like chalk and cheese. Read this description of Kostya and then fill in the missing words in the description of Kolya.

КОстя Очень интерЕсный, энергИчный человЕк. Он высОкий, худОй, и Очень лЮбит игрАть в бадминтОн. Он симпатИчный и Умный студЕнт и талАнтливый актЁр. У негО корОткие, свЕтлые вОлосы и он нОсит очкИ. Он всегдА весЁлый, и по суббОтам он хОдит в кинО.

КОля Очень (*boring, lazy*) человЕк. Он (*short*) и (*fat*) и (*doesn't like*) спорт. Он (*unpleasant*) и (*stupid*) студЕнт. У негО (*long, dark*) вОлосы (*and green eyes*). По суббОтам он хОдит в кинО.

Exercise 5

Read these excerpts from the 'lonely hearts' column in a newspaper. Which advertisement would you reply to if you were looking for **a** a cheerful, good-looking man who enjoys the theatre **б** an older woman with a family **в** a young blonde Ukrainian woman, good-natured **г** a music-loving man?

i ВАЛЕРИЙ МолодОй человЕк, 30 лет, рост 184 см., вес 98 кг., рУсский, не пью, не курЮ. ЛюблЮ мУзыку, спорт.

ii СЛАВИК 35 лет, 174 см., 65 кг., стрОйный брюнЕт, красИвый, спортИвный. ЖивУ в гОроде НОвгороде. ДОбрый, весЁлый харАктер. ЛюблЮ теАтр, кнИги.

iii ТАМАРА СимпатИчная дЕвушка, 25 лет, рост 165 см., вес 65 кг., блондИнка, украИнка, люблЮ цветЫ и сОлнце. По харАктеру дОбрая.

iv ЛЮДМИЛА ЖЕнщина, лет 53, рУсская, рост 153 см., вОлосы свЕтлые, глазА зелЁные, энергИчная. Сын и дочь.

Exercise 6

Match up the pictures with the descriptions opposite.

Лев ТолстОй   Юрий ГагАрин   Анна ПАвлова

а МолодАя жЕнщина, красИвая, стрОйная, энергИчная. ЛЮбит балЕт.

б ПожилОй человЕк с бородОй, энергИчный, Умный. ЛЮбит кнИги.

в МолодОй человЕк, красИвый, весЁлый. ЛЮбит путешЕствовать.

ПО-МОЕМУ . . . *In my opinion . . .*

Here are some expressions to use in conversation to express your opinions and feelings.

к сожалЕнию/к счАстью	*unfortunately/fortunately*
как ужАсно/интерЕсно/ скУчно	*how awful/interesting/boring*
навЕрно	*probably*
мОжет быть	*possibly, maybe*
кАжется	*it seems*
по-мОему	*in my opinion*
совсЕм	*quite (completely)*
довОльно	*quite (fairly)*
немнОжко/мнОго	*a bit/a lot*
прАвильно/непрАвильно	*that's right/not right*
лУчше/хУже	*better/worse*
я Очень люблЮ	*I really love*
я бОльше люблЮ	*I prefer (love more)*
бОльше всегО я люблЮ (bOl'she vsyivO)	*more than anything I love*
я совсЕм не люблЮ	*I really don't like*
вот почемУ	*that's why*
бОже мой!	*my God!*
как жаль!	*what a pity!*
кошмАр!	*what a nightmare!*
чудЕсно!	*wonderful!*
смешнО!	*that's funny!*
тОчно так!	*exactly!*
лАдно	*OK*

ДИАЛОГ 3 КАК ЖАЛЬ! *What a pity!*

Exercise 7

◀) CD 2, TR 10, 02:28

Read these brief dialogues and decide in which one Anatoly expresses **a** disappointment **б** horror **в** agreement.

i *Anatoly is visiting Deena at her flat.*

АнатОлий	ДИна, мОжно смотрЕть футбОл по телевИзору?
ДИна	ИзвинИ, к сожалЕнию, телевИзор сегОдня не рабОтает.
АнатОлий	Как жаль! БОльше всегО я люблЮ смотрЕть футбОл. А пОчему телевИзор не рабОтает?
ДИна	Я не знАю. НавЕрно потомУ, что он стАрый.
АнатОлий	По-мОему, нАдо купИть нОвый телевИзор.
ДИна	МОжет быть. Но скУчно смотрЕть телевИзор днём.

ii *Anatoly and Leonid are making plans for the evening.*

АнатОлий	Что ты хОчешь дЕлать сегОдня вЕчером?
ЛеонИд	Не знАю, но в университЕте идЁт хорОший концЕрт.
АнатОлий	Но ты знАешь, что я совсЕм не люблЮ мУзыку. ЛУчше идтИ в кинО, да?
ЛеонИд	Нет, довОльно скУчно. Я бОльше люблЮ теАтр. ПойдЁм на пьЕсу «Три сестрЫ». ЛАдно?
АнатОлий	ЛАдно.

iii *Vika rings Anatoly with a problem about tickets for their trip.*

АнатОлий	Алло! ВИка?
ВИка	Да, Это я. АнатОлий, извинИ, но я не могУ сегОдня купИть нАши билЕты на поЕзд.
АнатОлий	Как не мОжешь, ВИка?
ВИка	Я в больнИце, сломАла рУку.
АнатОлий	БОже мой! РукА болИт?
ВИка	КонЕчно, ужАсно болИт.
АнатОлий	КошмАр! Что дЕлать? Кто мОжет купИть билЕты, Если ты в больнИце?

Exercise 8

Match up each problem with a solution.

а Зал закрЫт! Что дЕлать?

i Не волнУйтесь. Он сломАл рУку. Вот почемУ он в больнИце.

б В машИне совсЕм грЯзно!

ii Вот идЁт экскурсовОд. Он, навЕрно, знАет.

в Я чУвствую себЯ хУже!

iii Вот водА и мЫло.

г Я не знАю, как попАсть в гостИницу!

iv МОжет быть, вАши билЕты в сУмке?

д КакОй кошмАр! Мы потерЯли билЕты!

v Вот таблЕтки. СкОро бУдет лУчше.

е Как ужАсно! ПочемУ ИвАн в больнИце?

vi Вот ключ.

Exercise 9

Read or listen to this letter written by a Russian in Minsk, Belarus. He is seeking a penfriend. Make brief notes in English, or write a reply in Russian.

Здравствуйте!

Меня зовут Саша Иванов, мне 18 лет, у меня сестра и брат. Их зовут Оля (10 лет) и Миша (3 года). Мы живём в квартире в Минске. Мой папа работает в поликлинике. Он - врач. Моя мама - учительница. Оля хорошая спортсменка и любит играть в теннис. Миша ещё не ходит в школу.

Я высокий, у меня тёмные волосы и чёрные глаза. Вы хотите фотографию? Я люблю читать и играть в шахматы, но я больше всего люблю ходить в театр. Зимой я люблю кататься на лыжах. Пожалуйста, напишите. Где вы живёте? Что вы любите делать в свободное время? У вас есть брат или сестра? Вы живёте в квартире или в доме?

Ваш Саша.

АНЕКДОТ *Anecdote*

Утром мать говорИт:

> – ПорА идтИ в шкОлу, сын.
> – Не хочУ, мама. НАдо идтИ?
> – НАдо, сын, ты учИтель.

And finally, a rhyming toast **тост** to congratulate you on finishing *Get started in Russian.*

ПорА и вЫпить!	*It's time to drink up!*
В дОбрый час!	*Good luck!*
За всЕх гостЕй!	*To all the guests!*
За всЕх за вас!	*To all of you!*

TEST YOURSELF

Well done! Your last ten questions will remind you how much you know about Russian life and language.

1 If you saw a sign saying В автОбусе нельзЯ курИть, would you
  i put your sandwiches away?
  ii get your bus ticket validated?
  iii put out your cigarette?

2 If you dialled the emergency number 01 to report пожАр, what would you get
  i an ambulance?
  ii a fire engine?
  iii the police?

3 Where would you meet a проводнИк?
  i on a train.
  ii in a bath house.
  iii in a restaurant.

4 What would you do at a sign saying ОбмЕн валЮты?
  i buy theatre tickets.
  ii pick up your left luggage.
  iii exchange currency.

5 If someone said to you ВходИте, раздевАйтесь, would you
  i come in and take your coat off?
  ii come in and sit down?
  iii shut the door as you leave?

6 If you saw От себЯ on a shop door, would you
  i push?
  ii conclude the shop was shut?
  iii pull?

7 If you had been invited to a friend's house for dinner would you take

   i an odd number of flowers?

   ii an even number of flowers?

8 If you were at the doctor's with a sore throat, would you say

   i у менЯ болИт ногА?

   ii у менЯ болИт гОрло?

   iii я плОхо сплю?

9 What is the correct order for these courses in a Russian meal?

   i пЕрвое блЮдо

   ii закУски

   iii вторОе блЮдо

   iv слАдкое

10 If you were in a café and you wanted to call the waiter over, would you say

   i дЕвушка?

   ii бАбушка?

   iii молодОй человЕк?

You are now a competent speaker of basic Russian. You should be able to handle most everyday situations on a visit to Russia and to communicate with Russian people sufficiently to make friends. If you would like to extend your ability so that you can develop your confidence, fluency and scope in the language, whether for social or business purposes, why not take your Russian a step further with *Complete Russian*?

I hope you enjoyed working your way through the course. I am always keen to receive feedback from people who have used my course, so why not contact me and let me know your reactions? I'll be particularly pleased to receive your praise, but I should also like to know if you think things could be improved. I always welcome comments and suggestions and I do my best to incorporate constructive suggestions into later editions.

You can contact me through the publishers at: Teach Yourself Books, Hodder Headline Ltd, 338 Euston Road, London NW1 3BH.

В дОбрый час! *Good luck!*

Rachel Farmer

Answers

Unit 1

1 **a** ii **b** iv **c** i **d** v **e** iii   **2 a** iii **b** iv **c** ii **d** v **e** i   **3** **a** iii **b** i **c** ii
4 **a** ii **b** i **c** iv **d** iii   **5** snooker, cricket, tennis, stadium, start, knockout, trainer, record, athletics, sport, sportsman   **6** **a** vi **b** i **c** viii **d** vii **e** iii
f iv **g** ix **h** v **i** ii   **7** visa, tractor, passport, taxi   **8** diplomat, tourist, cosmonaut, chemist, student, administrator, doctor, tractor driver, captain   **9** Ivan <u>Nina</u> Alexander Vladimir <u>Ekaterina</u> <u>Liza</u> Lev <u>Irina</u> Valentin <u>Larisa</u>   **11** atom, comet, meteor, climate, mechanism, microscope, sputnik, kilo, litre, planet, moon, kilometre   **12** television, cassette, monitor, cine camera, <u>lemonade</u>, radio, printer   **13** park, kiosk, grocer's, zoo, stadium, café, sauna, telephone, institute, casino, Internet café, university, antiques   **15** lamp, chair, corridor, sofa, mixer, vase, toaster, gas, lift   **16** saxophone, composer, guitar, piano, orchestra, soloist, opera, pianist, compact disc, heavy metal rock   **17** piano   **18** omelette, salad, <u>whisky</u>, fruit, <u>coffee</u>, muesli, cutlet, <u>wine</u>, <u>Pepsi-cola</u>, minestrone soup

TEST YOURSELF

1 33   **2** атомк   **3** London   **4** restaurant   **5** Nina   **6** Where?
7 drink it   **8** watch a match   **9** play it   **10** in a restaurant or café

Unit 2

1 **a** iii **b** vi **c** iv **d** i **e** v **f** ii   **2** **a** stewardess **b** platform
c excursion **d** bus **e** tram **f** airport **g** express **h** signal **i** Aeroflot
j trolleybus   **3** football, volleyball, badminton, marathon, arm-wrestling, boxing, gymnastics, ping-pong, surfing, final, rugby, paintball, hockey, basketball, bodybuilding   **4** symphony, ballerina,

poet, actress, best-seller, actor, ballet, thriller **5** energy, kilowatt, atmosphere, kilogram, electronics, experiment **6** America, Mexico, Africa, Pakistan, Argentina, England, Russia, Ukraine, Canada, India, Australia, Norway **8 a** bar **b** Melody (music shop) **c** Pizza Hut **d** museum **e** circus **f** bank **g** library **h** Kremlin **i** post office **j** Bolshoi Theatre **9** souvenirs, pet shop, militia, driving school, information, pizza, billiard club, provisions **10 a** cheeseburger **b** banana **c** cappuccino coffee **d** pizza 'super supreme' **11 a** manager **b** fax **c** briefing **d** marketing **e** floppy disk **f** businessman **g** know-how **h** broker **i** weekend **j** computer **k** notebook (computer) **13 a** Chekhov **b** Tolstoy **c** Pushkin **d** Tchaikovsky **e** Rachmaninov **f** Shostakovich **g** Lenin **h** Gorbachev **i** Yeltsin **14 a** temperature **b** bacterium **c** antibiotic **d** massage **e** tablet **f** diagnosis **g** penicillin **h** infection **15 a** iv **b** iii **c** v **d** ii **e** i **16** Игорь – футболИст. ЛарИса – студЕнтка. АнтОн – турИст. НатАша – балерИна. БорИс – теннисИст. **18 a** m **b** f **c** m **d** n **e** f **f** m **g** m **h** f **i** n **j** f **k** m **l** n **19** сестрА/стадиОн/саксофОн **20** суп омлЕт салАт (masculine) **21 a** сестрА **b** симфОния **c** АргентИна **d** библиотЕка **e** температУра

TEST YOURSELF

1 ch, b, ya **2** Australia **3** I don't know **4** grandfather **5** 3
6 feminine **7** masculine **8** neuter **9** Boris is a manager
10 Who is that?

Unit 3

1 a iii **b** i **c** ii **a** i **b** iii **c** ii Vladimir, Boris **2 a** дОброе Утро **b** дОбрый день **c** дОбрый вЕчер **3** МенЯ зовУт СтЮарт. Очень приЯтно. **4** e **5 a** iii **b** iv **c** i **d** ii **6 a** Hello **b** Thank you **c** I speak English **d** Good **e** Where is Boris? **f** I don't know **g** Slower, please **h** Excuse me/Sorry **7 a** iii **b** v **c** ii **d** i **e** iv **8 a** зовУт **b** ДОбрый **c** не **d** говорИте **e** человЕк **9 a** iii **b** ii **c** iii **10 a** iv **b** v **c** ii **d** iii **e** i

1 hello   **2** goodbye   **3** sorry / excuse me   **4** What are you called?
5 Do you speak English?   **6** я не понимАю   **7** ты   **8** вы
9 Очень приЯтно   **10** мЕдленнее, пожАлуйста

Unit 4

Before you start
автОбус (*m*) Опера (*f*) пианИно (*n*) метрО (*n*) мАма (*f*) банк (*m*)
2 a boulevard **b** avenue **c** campsite **d** taxi rank **e** café-bar **f** tourist
hotel **g** botanical garden **h** first-aid post **i** yacht club **j** tourist club
k canal **l** Red Square **m** swimming pool **n** tourist agency   **3 a** он
b онА **c** он **d** онО **e** онА **f** он **g** онА **h** онО   **5** 2-6, 7-5, 3-4, 8-1,
10-0, 9-10   **6 a** bus no. 5 **b** trolleybus no. 8 **c** tram no. 3 **d** bus no. 9
7 a Вот онО./ОнО вон там. **b** ИзвинИте, я не знАю. **c** Нет,
Это пОчта. **d** НЕ за что!   **8** крАсное винО, бЕлая таблЕтка,
зелёный салАт, жёлтый банАн, чёрный кот   **9** b d e c a
10 d c a e b

1 trolleybus   **2** three, five, ten   **3** flat   **4** What sort of city is
it?   **5** It's red wine   **6** шесть   **7** два   **8** Где метрО?   **9** Это
банк?   **10** Где ресторАн? Вот он

Unit 5

2 a i **b** ii **c** ii **d** i   *1* в ресторАн   *2* в инстИтут   *3* в универмАг
4 в бассЕйн   *5* в кафЕ   *6* в библиотЕку   *7* в шкОлу   *8* на
плОщадь   *9* в поликлИнику   *10* в цЕрковь   *11* в больнИцу
12 в музЕй   *13* в теАтр   *14* в аптЕку   *15* в цирк
16 на стАнцию метрО   *17* на пОчту   *18* в парк
19 на стадиОн   *20* в кинО   *21* в гастронОм   *22* в банк
23 на фАбрику   *24* в спрАвочное бюрО   *25* в гостИницу

26 на вокзАл   **3** Use same endings as Ex. 2, 1–26.   **4 a** Игорь хорОший футболИст. **b** ЛЕна красИвая балерИна. **c** Хард-Рок америкАнское кафЕ. **d** ЛОндон большОй гОрод. **e** ПрАвда рУсская газЕта.   **5** Tick **a** and **d**   **6 a** vi **b** iii/iv **c** i **d** iii **e** ii **f** v   **7** банАны, фрУкты, таблЕтки, сигарЕты, папирОсы, цветЫ, конфЕты   **8 a** 12-24-18 **b** 25-30-17 **c** 14-32-11 **d** 15-03-24 **e** 20-19-12   **9 a** ix **b** xi **c** vii **d** i **e** viii **f** iv **g** vi **h** iii **i** x **j** ii **k** v   **10 a** v theatre **b** iv library · **c** ii grocer's **d** iii station **e** vi restaurant **f** vii hotel **g** i café   **11 1** ii **2** v **3** iii **4** i **5** iv

TEST YOURSELF

1 How do I get to the centre?   **2** Do you have any flowers?   **3** The museum is closed   **4** Repeat that, please   **5** Is it far?
6 двАдцать шесть, тринАдцать, трИдцать   **7** ресторАны
8 как попАсть в музЕй?   **9** идИте прЯмо   **10** кудА вы идЁте?

Unit 6

1 a Где **b** Как **c** КудА **d** Что **e** Кто   **2** Suggested answers:
a Да, рУсская вОдка и матрёшки. **b** ИзвинИте, нет.
c Да, рУсские папирОсы и америкАнские сигарЕты. **d** Да, хорОшие банАны.   **3 a** iv **b** v **c** ii **d** iii **e** i   **4 a** ii **b** iv **c** vii **d** i **e** iii **f** v **g** vi   **5 a** вАше, моЁ **b** вАша, моЯ **c** вАши, моИ **d** ваш, мой   **6** Tick everything. Underline вОдка, пИцца, сметАна, Пепси-кОла.   **7** БольшОй теАтр, мАленькое рАдио, красИвые цветЫ, рУсские папирОсы, интерЕсная кнИга, молодОй человЕк, ботанИческий сад, хорОшие конфЕты, бЕлое винО
9   1 я хочУ чай с лимОном **2** я идУ в кинО **3** Это рУсская вОдка   **4** да, метрО закрЫто   **5** да, Это мой билЕт

TEST YOURSELF

1 What do you want to buy?   **2** What have you got?   **3** Show me, please   **4** How much does it cost?   **5** Give me a coffee, please **6** чай с лимОном **7** сто двАдцать **8** мой пАспорт **9** повторИте, пожАлуйста **10** молодОй человЕк

Unit 7

2 a ii b iv c vi d i e iii f v **3** a Scottish b Portuguese c Irish d Norwegian **4** a ii/4/C b iv/1/B c i/2/A d iii/3/D **5** a iii b v c ii d vii e i f iv g vi **6** a в больнИце в АрхАнгельске b на стадиОне c В гостИнице d в ресторАне **7** Эта книга, Этот паспорт, Эти сигарЕты, Это рАдио **8** a vi b x c vii d viii e i f iv g ii h ix i iii j v **9** the order is 4, 5, 2, 7, 8, 1, 6, 3

TEST YOURSELF

1 May I? / Do you mind? **2** Where do you work? **3** I live in Moscow **4** How is that spelled? **5** I am a Russian man **6** однУ минУточку **7** я рабОтаю в магазИне **8** вы говорИте по-англИйски? **9** магазИн открЫт? **10** пятьсОт девянОсто шесть

Unit 8

1 a 8.00 b 7.00 c 3.00 d 1.00 e 11.00 f 2.00 g 10.00 h 6.00 i 4.00 **2** a Час b Три часА c Пять часОв d дЕвять часОв трИдцать минУт e Два часА сОрок пять минУт f ОдИннадцать часОв дЕсять минУт g ДвенАдцать часОв пять минУт h Три часА двАдцать пять минУт i ЧетЫре часА пятьдесЯт минУт **3** a семь, встаЮ b вОсемь, зАвтракаю c дЕвять, идУ d обЕдаю e вОсемь f дЕвять, смотрЮ g одИннадцать **4** a МузЕй антрополОгии и этногрАфии открывАется в одИннадцать часОв. ВыходнОй день – суббОта. ТелефОн – двЕсти восемнАдцать – четЫрнадцать – двенАдцать. b МузЕй музыкАльных инструмЕнтов открывАется в двенАдцать часОв. ВыходнОй день – втОрник. ТелефОн – трИста четЫрнадцать – пятьдесЯт три – пятьдесЯт пять. c МузЕй-квартИра А. А. БлОка открывАется в одИннадцать часОв. ВыходнОй день – средА. ТелефОн – сто тринАдцать – вОсемьдесят шесть – трИдцать три. **d** МузЕй Арктики и АнтАрктики открывАется в дЕсять часОв. ВыходнОй день – понедЕльник. ТелефОн – трИста одИннадцать – двАдцать пять – сОрок дЕвять. **5 a** Чт. **b** Пн. **c** Вт. **d** Ср. **e** Сб. **f** Вс. **g** Пт. **6 a** 1st (ground floor) **b** 2nd **c** 3rd **d** 5th **e** 5th **f** 6th **g** 4th **h** 5th **i** 2nd **7 a** обЕд **b** зАвтрак **c** Ужин **8 a** в теАтре в НОвгороде **b** в библиотЕку **c** в университЕте, в шкОле **d** в инститУт **e** в поликлИнику **9 a** Wednesday **b** Friday **c** Tuesday **d** Monday **e** Thursday **f** Saturday **g** Sunday **10 a** Mon. **b** 13.00–14.00 **c** Sat. **d** Sun. **e** 16.00 **11** Friday

TEST YOURSELF

3 КогдА открывАется банк? **4** КогдА начинАется фильм? **5** ВстрЕтимся в семь часОв в ресторАне **6** porridge, muesli, bread, coffee **7** Я встаЮ в семь часОв **8** ВЕчером я смотрЮ телевИзор **9** Я рабОтаю в МосквЕ **10** Я идУ в теАтр

Unit 9

Dialogue

George – reading, jazz, languages, travel. Lyudmila – badminton, tennis, walking. George – saxophone. Jazz concert, this evening, 5th October.

1 суббОта пЕрвое октябрЯ, воскресЕнье вторОе октябрЯ, понедЕльник трЕтье октябрЯ, втОрник четвёртое октябрЯ, средА пЯтое октябрЯ, четвЕрг шестОе октябрЯ, пЯтница седьмОе октябрЯ. **a** Thurs. **b** Wed. **c** Three Sisters **d** Tues. **3 a** Likes library, reading books, newspapers. **b** Plays badminton. Likes sport. Plays guitar. **c** Likes travel. Speaks English and French well. Doesn't like going to opera or drinking champagne. **d** Likes going to theatre and concerts. Likes music, plays balalaika. Likes pizza. **4 a** пЕрвое январЯ **b** седьмОе январЯ **c** восьмОе мАрта **d** девЯтое мАя **g** тринАдцатого иЮня, двАдцать четвёртого декабрЯ, трИдцать пЕрвого октябрЯ **h** шестОго сентябрЯ, трЕтьего

октябрЯ, четЫрнадцатого февралЯ   **5 a** ix **b** vi **c** xi **d** v/x
e vii **f** v **g** iv **h** iii **i** ii **j** iii/vi/vii/viii **k** xii **l** i   **6 a** 6,000 **b** 14,500
c 20,380 **d** 5,346 **e** 19,923 **f** 2,411 **g** 1,298 **h** 10,531   **7 a** рабОтаю
b говорИте **c** понимАю **d** люблЮ **e** живЁте **f** зАвтракаю
g гулЯю   **8 a** Как вас зовУт? **b** Вы рУсский? **c** Где вы
живЁте? **d** Кто вы по профЕссии? **e** Где вы рабОтаете?
f У вас есть хОбби? **g** Вы лЮбите спорт?   **9 a** On Saturday
25 May, 6.00 **b** On Thursday 31 July, 9.25 **c** В понедЕльник
восьмОго февралЯ, в семь часОв трИдцать минУт.
d В пЯтницу шестнАдцатого мАрта, в пять часОв.
10 a Going to billiards clubs **b** Watching satellite TV **c** Playing
badminton and pool **d** Computer games **e** Going to the casino
f feng shui
АндрЕй **e** Очень люблЮ **c**, **f** люблЮ **a** не люблЮ **d** совсЕм не
люблЮ

TEST YOURSELF

A What hobbies do you have? B I really like reading the papers and
travelling A That's interesting B And you, do you have any hobbies? A
Yes, but I don't like reading at all! I like sport. In winter I play ice hockey
and in the summer I like walking B Do you like music? A No, not much.
How about you? B I really love music and like going to concerts

---

Unit 10

Dialogues
1 Two children. Parents live at dacha.   **2 a** БЕлла **b** СерЁжа **c** Tim
3 Anna prefers city, concerts, theatre, cinema, shops. Historical. Near
metro. Sasha prefers countryside. Peaceful. Walks in forest.

1 a 63 tram or 28 bus **b** 28 bus **c** 28 bus **d** 17 trolleybus **e** 63 tram
f 63 tram **g** 17 trolleybus **h** 28 bus   **2** Anya: Moscow. Pharmacy.
Mum and dad, sister. Cinema. Wants to speak German. Peter: Bristol.
Teacher, school. Son. Football. Wants to travel. Leonid: Yekaterinburg.
Train station. Wife. TV and sweets. Doesn't like sport. Wants to live in
Moscow. Zoya: St Petersburg. Ballerina. Theatre. Husband and brother.
Music. Wants to play piano.   **3** живЁт, магазИны, кУхня, её,

лЮбит, день, хОдит **4 a** iii **b** iv **c** ii **d** i **5** Boris: brother, flat. Nastya: cat, dacha. Liza: car, brother, flat, dacha. **6 a** знАю **b** идЁте, идУ **c** хочУ **d** говорИт **e** рабОтаешь **f** зАвтракаю **g** люблЮ **h** игрАем **i** Ужинают **7** Elite cottage. Prestige district. Electricity, water, gas. Jacuzzi and sauna. Fireplace. Satellite TV. 250 sq. m. Big garage.

TEST YOURSELF

1 ii **2** iii **3** i **4** ii **5** i **6** iii **7** ii **8** ii **9** iii **10** i

---

Unit 11

1 Sport: баскетбОл, футбОл, бокс, пинг-пОнг, тЕннис, рЕгби, хоккЕй. Food: хлеб, банАн, салАт, борщ, шоколАд, котлЕта. Family: мАма, дочь, бАбушка, дЯдя, пАпа, сын, брат, сестрА. **2** гитАра, инженЕр, больнИца **3** *1* теАтр *2* студЕнт *3* метрО *4* ресторАн *5* омлЕт *6* клИмат *7* пАспорт *8* входИте *9* трАктор *10* АмстердАм *11* октЯбрь *12* втОрник *13* телефОн **4** квартИра **5** Menu: Cold Starters: Salad / Mushrooms / Caviar / Salami sausage / Cheese; First Course (*literally* First Dishes): Borshch (beetroot soup) / Shshee (cabbage soup); Main course (*literally* Second Dishes): Fish / Cutlets / Chicken / Omelette / Pizza / Sausages; Sweet dishes: Fruit / Ice cream / Sweets; Drinks: Mineral water / Fruit juice / Beer / Wine / Vodka. **6 a** востОк **b** дЕдушка **c** Август **d** трИдцать **e** РоссИя

Unit 12

1 a 16«а» **б** white wine, бЕлое винО **в** 18:35, восемнАдцать часОв трИдцать пять минУт, 15 degrees, пятнАдцать грАдусов **2 a** ДевЯтое «б» налЕво. **б** У нас есть лимонАд, фруктОвый сок и кОфе с молокОм. **в** Дайте, пожАлуйста, фруктОвый сок. **г** У вас есть рУсский журнАл? **3 a** 4 «д» **б** 10 «г» **в** 25 «г» **г** 11 «в» **д** 2.08, +30 **е** 9.43, −5 **ж** 1.00, +7 **4 a** exit, no exit, boarding gate (exit to embarkation) **б** customs control, luggage reclaim, transit, passport control, flight number **в** check-in (registration), red channel, waiting room, entrance **5** дОллары, пистолЕт, дорОжные чЕки, фУнты стЕрлингов, кАмера, компьЮтер. **6 а** ЗдрАвствуй, ВалентИн? **б** Да, как делА? **в** В пЯтницу. **г** Да, шестОго иЮля. **д** В восемнАдцать часОв сОрок минУт. **е** Да, конЕчно. **ж** НОмер рЕйса SU двЕсти сОрок два. **з** До свидАния, ВалентИн. **7** НОмер рЕйса ВА восемьсОт сЕмьдесят вОсемь. Я буду в Санкт ПетербУрге в девятнАдцать часОв сОрок минУт, двАдцать шестОго январЯ. **8 а** Как приЯтно тебЯ вИдеть! **б** Как вы поживАете? **в** Я немнОжко устАл/а. **г** как всегдА **д** Мы скОро бУдем дОма. **9 а** шестнАдцатого Августа **в** двАдцать два часА трИдцать минУт **б** пЯтого ноябрЯ в дЕсять часОв пятнАдцать минУт **в** двАдцать девЯтого мАя в тринАдцать часОв пятьдесЯт минУт **г** десЯтого февралЯ в пятнАдцать часОв двАдцать минУт. **11 а** 165 **б** 392 **в** 78 **г** 413 **д** 521 **12 а** Что вы хотИте пить? **б** Как вАша фамИлия? **в** Где моЁ мЕсто? **г** У вас есть фУнты стЕрлингов? **д** Это ваш чемодАн и вАша сУмка? **13 а** 5 **б** 7 **в** 1 **г** 2 **д** 3 **е** 4 **ж** 6

ANECDOTE

1 food, transport, hospitals, schools **2** You mustn't grumble in the Soviet Union, but you can grumble in America.

TEST YOURSELF

1 22.18 **2** outside **3** Где моё мЕсто? **4** Да, Это мой чемодАн/Да, мой **5** That he will be in Washington on 4th July **6** Мы немнОжко устАли **7** Что вы хотИте есть и пить? **8** shorts **9** У вас есть англИйские газЕты? **10** Where are you from?

Unit 13

1 а 14 **б** on the right **в** 20–30 minutes **г** 10 minutes **д** 3 **е** на восьмОй автОбус **ж** прЯмо **з** ПешкОм трИдцать – сОрок минУт. А на автОбусе пятнАдцать. **и** ЧЕрез четЫре останОвки. **2** Smoke **3 а** «Парк КультУры» the Park of Culture **б** «УниверситЕт» University **в** 4 **4 а** АлексАндров-ский сад. **б** ПУшкинская **в** АрбАтская **г** БотанИческий сад **д** ПлОщадь РеволЮции. СкажИте, пожАлуйста, как попАсть в Кремль / в БотанИческий сад / на рЫнок / в Дом КнИги / в ГУМ? ДоЕдете до стАнции «АлексАндровский сад» / «БотанИческий сад» / «ПУшкинская» / «АрбАтская» / «ПлОщадь РеволЮции» **5 а** 6 August **б** train no. 7, carriage no. 13 **в** 10.30 **г** seat no. 2 **д** 11.00 **6** ПОезд нОмер пятьсОт одИннадцать в ПетербУрг отхОдит в дЕвять часОв трИдцать шесть. ПОезд нОмер девянОсто шесть в НОвгород отхОдит в двенАдцать часов пятьдесЯт пять. ПОезд нОмер семьсОт шестьнАдцать в ИванОво отхОдит в двАдцать часОв сОрок семь. ПОезд нОмер вОсемьдесят два в ТУлу отхОдит в двАдцать три часА пять. **7 а** 9.40 **б** Yes. **в** На КИевский вокзАл, пожАлуйста. В дЕсять часОв. **8 а** ii **б** iii **в** i **9 а** Как попАсть в Кремль? **б** Где останОвка автОбуса? **в** Вы сейчАс выхОдите? **г** Я Еду в БотанИческий сад на метрО. **д** КогдА отхОдит пОезд?

ANECDOTE 1

1 In case he loses the first and second ones. **2** He has a season ticket.

ANECDOTE 2

1 The train conductor **2** A forest

TEST YOURSELF

1 To the station on foot **2** a **3** Get on tram number 8 **4** b **5** What time the train leaves **6** c **7** b **8** Train 109 to Kiev is leaving at 5.11 **9** Не вольнУйтесь! **10** Я Еду в теАтр на автОбусе

Unit 14

1 Books about sport. **2 a** Estonia. 200 roubles per kilo **б МОжно посмотрЕть? в СкОлько вы хотИте? г** Всё? **д** НапрОтив
3 a Lemons and mandarins **б** Edam cheese from Holland **в** Ketchup **г** Indian **д** Stolichnaya, Smirnoff, Absolut **4** Underline all except МЯсо **5** Coffee, fruit-flavoured water, vodka, fruit tea, champagne. Luncheon meat, chocolate, caramel, sauces, ketchups, sweets.
6 a У вас есть колбасА? **б** ... чай? **в** ... торт? **г** ... рЫба? **д** ... молокО? **е** ... апельсИны? **ж** огурцЫ? **7** (аспирИн – аптЕка) (мАсло – молОчные продУкты/гастронОм/универсАм) (сАхар – гастронОм/универсАм) (винО – гастронОм/универсАм) (морОженое – киОск) (цветЫ – рЫнок) (хлЕб – бУлочная) (самовАр – сувенИры) (шАпка – универмАг/сувенИры) **8 a** Go round the shops. **б** Books, wooden toys, postcards and samovar. **в** No, not far. 3 stops by bus. **г** Opposite **д** онА говорИт, что **е** The salesgirl's aunt lives in London, and says they work there. **ж** Red, green, yellow. **9 a** Matryoshka doll. «СувенИр». Straight ahead, on the left. **б** Books. «Дом КнИги». Not far. Tram 31. 2 or 3 stops. **в** Cake. Grocer's on Улица МИра. Bus. **10 a** Оптика **б** ЧасЫ **в** БУлочная **г** АнтиквариАт **д** ДиетИческие продУкты **е** РЫба **ж** МузыкАльные инструмЕнты **з** Аудио-ВидеотЕхника **и** АвтомобИли
11 a Я хочУ купИть хлеб, сыр, помидОры и чай. **б** Где мОжно купИть газЕту? **в** Всё. **г** ПовторИте, пожАлуйста. **д** У вас есть бЕлое винО? **е** СкОлько стОит?

ANECDOTE

Fish is what they haven't got in the shop opposite.

TEST YOURSELF

1 мОжно посмотрЕть? **2** покажИте **3** скОлько стОит? **4** у вас есть конфЕты? **5** Это дОрого **6** повторИте, пожАлуйста **7** I'm listening **8** Can I help you? **9** How much do you want? **10** These?

Unit 15

1 a A room for one with bath **б** A big room for two with shower
в $120 **г** tomorrow **д** 7.00. 9.00. **e** yes **ж** suitcase and big bag
з straight ahead and right   **2 a** midnight **б** downstairs on left
3 a Room for two with shower. **б** Room for one for 7th January. **в** Room
for two for week.   **4 a** У вас есть свобОдный нОмер? **b** НОмер
на двоИх с вАнной, пожАлуйста. **c** ХорошО. В котОром часУ
начинАется обЕд? **d** Здесь есть лифт? У меня большОй
чемодАн. **e** Да, вИжу. **f** СпасИбо. НОмер трИдцать четЫре.
ПрАвильно? **g** СпасИбо большОе. До свидАния.   **7 a** Australia,
61. **б** Breakfast, tea with lemon and fruit. She feels unwell. **в** To the
station, 10.00 tomorrow.   **8 a** Edna's room is hot. Window shut,
because noisy outside on square. **б** Mark is cold. Another blanket
required. Room 73. Tap won't turn off and TV works badly. **в** Vanessa
says they have lost key. Room 16. Key at administrator's desk. Vanessa
delighted. **г** Bill wants the bill. Room for two for week. Very pleasant
stay, warm and quiet in room. Very pleased. **д** Gary is not happy.
Hot water not on, telephone not working, dirty room.   **9** Room 9, TV
needs mending. Room 14, telephone not working properly. Room 23,
tap won't turn off. Room 31, cold, window won't shut. Room 35, hot,
window won't open. Room 40, noisy. Room 52, dirty. Room 55, radio not
working.   **10** В нОмере хОлодно, грЯзно, шУмно. ТелевИзор
не рабОтает, кран не закрывАется, окнО выхОдит на
вокзАл. Я недовОлен/недовОльна.   **11 a** New, red, American
suitcase. **б** Old black bag containing visa and passport. **в** New
green coat. **г** Money: dollars, sterling and roubles.   **12** Ground floor:
cloakroom, lost property, restaurant. First floor: director, administrator,
service desk, newspaper kiosk, snack bar. Second floor: post office,
hairdresser's, bar.

TEST YOURSELF

1 pull   **2** unfortunately   **3** в нОмере хОлодно,
грЯзно и шУмно   **4** я хочУ заказАть таксИ   **5** мне
плОхо   **6** спасИбо большОе   **7** в чём дЕло?   **8** мы Очень

недовОльны   **9** телефОн не рабОтает   **10** у вас есть свобОдный нОмер?

Unit 16

1 a with lemon and sugar **б** sandwich (bread with salami sausage)
2 a ДАйте/покажИте, пожАлуйста, менЮ. **б** ДАйте, пожАлуйста, кОфе и морОженое. **в** Нет, кОфе с молокОм и с сАхаром. **г** Я не понимАю. ПовторИте, пожАлуйста.
д ПонЯтно. ДАйте, пожАлуйста, ванИльное морОженое.
е СпасИбо. СкОлько с менЯ? **3** First (ground) floor, restaurant. Breakfast, 8.00 – 10.00. ЗАвтрак начинАется в вОсемь часОв и кончАется в дЕсять часОв. Dinner, 13.00–15.00. ОбЕд начинАется в тринАдцать часОв и кончАется в пятнАдцать часОв. Evening meal, 18.00 – 20.00. Ужин начинАется в восемнАдцать часОв и кончАется в двАдцать часОв. Second (first) floor grill-bar, where coffee and sandwiches can be ordered.
4 a Moscow salad and borshsh (beetroot soup). **б** Mushrooms in sour cream, shshee (cabbage soup), kebab (shashlik) with rice, fruit, white wine, tea with lemon but no sugar. **в** Her brother. Asks for extra wine-glass and plate. **5** ДАйте, пожАлуйста, ещЁ чАшку, лОжку, нож и стул. **6** Mushrooms in sour cream, cabbage soup, shashlik, rice, red wine, bread. Another fork. ГрибЫ в сметАне, щи, шашлЫк, рис и красное винО. Хлеб. ЕщЁ вИлка. **7** На столЕ – тарЕлка, нож, вИлка, лОжка, рЮмка, салфЕтка, бутЫлка винА, хлеб, кУрица. **8** ДАйте, пожАлуйста, москОвский салАт, суп с грибАми, беф-стрОганов, рис, шоколАдное морОженое, бЕлое винО и кОфе с молокОм. ДАйте, пожАлуйста, счЁт. **9** ж б з а д г и е в **11** КАша рИсовая молОчная: рис – сто грамм; мАсло – двАдцать пять грамм; сАхар – двАдцать грамм; соль – пять грамм; молокО – двЕсти шестьдесЯт миллилИтров; водА – двЕсти миллилИтров **12 a** Champagne and flowers (roses). **б** Fine. **в** Mushrooms in sour cream and caviar. **г** Yes, very tasty. **д** Vodka. **е** It's late. **13 a** Я Очень люблЮ шампАнское. **б** За вАше здорОвье! **в** КакИе красИвые рЮмки! **г** Как делА?

ANECDOTE

Someone has stolen his bike, so he does not need to avoid alcohol.

TEST YOURSELF

1 Bon appétit! **2** What would you like? **3** What do you recommend? **4** How much do I owe you? **5** Everything is really tasty **6** нож, вИлка, лОжка **7** за вАше здорОвье! **8** дАйте, пожАлуйста, менЮ **9** слАдкое **10** шампАнское

Unit 17

1 a iii **б** ii **в** iii **2 a** ii **б** iii **в** v **г** i **д** iv **3 a** Krasnodar. 861-992-54-16. Tomorrow at 10.00. Three minutes. **б** Nottingham, England. 0115-923-44-19. Today at 11.00. Eight minutes. **в** Novgorod. 816-25-13-67. Tomorrow evening at 7.00. Five minutes. **4 a** v **б** ix **в** x **г** i **д** iv **е** iii **ж** vi **з** ii **и** vii **к** viii **5 a** stamps, envelopes, postcards **б** 4 stamps at 4 roubles for letter to UK **в** fill in form **г** books and toys

6 a Три мАрки по дЕсять рублЕй. **б** Что нАдо дЕлать? **в** КонЕчно мОжно. **г** ПрАвильно. **д** СпасИбо вам большОе. **е** мОжно **ж** хотИте **з** запОлнить **и** Это **к** свидАния

7 a Как **б** Где **в** КудА **г** Кто **д** СкОлько **е** Как **ж** Что **з** КогдА

8 КудА, комУ ... МосквА, ПроспЕкт МИра, дом 26, квартИра 9, ИванОв, А. Текст ... Я в МосквЕ в гостИнице «РоссИя», Улица ВарвАрка, нОмер 331. ФамИлия и Адрес отправИтеля ... МосквА, гостИница «РоссИя», Улица ВарвАрка, нОмер 331, your surname and initials in Cyrillic script. **9** сын/дочь, соль/пЕрец, стол/стул, вокзАл/пОезд, Яблоки/грУши, мАма/пАпа, теАтр/пьЕса, дЕвушка/молодОй человЕк **10** РоссИя 194358, Санкт ПетербУрг, ПроспЕкт Энгельса, дом 121, кОрпус 2, квартИра 69, КузнецОва, Т. И.

TEST YOURSELF

1 letter, postcard, stamp, envelope **2** How much is a stamp for a letter to the UK? **3** How do you get to the post office? **4** international conversation   **5** What is the telephone number?   **6** извинИте, пожАлуйста   **7** да, понЯтно   **8** спрАвочное бюрО   **9** милИция   **10** кто говорИт?

Unit 18

Holiday advert:
Cyprus. Aeroflot flights. 3 star hotel, twin rooms, bar, café, discos, tennis, pool, shopping tour, casino, excursions, diving. Staff speak Russian.
1 а Go skiing in forest.   **б** Cold, frosty, sunny, minus 10.   **в** Sit at home and watch TV.   **г** Summer, hot, can walk on beach, eat ice cream.   **д** To ring Andrew.   **е** 739-15-42.   **2 а** 3 **б** 4 **в** 2 **г** 5 **д** 1   **3** Tomorrow: cold, air temperature −7°, northerly wind, snow and frost.   **4** На зАпаде пАсмурно и идЁт дождь. На сЕвере тумАнно. На востОке мИнус 10 грАдусов и идЁт снег. На Юге теплО, плюс 20 грАдусов и сОлнце свЕтит.   **5** Helen is from Lancaster. Likes radio, chess, reading, films and concerts. Yura is from Krasnodar. Plays hockey, skis, walks in country, plays tennis, swims in sea, collects mushrooms.   **6** Здесь мОжно ловИть рЫбу, купАться в мОре, загорАть на плЯже, катАться на велосипЕде, катАться на лОдке, игрАть в тЕннис.   **7 i** б **ii** в **iii** а   **8** Almost any excuse will do!   **9 а** Tomorrow. **б** Eight. **в** 8 a.m.   **10 1** Enquiry office **2** tourist complex **3** hotel **4** campsite **5** architectural monument **6** museum **7** archeological monument **8** theatre, concert hall **9** stadium **10** restaurant, café, bar **11** department store **12** market **13** taxi rank **14** petrol station **15** train station **16** beach **17** garden, park.   **11 а** Sochi, in hotel at beach. **б** Sunny and hot. **в** Eats ice cream and plays volleyball on beach.   **12 а** 8.30, 12.30, 16.55, 19.20, 21.00, 23.50 **б** 9.55, 21.40 **в** 14.20, 16.30, 20.40 **г** 11.10, 18.20 **д** 9.20, 14.00, 20.00   **13 а** i **б** iii

TEST YOURSELF

1 What is the weather like today?   **2** What is your favourite season? **3** What do you do in your spare time?   **4** It's raining   **5** Do you want to go to the cinema?   **6** с удовОльствием   **7** я люблЮ смотрЕть фИльмы   **8** сегОдня слИшком жАрко   **9** мОжно заказАть экскУрсию?   **10** нет, я не Очень хочУ

Unit 19

1 Vadim has run a marathon, Tanya has flu, Anton has food poisoning
2 **1** нос **2** ногА **3** головА **4** сЕрдце **5** Ухо **6** живОт **7** гОрло
8 глаз **9** зУбы **10** рукА **11** спинА   **3** **а** Brian Wilkinson.
б Headache, hot and cold, temperature, sore throat. **в** No. **г** To rest at home and take medicine three times a day.   **4** **а** Broken his right leg. **б** Ambulance. **в** Take an aspirin.   **5** **а** Hotel Izmailovo **б** Feels bad, heart hurting. **в** Soon, in three minutes.   **6** **а** Я принимАю таблЕтку. **б** Я идУ к врачУ. **в** Я Еду в больнИцу. **г** Я принимАю лекАрство.   **7** **а** vii **б** iv **в** i **г** v **д** ii **e** vi **ж** iii   **8** Suggested answer: ЛеонИд **а** × **б** ✓ **в** ✓ **г** ×   ИрИна **а** × **б** × **в** ✓ **г** ✓
АркАдий **а** × **б** ✓ **в** × **г** ×   МариАнна **а** × **б** ✓ **в** × **г** ×
9 **а** гОда **б** лет **в** гОда **г** лет **д** год   **10** **а** Nina Andryeyevna.
27. Back hurts. **б** Nikolay Vladimirovich. 53. Temperature. Feels sick.
в Sergey Sergeyevich. Toothache.

ANECDOTE

Doctor tells her she will live to 90 if she doesn't drink and smoke. She is already 93.

TEST YOURSELF

1 What hurts?   **2** What symptoms do you have?   **3** How old are you?   **4** Do you smoke?   **5** Open your mouth   **6** я чУвствую себЯ плОхо   **7** у менЯ температУра   **8** у менЯ болИт спинА   **9** Это серьЁзно?   **10** МенЯ тошнИт

Unit 20

1 **а** On a train. **б** Wears spectacles, dressed in coat, boots and hat. Beautiful. 23 years old. **в** In restaurant 'Vostok' at 7.00. **г** Victor will

wear a suit. 40 years old, smokes cigars. **2** Vanya: ✓ **в д ж к**. Galya:
✓ **а б в д е**. **3** Это молодОй человЕк. ЕмУ лет девятнАдцать.
Да, высОкий и худОй. У негО корОткие, тЁмные вОлосы. Он
в джИнсах и в рубАшке. **4** скУчный, ленИвый, невысОкий,
тОлстый, не лЮбит, неприЯтный, глУпый, длИнные, тЁмные,
ЗелЁные глазА. **5 а** ii **б** iv **в** iii **г** i **6** 1 б 2 в 3 а **7 а** i
б iii **в** ii **8 а** vi **б** iii **в** v **г** ii **д** iv **е** i **9** Sasha Nikolayevich Ivanov,
18, has sister and brother. Olya 10, Misha 3. Live in flat, Minsk. Father
is doctor, mother is teacher. Olya likes sport, tennis. Misha not yet at
school. Tall, dark hair, black eyes. Do you want photo? Likes reading and
chess most of all, going to theatre. Skiing. Please write. Where do you
live? What do you like to do? Brothers or sisters? Do you live in a flat or a
house?

TEST YOURSELF

1 iii   **2** ii   **3** i   **4** iii   **5** i   **6** i   **7** i   **8** ii   **9** ii, i, iii, iv   **10** iii

Numbers

Cardinal numbers

0	ноль		
1	одИн	11	одИннадцать
2	два	12	двенАдцать
3	три	13	тринАдцать
4	четЫре	14	четЫрнадцать
5	пять	15	пятнАдцать
6	шесть	16	шестнАдцать
7	семь	17	семнАдцать
8	вОсемь	18	восемнАдцать
9	дЕвять	19	девятнАдцать
10	дЕсять	20	двАдцать

21	двАдцать одИн		
30	трИдцать	200	двЕсти
40	сОрок	300	трИста
50	пятьдесЯт	400	четЫреста
60	шестьдесЯт	500	пятьсОт
70	сЕмьдесят	600	шестьсОт
80	вОсемьдесят	700	семьсОт
90	девянОсто	800	восемьсОт
100	сто	900	девятьсОт

1,000	тЫсяча	6,000	шесть тЫсяч
2,000	две тЫсячи	7,000	семь тЫсяч
3,000	три тЫсячи	8,000	вОсемь тЫсяч
4,000	четЫре тЫсячи	9,000	дЕвять тЫсяч
5,000	пять тЫсяч	10,000	дЕсять тЫсяч
		20,000	двАдцать тЫсяч

Ordinal numbers

1st	пЕрвый	11th	одИннадцатый
2nd	вторОй	12th	двенАдцатый
3rd	трЕтий	13th	тринАдцатый
4th	четвЁртый	14th	четЫрнадцатый
5th	пЯтый	15th	пятнАдцатый
6th	шестОй	16th	шестнАдцатый
7th	седьмОй	17th	семнАдцатый
8th	восьмОй	18th	восемнАдцатый
9th	девЯтый	19th	девятнАдцатый
10th	десЯтый	20th	двадцАтый
		21st	двАдцать пЕрвый
		30th	тридцАтый

Summary of language patterns

The/a

There are no words in Russian for *the* and *a*.

To be

The verb *to be* is not used in the present tense.

Spelling rules

1 Do not use **ы** after **г, к, х, ж, ч, ш, щ**. Instead, use **и**.
2 Do not use unstressed **о** after **ж, ч, ш, щ, ц**. Instead, use **е**.

Gender of singular nouns

Masculine nouns end in	**a** consonant	**парк**
	й	**музЕй**
	ь	**Кремль**
	а	**пАпа**
Feminine nouns end in	**а**	**рекА**
	я	**энЕргия**
	ь	**дочь**
Neuter nouns end in	**о**	**метрО**
	е	**кафЕ**

Plural forms of nouns

Masculine
рестарАн/рестарАны *restaurant/s*
киОск/киОски *kiosk/s*
рубль/рублИ *rouble/s*

Feminine
гостИница/гостИницы *hotel/s*
библиотЕка/библиотЕки *library/libraries*
плОщадь/плОщади *square/s*

Neuter
Утро/Утра *morning/s*

Many neuter nouns (**бюрО, какАо, кафЕ, килО, кинО, метрО, пианИно, рАдио**) do not change.

Adjectives

Masculine singular	Это красИв**ый** парк.	*It's a beautiful park.*
Feminine singular	Это красИв**ая** вАза.	*It's a beautiful vase.*
Neuter singular	Это красИв**ое** рАдио.	*It's a beautiful radio.*
Plural	Это красИв**ые** мАрки.	*They are beautiful stamps.*

Most common endings are **–ый –ий –Ой** (*m*), **–ая –яя** (*f*), **–ое –ее** (*n*) and **–ые –ие** (*pl*).

Possessive pronouns

Мой (*my/mine*), **твой** (*your/yours*), **наш** (*our/ours*), **ваш** (*your/yours*) change form to agree with nouns to which they refer.

Masculine	Feminine	Neuter	Plural
мой пАспорт	моЯ балалАйка	моЁ пианИно	моИ дЕньги
твой пАспорт	твоЯ балалАйка	твоЁ пианИно	твоИ дЕньги
наш пАспорт	нАша балалАйка	нАше пианИно	нАши дЕньги
ваш пАспорт	вАша балалАйка	вАше пианИно	вАши дЕньги

ЕгО (*his*), **еЁ** (*her/hers*), **их** (*their/theirs*) do not change form.

егО пАспорт	егО балалАйка	егО пианИно	егО дЕньги

Pronouns

Где автОбус?	*Where is the bus?*	Вот **он.**	There **it** is. (*m*)
Где вАза?	*Where is the vase?*	Вот **онА.**	There **it** is. (*f*)
Где рАдио?	*Where is the radio?*	Вот **онО.**	There **it** is. (*n*)
Где конфЕты?	*Where are the sweets?*	Вот **онИ.**	There **they** are. (*pl*)

Demonstrative pronouns

ДАйте, пожАлуйста, **Этот** чемодАн.	*Please give me **that** suitcase.*
Эта дЕвушка – моЯ дочь.	***This** girl is my daughter.*
ПокажИте, пожАлуйста, **Это** рАдио.	*Please show me **that** radio.*
Эти билЕты – моИ.	***These** tickets are mine.*

Personal pronouns

singular		plural	
Я	*I*	МЫ	*we*
ТЫ	*you* (informal)	ВЫ	*you* (plural or formal)
ОН	*he/it*	ОНИ	*they*
ОНА	*she/it*		
ОНО	*it*		

As well as meaning *his, her* and *their,* the words **его, еЁ** and **их** mean *him, her* and *them* in phrases where personal pronouns are the direct object of the verb.

ты лЮбишь **менЯ**	*you love me*	вы лЮбите **нас**	*you love us*
я люблЮ **тебЯ**	*I love you*	онИ лЮбят **вас**	*they love you*
онА лЮбит **егО**	*she loves him*	мы лЮбим **их**	*we love them*
он лЮбит **еЁ**	*he loves her*		

У ВАС ЕСТЬ ...? *Do you have ...?*

у менЯ	*I have*	у нас	*we have*
у тебЯ	*you have*	у вас	*you have*
у негО	*he/it has*	у них	*they have*
у неЁ	*she has*		

Accusative case after в and на (into/to)

Masculine and neuter singular nouns do not change after **в** and **на** when motion is indicated, but feminine singular nouns change their endings from -**а** to -**у** and -**я** to -**ю**.

Masculine	**Feminine**	**Neuter**
Как попАсть в теАтр?	Как попАсть на пОчту?	Как попАсть в кафЕ?
		Как попАсть в галерЕю?

Accusative case with direct objects

The accusative case is used when an inanimate noun is the direct
object of a verb. Only the feminine singular ending changes.

(m)	Я люблЮ **спорт**.	*I love sport.*
(f)	Я люблЮ **мУзыку**.	*I love music.*
(n)	Я люблЮ **кинО**.	*I love cinema.*
(pl)	Я люблЮ **кнИги**.	*I love books.*

Prepositional case after в and на (in)

When **в** and **на** mean *in* or *at* a certain place, they trigger the
prepositional case in the following word.

Masculine	Feminine	Neuter
(инститУт) в инститУте	(шкОла) в шкОле	(письмО) в письмЕ
(Кремль) в КремлЕ		
(музЕй) в музЕе		

Verbs in present tense

Group 1 verbs
рабОтать *to work*

я рабОтаю	мы рабОтаем
ты рабОтаешь	вы рабОтаете
он/онА/онО рабОтает	онИ рабОтают

идтИ *to go on foot on one occasion*

я идУ	мы идЁм
ты идЁшь	вы идЁте
он/онА идЁт	онИ идУт

быть *to be* (future tense)

я бУду	мы бУдем
ты бУдешь	вы бУдете
он/онА бУдет	онИ бУдут

пить   *to drink*

я пью	мы пьЕм
ты пьЁшь	вы пьЕте
он/онА пьЕт	онИ пьют

мочь   *to be able*

я могУ	мы мОжем
ты мОжешь	вы мОжете
он/онА мОжет	онИ мОгут

Group 2 verbs

говорИть   *to speak/talk*

я говорЮ	мы говорИм
ты говорИшь	вы говорИте
он/онА говорИт	онИ говорЯт

ходИть   *to go on foot habitually*

я хожУ	мы хОдим
ты хОдишь	вы хОдите
он/онА хОдит	онИ хОдят

любИть   *to love*

я люблЮ	мы лЮбим
ты лЮбишь	вы лЮбите
он/онА лЮбит	онИ лЮбят

Irregular verbs

хотЕть   *to want*

я хочУ	мы хотИм
ты хОчешь	вы хотИте
он/онА хОчет	онИ хотЯт

есть   *to eat*

я ем	мы едИм
ты ешь	вы едИте
он/онА ест	онИ едЯт

Vocabulary

1 The English translations apply only to the meaning of the words as used in this book.

2 Nouns ending in a consonant or **-й** are masculine. A few nouns ending in **-a** are also masculine, but this will be clear from their meaning, e.g. **дЕдушка** – *grandfather*. Other nouns ending in **-a** or **-я** are feminine. Nouns ending in **-ь** may be masculine or feminine. This will be indicated by (*m*) or (*f*). Nouns ending in **-o** or **-e** are neuter.

3 Adjectives are shown in their masculine singular form, ending **-ый, -ий** or **-ой**.

4 Verbs are shown in their infinitive form unless otherwise stated. If they are straightforward verbs it will be shown whether they belong to Group 1 or Group 2.

English–Russian

be able **мочь 1**
all right, fine **нормАльно**
already **ужЕ**
also **тОже**
always **всегдА**
and **и**
another **ещЁ**
at **на**
at home **дОма**
at last **наконЕц**
awful **ужАсно**

bad **плОхо**
be **быть**
beautiful **красИвый**
because **потомУ, что**
better **лУчше**

big **большОй**
to have breakfast **зАвтракать 1**
brother **брат**
but **а, но**

closed **закрЫт**
cold **хОлодно**

daughter **дочь (f)**
to do **дЕлать 1**
to have dinner **обЕдать 1**
don't mention it! **нЕ за что!**
to drink **пить 1**

each, every **кАждый**
early **рАно**
to eat **есть**

entrance **вход**
everything **всё**
excuse me **извинИте**
exit **вЫход**
it's expensive **дОрого**

fairly, quite **довОльно**
far, a long way **далекО**
father **отЕц**
favourite **любИмый**
it's fine **прекрАсно**
fine **прекрАсный**
flat **квартИра**
fortunately **к счАстью**
funny **смешнО**

to get to **попАсть**
girl, young woman **дЕвушка**
give me **дАйте**
go (imperative) **идИте**
to go on foot **идтИ 1**
to go on foot (habitually) **ходИть 2**
it's good **хорошО**
good **хорОший**
good day **дОбрый день**
good evening **дОбрый вЕчер**
good morning **дОброе Утро**
good night **спокОйной нОчи**
goodbye **до свидАния**
grandfather **дЕдушка**
grandmother **бАбушка**

do you have? **у вас есть?**
he **он**
hello **здрАвствуйте**
her **еЁ**
here **здесь**
him **егО**
his **егО**
house, block of flats **дом**
how **как**

how is that written? **как Это пИшется?**
how much do I owe? **скОлько с менЯ?**
how much does it cost? **скОлько стОит?**
how much? how many? **скОлько**
how old are you? **скОлько вам лет?**
husband **муж**

I **я**
if **Если**
in, into **в**
in English **по-англИйски**
in my opinion **по-мОему**
in Russian **по-рУсски**
in the afternoon **днём**
in the evening **вЕчером**
in the morning **Утром**
it's interesting **интерЕсно**
interesting **интерЕсный**
it **он, онА, онО**
it is **Это**

just so! **тОчно так!**

to know **знать 1**

late **пОздно**
left **лЕвый**
to the left **налЕво**
let's go (by transport) **поЕдем**
let's go (on foot) **пойдЁм**
let's meet **встрЕтимся**
a little bit **немнОжко**
to live **жить 1**
look (imperative) **посмотрИте**
to look, watch **смотрЕть 2**
a lot **мнОго**
to love **любИть 2**

man **мужчИна**
man, person **человЕк**
may I help you? **вам помОчь?**
maybe **мОжет быть**
me **менЯ**
mobile phone **мобИльный телефОн**
more **бОльше**
most of all **бОльше всегО**
mother **мать**
my **мой**

name **Имя**
it's necessary **нАдо**
new **нОвый**
no **нет**
it's noisy **шУмно**
not **не**
not allowed, mustn't **нельзЯ**
not far **недалекО**
now **сейчАс**
numbers **цИфры**

of course **конЕчно**
often **чАсто**
old **стАрый**
only **тОлько**
open **открЫт**
opposite **напрОтив**
or **Или**
our **наш**

patronymic name **Отчество**
it's peaceful **спокОйно**
pity (what a pity!) **жаль (как жаль!)**
to play **игрАть 1**
please **пожАлуйста**
with pleasure **с удовОльствием**

it's possible **мОжно**
probably **навЕрно**

it's quiet **тИхо**
quite, entirely **совсЕм**

to read **читАть 1**
repeat (imperative) **повторИте**
right **прАвый**
to the right **напрАво**
rouble **рубль**
Russian **рУсский, рУсская**

to say, talk **говорИть 2**
say, tell me **скажИте**
to see **вИдеть 2**
it seems **кАжется**
she **онА**
shop **магазИн**
show me (imperative) **покажИте**
sit down (imperative) **садИтесь**
slower **мЕдленнее**
small **мАленький**
so **так**
son **сын**
straight ahead **прЯмо**
street **Улица**
to have supper **Ужинать 1**
surname **фамИлия**

thank you **спасИбо**
that **что**
that's nice **приЯтно**
that's right **прАвильно**
their **их**
them **их**
then **потОм**
there **вот, там**
there is, there are **есть**

these **Эти**
they **онИ**
to think **дУмать 1**
this (m), (f), (n) **Этот, Эта, Это**
it's time **порА**
today **сегОдня**
tomorrow **зАвтра**
too, too much **слИшком**
town **гОрод**

to understand **понимАть 1**
understood **понЯтно**
unfortunately **к сожалЕнию**
us **нас**
usually **обЫчно**

very **Очень**

to want **хотЕть** (irreg)
it's warm **теплО**
we **мы**
what **что**
what have you got? **что у вас есть?**

what is your name? **как вас зовУт?**
what sort of . . .? **какОй . . .?**
what time is it? **котОрый час?/ скОлько сейчАс врЕмени?**
what's the matter? **в чём дЕло? что с вАми?**
where **где**
where from **откУда**
where to **кудА**
who **кто**
wife **женА**
woman **жЕнщина**
it's wonderful **чудЕсно**
to work **рабОтать 1**
worse **хУже**

yes **да**
yesterday **вчерА**
you (pl, formal) **вы**
you (pl object) **вас**
you (sing. informal) **ты**
you (sing. object) **тебЯ**
young **молодОй**
your **ваш** (pl), **твой** (sing.)

Russian–English

а but
Август August
авиаписьмО airmail letter
автОбус bus
автомобИль (m) car
автошкОла driving school
администрАтор administrator
Адрес address
Адрес отправИтеля address of sender

аккордеОн accordion
актЁр actor
актИвный active
актрИса actress
аллО hello (on phone)
альбОм album
АмЕрика America
америкАнец, америкАнка American (m, f)
америкАнский American (adj)

америкАнскйи пул *pool*
англИйский *English*
англичАнин, англичАнка
   Englishman, woman
Англия *England*
анекдОт *anecdote*
анкЕта *questionnaire*
антибиОтик *antibiotic*
антиквариАт *antiques*
апельсИн *orange*
аптЕка *pharmacy*
армрЕстлинг *arm wrestling*
аспирИн *aspirin*
атлЕтика *athletics*
атмосфЕра *atmosphere*
Атом *atom*
аэропОрт *airport*
АэрофлОт *Aeroflot*

бАбушка *grandmother*
багАж *luggage*
бадминтОн *badminton*
бактЕрия *bacterium*
балалАйка *balalaika*
балерИна *ballerina*
балЕт *ballet*
банАн *banana*
банк *bank*
бАнка *tin, jar*
бАня *steam bath*
бар *bar*
баскетбОл *basketball*
бассЕйн *swimming pool*
батОн *long loaf*
бЕлый *white*
бЕрег *bank, shore*
берИте *take (imperative)*
(не) беспокОйтесь *(don't)*
   worry (imperative)
бестсЕллер *bestseller*
библиотЕка *library*

бизнесмЕн *businessman*
билЕт *ticket*
бильЯрдный клуб *billiard club*
бланк *form*
блондИн, блондИнка *blond*
   man, blonde woman
блУза *blouse*
блЮдо *dish*
бОдибилдинг *bodybuilding*
бОже мой! *my God!*
бокс *boxing*
болИт, болЯт *it hurts,*
   they hurt
больнИца *hospital*
бОльше *more*
бОльше всегО *most of all*
большОй *big*
бородА *beard*
борщ *borshsh (beetroot soup)*
ботанИческий *botanical*
ботИнки *ankle boots*
брат *brother*
брИфинг *briefing*
брОкер *broker*
брЮки *trousers*
брюнЕт, брюнЕтка *brown-*
   haired man, woman
бУдет *will be*
бУлка *sweet bread roll*
бУлочная *bakery*
бульвАр *boulevard*
бумАжник *wallet*
бутербрОд *sandwich*
бутЫлка *bottle*
буфЕт *snack bar*
был *(m) was*
быть *to be*
бюрО нахОдок *lost property*
   office
бюрО обслУживания *service*
   desk

в in, into
вагОн train carriage
вагОн-рестОрАн restaurant car
вАза vase
вАленки felt boots
вам помОчь? may I help you?
ванИльный vanilla
вАнна bath
вАнная bathroom
варЕнье fruit preserve
вас you (object)
ваш your
велосипЕд bicycle
вес weight
веснА spring
веснОй in spring
вЕтрено windy
вЕчером in the evening
вид view
вИдеть 2 (вИжу, вИдишь) to see
вИза visa
вИлка fork
винО wine
вИски whisky
вкУсный tasty
внизУ downstairs
водА water
вОдка vodka
вОздух air
вОзраст age
вокзАл (на) train station
волейбОл volleyball
вОлосы hair
вон там over there
воскресЕнье Sunday
востОк (на) east
востОчный eastern
вот there
врач doctor
врЕмя time
всё everything

всегдА always
встаЮ I get up
встрЕтимся let's meet
втОрник Tuesday
вторОе блЮдо second (main) course
вход entrance
входИте come in (imperative)
в чём дЕло? what's the matter?
вчерА yesterday
вы you (pl, formal)
вЫдача багажА luggage reclaim
вЫзвать to send for
высОкий tall
вЫход exit
вЫход на посАдку boarding gate
выходИть to go out
выходнОй день closing day

газ gas
газЕта newspaper
газирОванный sparkling, fizzy
галерЕя gallery
гАлстук tie
гардерОб cloakroom
гарнИр side dishes
гастронОм grocer's
где where
ГермАния Germany
гимнАстика gymnastics
гитАра guitar
глаз eye
говорИть 2 to say, talk
год year
головА head
голубОй blue
гольф golf
гомеопатИческая аптЕка homeopathic chemist

гOрло throat
гOрод town
городскOй urban
горЯчий hot
господИн Mr
госпожA Mrs, Miss
гостИная lounge
гостИница hotel
готOвить 2 (готOвлю, готOвишь) to prepare, cook
грAдус degree
граждAнство nationality
грамм gram
гриб mushroom
грипп flu
грУша pear
грЯзный dirty
гулЯть 1 to go for a walk

да yes
дAйвинг diving
дAйте give (imperative)
далекO far, a long way
дAча dacha (country house)
дверь (f) door
дEвушка girl, young woman
дEдушка grandfather
дежУрная woman on duty
декАбрь (m) December
деклаpАция declaration
как делA? how are things?
дEлать 1 to do
дEньги money
дерEвня village, countryside
деревЯнный wooden
дEти children
дEтский сад kindergarten
джаз jazz
джакУзи jacuzzi
джИнсы jeans
диАгноз diagnosis

дивАн couch
дизАйн-стУдия design studio
дипломAт diplomat
длИнный long
для курЯщих for smokers
днём in the afternoon
до свидАния goodbye
дOброе Утро good morning
дOбрый вЕчер good evening
дOбрый день good day
довОлен happy
довOльно fairly, quite
доEдете до travel as far as
дождь (m) rain
дOктор doctor
докумЕнт document
как вы долетЕли? how was your flight?
дOллар dollar
дом house, block of flats
Дом КнИги House of the Book (bookshop)
дOма at home
домофOн entry phone
дOрого it's expensive
дорOжный чек traveller's cheque
дочь (f) daughter
дУмать 1 to think
дурАк fool
душ shower
дУшно it's humid
дЯдя uncle

едИный билЕт season ticket
Ёлка fir tree
Если if
есть there is, there are
есть to eat
Ехать 1 (Еду, Едешь) to go by transport
ещЁ another

жаль (как жаль!) *pity (what a pity!)*

жАрко *it's hot*

ждать 1 (жду, ждёшь) *to wait*

жЁлтый *yellow*

женА *wife*

жЕнщина *woman*

живОт *stomach*

жить 1 (живУ, живёшь) *to live*

журнАл *magazine*

за вАше здорОвье! *your health!*

за грьанИцей *abroad*

за окнОм *through the window*

зАвтра *tomorrow*

зАвтрак *breakfast*

зАвтракать 1 *to have breakfast*

загорАть 1 *to sunbathe*

заказАть *to order*

закрывАется, закрывАются *it closes, they close*

закрЫт *closed*

закУски *starters*

зал *hall*

зал ожидАния *waiting room*

зАпад (на) *west*

запОлните *fill in (imperative)*

застегнИте *fasten (imperative)*

здесь *here*

здрАвствуйте *hello*

зелЁный *green*

зЕркало *mirror*

зимА *winter*

зИмний *winter (adj)*

зимОй *in winter*

знать 1 *to know*

зовУт (как вас зовУт?) *they call (what are you called?)*

зоологИческий *zoological*

зоомагазИн *pet shop*

зоопАрк *zoo*

зуб *tooth*

и *and*

игрАть 1 *to play*

игрУшка *toy*

идИте *go (imperative)*

идтИ 1 (идУ, идёшь) *to go on foot*

извинИте *excuse me (imperative)*

икрА *caviar*

Или *or*

Имя *name*

инженЕр *engineer*

инститУт *institute*

интерЕсно *it's interesting*

интерЕсный *interesting*

интернЕт кафЕ *Internet café*

инфЕкция *infection*

информАция *information*

ирлАндец, ирлАндка *Irish man, woman*

испАнец, испАнка *Spanish man, woman*

ИспАния *Spain*

исторИческий *historical*

ищУ *I'm looking for*

иЮль (m) *July*

иЮнь (m) *June*

к себЕ *pull*

к сожалЕнию *unfortunately*

к счАстью *fortunately*

кабинЕт *study, consulting room*

кАждый *each, every*

кАжется *it seems*

казинО *casino*

как *how*

как Это мОжет быть? *how can this be?*

как Это пИшется? *how is that written?*

какАо *cocoa*

какОй *what sort of*

кАмера *camera*

камИн *fireplace*

канАл *canal*

канИкулы *school holidays*

капитАн *captain*

кАрий *brown (eyes)*

картОшка *potato*

кАсса *cash desk*

кассЕта *cassette*

катАться на лЫжах, конькАх, сАнках *to ski, skate, sledge*

кафЕ *café*

кАша *porridge*

квадрАтный метр *square metre*

квартИра *flat*

кЕмпинг *camping*

килО *kilo*

киловАтт *kilowatt*

килогрАмм *kilogram*

киломЕтр *kilometre*

кинО *cinema*

киноаппарАт *cine-camera*

кинотеАтр *cinema*

киОск *kiosk*

клИмат *climate*

ключ *key*

кнИга *book*

код *code*

колбасА *salami sausage*

комЕта *comet*

кОмната *room*

компАкт-дИск *compact disc*

композИтор *composer*

компОт *stewed fruit*

компьЮтер *computer*

компьЮтерные Игры *computer games*

комУ *to whom*

комфОрт *comfort*

конвЕрт *envelope*

конЕчно *of course*

консультАция *consultation*

консьЕрж *concierge*

конфЕта *sweet*

кончАется *it finishes*

коридОр *corridor*

корОткий *short*

кОрпус *section of housing block*

космонАвт *cosmonaut*

костЮм *suit*

кот *cat*

котлЕта *cutlet (flat meatball)*

котОрый час? *what time is it?*

кОттедж *cottage*

кОфе *coffee*

кошелЁк *purse*

кошмАр *nightmare*

кран *tap*

красИвый *beautiful*

КрАсная плОщадь *Red Square*

крАсный *red*

Кремль *(m) Kremlin*

крЕсло *armchair*

крИкет *cricket*

кровАть *(f) bed*

кто *who*

кудА *where to*

купАться *to swim*

купЕ *compartment*

купИть *to buy*

курИть *to smoke*

кУрица *chicken*

курс *exchange rate*

кУхня *kitchen*

лАдно *OK*

лАмпа *lamp*

лЕвый *left*

лекАрство *medicine*
лес *forest*
лЕто *summer*
лЕтом *in summer*
лимонАд *lemonade*
литр *litre*
лифт *lift*
ловИть рЫбу *to catch fish*
лОдка *boat*
лОжка *spoon*
ложУсь спать *I go to bed*
лОшадь *(f) horse*
лунА *moon*
лУчше *better*
лЫсый *bald*
любИмый *favourite*
любИть 2 (люблЮ, лЮбишь) *to love*

магазИн *shop*
май *May*
мАленький *small*
мАльчик *boy*
мАма *mum*
марафОн *marathon*
мАрка *stamp*
мАркетинг *marketing*
март *March*
маршрУт *route*
маршрУтка *fixed route taxi*
мАсло *butter*
массАж *massage*
матрЁшка *matryoshka doll*
мать *(f) mother*
машИна *car*
медАль *(f) medal*
мЕдленнее *slower*
медпУнкт *first-aid post*
медсестрА *nurse*
междугорОдный *intercity*
междунарОдный *international*

мЕнеджер *manager*
менЮ *menu*
менЯ *me*
мЕсто *place, seat*
мЕсяц *month*
метеОр *meteor*
метр *metre*
метрО *metro*
механИзм *mechanism*
микроскОп *microscope*
мИксер *mixer*
милИция *police*
минерАльная водА *mineral water*
мИнус *minus*
минУта *minute*
мнОго *a lot*
мобИльный телефОн *mobile phone*
мОжет быть *maybe*
мОжно *it's possible*
мой *my*
молодОй *young*
молокО *milk*
молОчные продУкты *dairy products*
монитОр *monitor*
мОре *sea*
морОженое *ice cream*
морОз *frost*
МосквА *Moscow*
москвИч, москвИчка *Muscovite (m, f)*
мост *bridge*
мочь 1 (могУ, мОжешь) *to be able*
мужчИна *man*
музЕй *museum*
мУзыка *music*
мы *we*
мЫло *soap*

мЮсли muesli
мЯгкий soft
мЯсо meat

на at, to, on
нАбережная embankment
навЕрно probably
нАдо it's necessary
наконЕц at last
налЕво to the left
напИток drink
напишИте write (imperative)
напрАво to the right
напрОтив opposite
наркОтик narcotics
начинАется it starts
наш our
не not
нЕ за что! don't mention it!
невАжно not very well
невысОкий short, not tall
недалекО not far
недЕля week
недОрого it's inexpensive
некрасИвый ugly
нельзЯ it is not allowed, mustn't
нЕмец, нЕмка German man, woman
немнОжко a little bit
нет no
но but
нОвый new
ногА leg, foot
нож knife
нокАут knock-out
нОмер number, hotel room
норвЕжец, норвЕжка Norwegian man, woman
нормАльно all right, fine
нос nose
нОутбук notebook (computer)

нОчью at night
ноЯбрь (m) November

о about
обЕд dinner
обЕдать 1 to have dinner
обмЕн валЮты currency exchange
обрАтный билЕт return ticket
Обувь (f) footwear
объЕкт object
обЫчно usually
Овощи vegetables
огурЕц, огУрчик cucumber, gherkin
одЕжда clothes
одЕт dressed
одеЯло blanket
однУ минУточку wait a minute
окнО window
октЯбрь (m) October
омлЕт omelette
он he, it
онА she, it
онИ they
онО it
Опера opera
оркЕстр orchestra
Осень (f) autumn
Осенью in autumn
останОвка stop (bus)
осторОжно carefully
от себЯ push
отдЕл department
отдыхАть 1 to rest, holiday
отЕц father
открОйте open (imperative)
открывАется it opens
открЫт open
открЫтка postcard
откУда where from

отправлЕние *departure*
Отпуск *holiday*
отхОдит (пОезд) *departs (train)*
Отчество *patronymic name*
официАнт, официАнтка
   waiter, waitress
Очень *very*
Очередь *(f) queue*
очкИ *spectacles*

пальтО *coat*
пАпа *dad*
папирОса *cigarette with card-*
   board mouthpiece
парикмАхерская *hairdresser's*
парк *park*
парфюмЕрия *perfumery*
пАсмурно *it's overcast*
пАспорт *passport*
пАспортный контрОль
   passport control
пассажИр *passenger*
пассажИрский *passenger (adj)*
пАчка *packet*
пеницеллИн *penicillin*
пЕнсия *pension*
Пепси-кОла *Pepsi-cola*
пЕрвое блЮдо *first (soup)*
   course
пересАдка *change (train)*
перехОд *crossing*
пЕрец *pepper*
печАть *(f) print: newspapers for*
   sale
пешкОм *on foot*
пианИно *piano*
пианИст *pianist*
пИво *beer*
пинг-пОнг *table tennis*
пистолЕт *pistol*
письмО *letter*

пить 1 (пью, пьёшь) *to drink*
пИцца *pizza*
пишУ *I write*
план *plan*
планЕта *planet*
платИть *to pay*
платОк *shawl*
платфОрма *platform*
плАтье *dress*
плОхо *it's bad*
плОщадь *(f) (на) square*
плюс *plus*
пляж *beach*
по *by, on, at, along*
по-англИйски *in English*
повторИте *repeat (imperative)*
погОда *weather*
подАрок *present*
пОдпись *(f) signature*
подУшка *pillow*
поЕдем *let's go (by transport)*
пОезд *train*
пожАлуйста *please*
пожАр *fire*
(как вы) поживАете? *how are*
   you?
пожилОй *elderly*
позвонИть *to telephone*
пОздно *it's late*
по-испАнски *in Spanish*
пойдЁм *let's go (on foot)*
пойтИ *to go (on foot)*
покажИте *show (imperative)*
пОлдень *(m) midday*
поликлИника *health centre*
пОлночь *(f) midnight*
пОлный *chubby*
полотЕнце *towel*
помидОр *tomato*
пОмню *I remember*
по-мОему *in my opinion*

понедЕльник Monday
по-немЕцки in German
понимАть 1 to understand
понЯтно it's understood
попАсть to get to
порА it's time
португАлец, португАлка Portuguese man, woman
по-рУсски in Russian
послАть to send
посмотрЕть to have a look
посмотрИте look (imperative)
посЫлка parcel
(мы) потерЯли (we) lost
потОм then
потомУ, что because
пОчта (на) post office
почтОвый Ящик post box
поЭт poet
по-япОнски in Japanese
прАвда truth (newspaper)
прАвильно that's right
прАвый right
прАздник public holiday, festive occasion
прекрАсно it's fine
прекрАсный fine (adj)
престИжный райОн prestige district
приезжАйте к нам в гОсти come and visit us (imperative)
принестИ to bring
принимАть 1 (лекАрство) to take (medicine)
прИнтер printer
приЯтно that's nice
приЯтного аппетИта bon appétit, enjoy your meal
пробЕйте талОн punch ticket (imperative)

проводнИк, проводнИца conductor, conductress
прогнОз forecast
продавЕц, продавщИца shop assistant (m, f)
продаЁтся, продаЮтся is for sale, are for sale
продУкты provisions
(у менЯ) пропАл (I've) lost
проспЕкт avenue
профЕссия profession
прохлАдно it's cool
прЯмо straight ahead
путешЕствовать to travel
пьЕса play
пэйнтбОл paintball
пЯтница Friday

рабОта (на) work
рабОтать 1 to work
рАдио radio
раз once, time
разговОр conversation
раздевАйтесь take your coat off (imperative)
рАно early
расписАние timetable
рЕгби rugby
регистрАция registration
рейс flight
рекА river
(вы) рекомендУете (you) recommend
рекОрд record
рЕмни seat belts
ремОнт repair
ресторАн restaurant
рецЕпт prescription, recipe
рис rice
рисовАть to draw
рождествО Christmas

рОза rose
ромАн novel
РоссИя Russia
рот mouth
рубАшка shirt
рубль (m) rouble
рукА arm, hand
рУсский, рУсская Russian man, woman (adj)
рЫба fish
рЫжий red haired
рЫнок market
рЮмка wine glass

с with
с удовОльствием with pleasure
сад garden
садИтесь sit down (imperative)
саксофОн saxophone
салАт salad
салфЕтка napkin
самовАр samovar
самолЁт aeroplane
сАуна sauna
сАхар sugar
свЕжий fresh
свЕтлый light
свИтер sweater
свобОдный free
сЕвер (на) north
сегОдня today
сейчАс now
семьЯ family
сентЯбрь (m) September
сЕрдце heart
сЕрфинг surfing
сЕрый grey
серьЁзный serious
сестрА sister
сигарЕта cigarette
сигнАл signal

симптОм symptom
симфОния symphony
скажИте say, tell me (imperative)
скОлько how much, how many
скОлько вам лет? how old are you?
скОлько с менЯ? how much do I owe?
скОлько сейчАс врЕмени? what's the time?
скОлько стОит, стОят? how much does it, do they cost?
скОрая медицИнская пОмощь ambulance
скОрый fast
скУчный boring
слЕдующий next
слИшком too, too much
слОво word
сломАть to break
слУшать 1 to listen
слУшаю вас I'm listening
сметАна smetana (sour cream)
смешнО it's funny
смотрЕть 2 to look, watch
снег snow
снУкер snooker
собирАть 1 to collect
совсЕм quite, entirely
сок juice
солИст soloist
сОлнце свЕтит the sun is shining
соль (f) salt
сосИска sausage
спАльня bedroom
спасИбо thank you
спать to sleep
спинА back
спокОйно it's peaceful

спокОйной нОчи good night
спорт sport
спортсмЕн, спортсмЕнка
sportsman, sportswoman
спрАвочное бюрО
information bureau
спУтник sputnik
спУтниковое ТВ satellite TV
средА Wednesday
стадиОн (на) stadium
стакАн glass
стАнция (на) station (bus, metro)
старт start
стАрый old
стол table
столОвая dining room
стоп stop
стоЯнка таксИ taxi rank
стрОйный slim
студЕнт, студЕнтка student (m, f)
стул chair
стюардЕсса stewardess
суббОта Saturday
сувенИр souvenir
сУмка bag
суп soup
супермАркет supermarket
сУшка dry ring-shaped biscuit
счёт bill
сын son
сыр cheese
сюдА here (motion)

табАк tobacco
таблЕтка tablet
так so
таксИ taxi
талОн ticket (transport)
там there
тамОженный контрОль
customs control

танцевАть to dance
тарЕлка plate
теАтр theatre
текст text
телевИзор television
телегрАмма telegram
телефОн telephone
телефОн-автомАт public pay
phone
телефонкАрта phonecard
тёмный dark
температУра temperature
тЕннис tennis
теннисИст, теннисИстка
tennis player (m, f)
теплО it's warm
терЯть to lose
тётя aunt
тИхо it's quiet
то . . ., то . . . now this, now the
other
товАрищ comrade
тОже also
тОлстый fat
тОлько only
торгОвый центр shopping
centre
торт cake
тОстер toaster
тОчно так! just so!
(менЯ) тошнИт (I) feel sick
трАктор tractor
трактор И́ст, трактор Истка
tractor driver (m, f)
трамвАй tram
трамплИн ski jump
транзИт transit
трАнспорт transport
трЕнер trainer
трИллер thriller
троллЕйбус trolleybus

туалЕт toilet
тумАнно it's foggy, misty
турИст, турИстка tourist (m, f)
туристИческое агЕнтство tourist agency
тУфли shoes
ты you (singular, informal)

у вас есть? do you have?
угощАйтесь help yourself (imperative)
ужАсно it's awful
ужАсный awful
ужЕ already
Ужин supper
Ужинать 1 to have supper
Улица (на) street
универмАг department store
универсАм supermarket
университЕт university
устАл tired
Утром in the morning
Ухо, Уши ear, ears
учИтель, учИтельница teacher (m, f)

фАбрика (на) factory
факс fax
фамИлия surname
феврАль (m) February
фен-шУй feng shui
финАл final
фотоаппарАт camera
ФрАнция France
францУз, францУженка French man, woman
фрУкты fruit
фунт стЕрлингов pound sterling
футбОл football
футболИст footballer

хЕви металл-рОк heavy metal rock
хИмик chemist
хлеб bread
ходИть 2 (хожУ, хОдишь) to go on foot (habitually)
хоккЕй ice hockey
хОлодно it's cold
холОдный cold
хорОший good
хорошО it's good
хотЕть (хочУ, хОчешь, хОчет, хотИм, хотИте, хотЯт) to want
храм church
худОй thin
хУже worse

цветЫ flowers
центр centre
цЕрковь (f) church
цирк circus
цИфры numbers

чай tea
час hour, o'clock
чАсто often
часЫ watch, clock
чАшка cup
чек receipt, chit
человЕк man, person
чемодАн suitcase
чЕрез after
чЁрный black
четвЕрг Thursday
числО number, date
читАть 1 to read
что what, that
что вы! what on earth!
что с вАми? what's the matter?

что у вас есть? what have you got?

я чУвствую себЯ I feel

чудЕсно it's wonderful

шампУнь (m) shampoo

шАпка hat

шашлЫк kebab (shashlik)

шкаф cupboard

шкОла school

шоколАд chocolate

шоколАдный chocolate (adj)

шотлАндец, шотлАндка Scot (m, f)

шУмно it's noisy

щи shshee (cabbage soup)

экскУрсия excursion

эксперимЕнт experiment

экспрЕсс express

электрИческий electric

электрИчество electricity

электрИчка suburban train

электрОника electronics

элИтная квартИра elite apartment

энергИчный energetic

энЕргия energy

этАж floor, storey

Эта this (f)

Эти these

Это it is, this (n)

Этот this (m)

Юбка skirt

юг (на) south

я I

Яблоко apple

янвАрь (m) January

япОнец, япОнка Japanese man, woman

ЯпОния Japan

Ясли day nursery

яхт yacht